40

GREAT ESCAPES

GREAT ESCAPES

The stories behind 50 remarkable journeys to freedom

Scott Christianson

FIREFLY BOOKS

A FIREFLY BOOK

Published by Firefly Books Ltd. 2009

First printing

Project Editor: Frank Hopkinson
Designer: Cara Rogers

Publisher Cataloging-in-Publication Data (U.S.)

Christianson, Scott.
    Great escapes : 50 journeys to freedom / Scott Christianson.
[256] p. : ill., photos. (some col.) ; cm.
Includes index.
Summary: Fifty stories of escape from a variety of international imprisonments.
ISBN-13: 978-1-55407-506-5
ISBN-10: 1-55407-506-8
1. Escapes. I. Great escapes : fifty journeys to freedom. II. Title.
365.641 dc22   HV8657.C575 2009

Library and Archives Canada Cataloguing in Publication

Christianson, Scott
    Great escapes : 50 journeys to freedom / Scott Christianson.
ISBN-13: 978-1-55407-506-5
ISBN-10: 1-55407-506-8
    1. Escapes. I. Title.
HV8657.C46 2009   365'.641   C2009-901074-7

Published in the United States by
Firefly Books (U.S.) Inc.
P.O. Box 1338, Ellicott Station
Buffalo, New York 14205

Published in Canada by
Firefly Books Ltd.
66 Leek Crescent
Richmond Hill, Ontario L4B 1H1

Reproduction by Rival Colour Ltd, London
Printed in China by C.T. Printing Ltd.

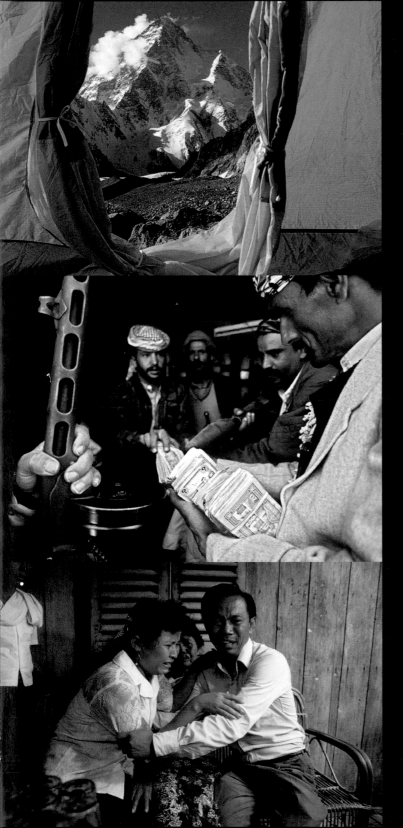

Introduction

They say a journey of a thousand miles must begin with a single step. The same is true for any escape. Unfortunately, sometimes victims are unable to take that crucial step in time to save themselves; others try mightily but fail to defeat the force that holds them. It is often only the luckier ones who can and do escape from something truly monstrous.

This book is about Great Escapes — notable, amazing, incredible, inspiring tales of individuals who are thrust into life-threatening situations. Faced with natural disasters or man-made hells, these individuals prevail against enormous odds to get away. What makes them all so extraordinary is that they are true stories, based on authentic accounts. Some are famous episodes in recent history; a few incidents are not so widely known. But all of them involve real individuals, caught in a terrible bind, many with life-or-death decisions to make. Each story seeks to describe how the fly caught in the cobweb managed to break free, and in some instances, save others.

How did anyone escape from Auschwitz or survive inside the collapsing World Trade Center towers? What happens when a hapless and lone individual is faced with the most gigantic tsunami of modern times or the crash of his balloon from 30,000 feet (9,144 m)?

Whether it is an Australian kayaker trapped underwater, or a Middle East terrorists' hostage faced with imminent execution, many of these predicaments entail a split-second decision or an instinctive, conditioned response that makes the difference between survival and death. Others, such as a breakout from an "escape-proof prison" or the return of a crippled spaceship to Earth, require exceptional intelligence, planning and execution of a complex series of actions all of which must be done to perfection under great stress.

All involve an element of good fortune that sometimes appears almost miraculous in its beneficence.

These stories span every continent, as well as some of the seas and space. People of many nationalities and groups are also represented. The settings range from mountain peaks and arctic wilderness to teeming jungles and sun-baked deserts, modern cities and primitive villages. The protagonists are soldiers, fire fighters, rock climbers, adventurers, tourists, runaway Aboriginal children, Chinese orphans and Cambodian refugees from Pol Pot's genocide — and many more.

There are examples of conflict and resistance that remind us how much some individuals will struggle against adversity to try to control their own fate. There are prisoners of war who defy their captors and risk everything to bust out from their dismal camp; slaves who hunger for freedom and devise bold schemes to break the chains that bind them; a terrified captive of a serial murderer or rapist who refuses to capitulate to demonic abuse.

In some instances, the escapee manages to extend a helping hand to others — to save another person as well, maybe even a stranger and perhaps even an oppressor. Without accomplices, mission control, fellow members of the underground or good samaritans, many of these trapped individuals would never have escaped. Sadly, it is sometimes the bravest and most virtuous who are lost trying to rescue others. Sometimes it is not the noblest that get away.

Each of us must at some time confront our own close call or near-disaster, our dangerous or horrifying bind. Perhaps there is something to be learned from reading about what someone else has done to affect his or her great escape.

The greatest escape from space: Apollo 13 astronauts James Lovell, Fred Haise and John Swigert (left to right), bow heads in a prayer offered by Navy Chaplain Lt. Commander Phillip Jerauld moments after they arrived on deck of the carrier USS *Iwo Jima*, after a successful splashdown. Their mission had been wrecked by a loss of oxygen en route to the moon.

1 Nature

Shackleton's endurance

ERNEST SHACKLETON	1914–1916

On August 1, 1914, British explorer Ernest Shackleton set out on an unprecedented expedition — the first crossing of Antarctica. Despite his crew of highly skilled seamen and his sturdy vessel (the aptly named *Endurance*), Shackleton's ambitious expedition became a fight for survival.

By 1914, British explorer Sir Ernest Henry Shackleton (b. 1874) had already been knighted for his heroic maritime feats that had contributed much to national pride. But he was never one to rest on his laurels.

Portrait of a hero: Sir Ernest Shackleton, photographed before departing for the Antarctic. **Top right:** Waving farewell from HMS *Endurance* at Millwall Docks, London, August 1914.

Now his plan was to make the first crossing of Antarctica by traveling from the Weddell Sea to the Ross Sea via the South Pole; an almost impossible distance of 1,800 miles (2,897 km). A charismatic Anglo-Irish merchant seaman, Shackleton raised the necessary funds to mount an expedition, then placed an ad in the newspapers that read: "MEN WANTED FOR HAZARDOUS JOURNEY. Small wages, bitter cold, long months of complete darkness, constant danger, safe return doubtful. Honour and recognition in case of success." From those who applied, he selected 27 exceptional seamen.

Their vessel would be *Endurance*, a 300-ton, 144-foot (44 m) sailing ship — a barquentine — that was built of planks of sturdy oak and Norwegian fir up to 2.5 feet (0.8 m) thick, which were sheathed in extra-strong greenheart wood. Its engines burned coal or oil and its top speed under steam was 9–10 knots. Shackleton had it specially outfitted for an Antarctic voyage, with kennels for the sled dogs and other features, and added a wireless receiver (but no transmitter), a gramophone and a darkroom for the expedition's photographer. Also aboard the vessel were four scientists: a biologist, a geologist, a meteorologist and a physicist. Among their many tasks would be carefully to record the perilous ice drift that threatened maritime traffic.

The expedition seemed jinxed from the start: three days after *Endurance* set out from London on August 1, 1914, Britain entered into the Great War with Germany, and Shackleton had to await approval from the Admiralty

SIR ERNEST SHACKLETON (1874–1922)

Born in Ireland as the second of 10 children and the eldest son — a fact that later helped prepare him for taking care of his crew — Shackleton grew up in suburban London and did well enough in his studies. But he left school at age 16 to go to sea.

By 1901 he had worked his way up in the merchant marine to become the third officer on the daring National Antarctic Expedition, serving on the *Discovery* under Commander Robert Falcon Scott. However, he was sent home early in 1904 for health reasons.

The ambitious young adventurer later sought to make amends for his personal failure by serving as leader of the harrowing Nimrod Expedition (1907–1909), wherein he established a record for reaching the southern-most point of any explorer in history at that time. As a result, Shackleton was knighted by King Edward VII.

After the glorious failure of the *Endurance* expedition, he returned to the Antarctic in 1921 for the fourth time with the Shackleton-Rowett Expedition. But before it got fully underway, he suffered a heart attack in his bunk and died on January 5, 1922. His wife had him buried on the before proceeding further. After getting the order to continue, he sailed on to the South Atlantic and arrived at his last port of call, the mountainous island of South Georgia which was the site of a last, lonely Norwegian whaling station.

Although some of the whalers warned that the pack ice (ice floes driven into large piles) was already appearing farther north than usual — a fact that did not bode well for the voyage — Shackleton insisted on going ahead, and *Endurance* departed in early December, heading for Vahsel Bay. Only three ships before it had ever ventured into the Weddell Sea and two of them had

Sinking: The reinforced planking of the Norwegian-built hull finally succumbed to the pressure of pack ice in the Weddell Sea. The team would be forced to slaughter the sled dogs as conditions worsened.

become trapped there; precious little information was available about how to successfully navigate its treacherous expanse. Yet Shackleton was determined to move ahead with his expedition.

Icebound: One of the classic images of the expedition captured by New Zealand photographer Frank Hurley. HMS *Endurance* is trapped in ice and is forced to drift with the pack for ten months before being crushed near the Caird Coast.

As the ship moved southward, however, the early ice slowed its progress, causing Shackleton to weave and push the ship through a seemingly never-ending obstacle course. Conditions in the Weddell Sea gradually got so bad that on January 19, 1915, the ship became frozen fast in an ice floe and it appeared they might be stuck for a long time, slowly drifting northward with the pack.

On February 24, realizing that the vessel would be

Provisions: Though Shackleton didn't lose a man on his team, the seven-man crew of the supply ship *Aurora* lost three supplying provisions to Shackleton's intended destination camp.

Trapped

On October 24, 1915, *Endurance* was being crushed by the ice floes, "wringing animal-like screams from her as they sought to break her back," as one witness put it, and water began pouring in. At 5 p.m. Shackleton gave the order to abandon ship, requiring the men to transfer all provisions and equipment they could salvage to camps on the ice. All of them would have to try to survive on the ice floes. Finally, on November 21, 1915, the mangled wreck slipped beneath the surface, leaving them stranded and alone in the vast, white wilderness.

Their exploratory expedition was over, but now their battle for survival was just beginning. Making matters worse, the ice was now drifting east, probably carrying them into the South Atlantic where their chances of survival would be few.

Encamped in the open air, the party faced temperatures that dropped to -31°F (-35°C). The men had to drag their boats and provisions over the ice. But Shackleton didn't seem discouraged. "He never appears to be anything but the acme of good humour and hopefulness," one of the expedition's scientists, Thomas Orde-Lees, wrote in his diary. Notwithstanding his own royal status, he treated the men as equals and led by example. As a result, the crew remained well disciplined and cohesive.

Each day brought new trials: one day the men were attacked by sea leopards. Subsisting on penguins and seals, they had to kill their beloved dogs. Many developed terrible frostbite; in one instance a man had to have his foot amputated.

> **❝ He never appears to be anything but the acme of good humour and hopefulness. ❞**
>
> Thomas Orde-Lees, one of the expedition's scientists, in a diary entry on Shackleton

For almost two months Shackleton and his party remained camped on a large, flat floe, hoping that it would drift towards Paulet Island, approximately 250 miles (402 km) away, where they might be safe and use the stores that had been cached there. But that did not appear to be happening. So after making several failed attempts to march across the ice to Paulet, Shackleton

trapped until the following spring, Shackleton ordered the ship's conversion to a winter station. The ship kept moving slowly northward with the ice through the following months, preserving the hope that they might eventually reach open water.

By the time total darkness descended in June they had already been trapped for four and a half months. The ice's grip on *Endurance* tightened like a vise. When spring arrived in September, the breaking ice put even more extreme pressures on the ship's creaking hull, throwing it violently onto the starboard beam and causing leaks to break out from the squealing timbers.

Sitting it out: Expedition photographer Frank Hurley (left) and Shackleton (right) sit outside their makeshift camp on the ice of the Weddell Sea. Once the *Endurance* became crushed by the ice it was too dangerous to remain billeted on the ship.

Departure: Shackleton and his carefully chosen crew set off from Elephant Island in the lifeboat *James Caird*. Shackleton's mission was to reach the whaling station on South Georgia 800 miles (1,287 km) across the South Atlantic.

decided to set up another more permanent camp on a different floe, banking that the drift of the ice would take them in that direction. By March 17 they determined that their ice camp was within 60 miles (97 km) of Paulet, yet separated from it by brutal, impassable ice.

Lifeboat launch

On April 9, the end of the Southern Hemisphere summer, their ice floe broke into two and Shackleton ordered his crew into the three open lifeboats to head for the nearest land. It was not a good situation. Soaked to the bone and suffering from dysentery, they rowed for a week until they reached Elephant Island, a desolate rocky outcrop off the tip of the Antarctic peninsula and the last piece of land before the open sea. Shackleton realized that, if he and his men stayed there, they had little hope

of rescue and it was doubtful whether many of them would survive.

Therefore, he made a command decision. He selected the strongest of the lifeboats, *James Caird*, and had the ship's carpenter make various improvements to strengthen it for an arduous voyage, including sled runners so it could glide on the ice. Then he carefully chose five companions for the journey, with the goal of finding help to rescue his crew.

On April 15 they set off in the 22-foot (6.7 m) lifeboat in an effort to get to South Georgia, 800 miles (1,287 km) away. It would be their only hope. But they were already reaching the end of their endurance.

On May 8, after 16 grueling days, his navigator succeeded in steering them to within sight of the cliffs of South Georgia. But hurricane-force winds prevented the possibility of landing and they struggled to ride out the monstrous waves without being dashed against the rocks. Somehow, they succeeded in staying afloat.

The final push

The next day they were able to land on the barren southern shore. But to reach their destination, they still faced a 22-mile (35 km) trek across the uncharted mountainous interior — something that had never been done before — and a journey for which they were woefully ill-equipped. All told, they had only 48 matches, an axe, a coil of rope and two compasses.

Shackleton took two men with him and headed off into the interior. Thirty-eight sleepless and grueling hours later, after becoming beset with hallucinations, they finally reached the whaling station of Stromness, just ahead of another storm.

Shackleton and his companions had made it. Soon afterward a ship picked up the remaining three men on the other side of South Georgia. But that still left the others in urgent need of rescue. After making three unsuccessful attempts to reach the rest of his stranded crew on Elephant Island, the ice finally allowed a Chilean ship to reach them on August 30, 1916. Despite being trapped there for four months, they too had survived.

Although his Imperial Trans-Antarctic Expedition had failed to ever reach Antarctica, Shackleton's incredible endurance and rescue established the episode as one of history's greatest escapes. Shackleton died of a heart attack in 1922. He was 47 years old.

Goal achieved: The abandoned whaling station at Stromness as it looks today. Shackleton had to scale the mountain range behind the village with no specialist climbing equipment — just a coil of rope, a carpenter's adze (used as an ice axe), three days' food, a stove and 48 matches.

Sudden descent

STEVE FOSSETT	August 1998

After three failed attempts, in 1998 Steve Fossett was determined to become the first man in history to fly non-stop around the world in a balloon. After flying for more than 15,200 miles (24,462 km), Fossett's balloon plummeted into shark-infested waters east of Australia.

By 1998 the American millionaire Steve Fossett had already established himself as the world's greatest adventurer and the champion world-record setter in a variety of fields including aviation, gliding, airships, sailing and ballooning. Rich, fearless, super-competitive and extraordinarily enterprising, there simply were not enough adjectives to describe his amazing qualities of derring-do. But his latest adventure would test him on many counts.

One of his most elusive challenges was to become the first person in history to fly non-stop around the world in a balloon. He had already tried it and failed on three different expeditions. Most recently, in January 1997 he had broken the distance record for non-stop ballooning around the world when he traveled 10,360 miles (16,673 km) from St. Louis, Missouri before crash-landing in a field in India. Now he was trying again.

Solo spirit

Named the *Solo Spirit*, his Rozière-style craft had separate chambers for both helium and heated air, being designed to allow its flyer some control of buoyancy with much less use of fuel than a typical hot air balloon. With a white-and-blue-crowned canopy that was shaped like a giant top, and a tiny yellow gondola made of Kevlar and carbon fitted with a plastic bubble hatch that was called the carbon fiber capsule, Fossett's airship was loaded with high-tech communications gear, but low on comfort.

On August 7 he launched his craft from Mendoza, Argentina on the South American coast. But on the first

Round one: Early in 1997 Fossett attempted to be the first person to fly a balloon around the world non-stop, launching from Busch Stadium in St. Louis. It was a trip that would end in India.

Six days later: Journey's end for the first Solo Spirit adventure in a field in India. Fossett would try again in December 1997 but a faulty heater ended his attempt in Novokiporovskaya, Russia, after 7,300 miles (11,750 km). His next flight would depart from the Southern Hemisphere.

day, the balloon began to have some problems, which may have been due to a broken fuel line. In the course of putting out an external fire and making repairs, he sustained minor burns and lost three of the four burners that provided heat for the hot air portion of the craft.

Several hours later, with input he received from his ground crew, one of the burners got going again.

His route took him over the coast of Africa, making him the first person to ever cross the South Atlantic Ocean in a balloon. He continued by crossing the Indian Ocean to Australia. He floated over Australia and headed out into the southern Pacific — a phenomenal feat.

> **❝ You have to believe that you are going to succeed ... because a water landing would be very dangerous. ❞**
>
> Steve Fossett

Of all his adventurous activities, Fossett considered ballooning the most dangerous. He often had to climb outside his cramped quarters in sub-zero temperatures to check the fuel tanks and burners. This left him with only a couple of hours sleep per day.

Nine days into the flight, a line of fierce thunderstorms rose in his path. All he could do was try to rise over them, but at an altitude of 29,000 feet (8,839 m), a violent downdraft with hail and lightning punctured the skin of his balloon. Severely damaged, the craft plummeted toward the sea, 5.5 miles (8.9 km) below, leaving him to wonder if he could possibly survive the crash.

Addicted to records: Fossett was a phenomenal collector of records. In 2002 he attempted to set a new gliding altitude record at Omarama in New Zealand but was forced down by turbulence.

Crash landing

Upon hitting the rock-hard waves, the exterior of the capsule burst into flames and turned upside down, filling with water. Fossett survived the G-forces of the impact but was almost overwhelmed by suffocating fumes from the burning resins lining the exterior of the capsule. But by seizing his 12-pound (5.4 kg) life raft and EPIRB beacon, which he had triggered during the descent, he found a way out of the capsule's submerged hatch, dragging the lifesaving equipment behind him. Somehow he clambered into the tiny life raft and hung on for dear life as it plunged down and up on the monstrous waves.

At 9:23 a.m. (CST) on August 16 his ground crew back in the United States received his warning signal: the emergency locator beacon sounded twice, indicating a serious problem. At 11:02 a.m. (CST) it sounded again,

indicating Fossett was in the water approximately 500 miles (805 km) east of Australia.

Fossett's tiny raft continued to bob in the shark-infested water.

Eight hours later, a reconnaissance plane — sent from New Caledonia and guided to the raft by emergency locator beacons whose signals were picked up by satellite — spotted him in the water and dropped some emergency supplies. Several hours after that and following 23 hours in the life raft, a private Australian yacht, the *Atlanta*, picked him up in good condition.

More records

The *Solo Spirit* flight had ended two-thirds of the way through its flight, approximately 15,200 miles (24,462 km) past the initial launch site, breaking the distance record for manned balloon flight he had set during his second global attempt.

While still on the rescue boat he was already on the satellite phone with his rival and friend, Sir Richard Branson, scheming about his next adventure.

Out of adversity: Fossett with the *Solo Spirit* gondola that would take him to his coveted global first in 2002. The capsule now resides in the Smithsonian Museum in Washington, D.C.

The greatest long-distance pilot

In 2002, on his sixth attempt, Steve Fossett launched his new 10-story-high balloon, *Spirit of Freedom,* from Northam, Western Australia, and subsequently landed in Queensland, Australia, finally becoming the first person in history to circumnavigate the globe alone in a balloon. The record flight took 13 days, 8 hours, 33 minutes (14 days, 19 hours, 50 minutes to landing), and covered 20,626.48 statute miles (33,195.10 km).

"I feel a tremendous sense of satisfaction," he said afterwards. "I've worked towards this goal for 10 years. This is the reason I took up ballooning."

Fossett went on to set a final total of 116 world records, 23 of them on water and 93 in balloons, gliders and powered aircraft — more than half of which still stand. He was recognized as the "world's most accomplished speed sailor," the greatest long-distance pilot, the fastest east-to-west non-supersonic flyer and a host of other titles.

Throughout his lifetime he had many stirring adventures. He swam the treacherous waters from San Francisco to Alcatraz, completed the Hawaii Ironman Triathlon, swam the English Channel, participated in the Iditarod dog sled race, ran the Leadville Trail 100, set some Colorado distance records in cross-country skiing, drove in the 24 Hours of the LeMans car race and climbed six of the seven continental summits.

On September 3, 2007, however, Fossett took off for a routine flight over the Nevada desert and was never heard from again. A massive month-long search failed to find any wreckage or trace of him. On September 29, 2008, a hiker found Fossett's identification cards in the Sierra Nevada Mountains in California, and the crash site was discovered a few days later. On November 3, 2008, DNA tests conducted on bones recovered near the site of the crash confirmed his death at age 63. In the end, he had reached his limit of great escapes.

Trapped between a rock and a hard place

ARON RALSTON	April–May 2003

When Aron Ralston gave up his high-paying corporate job to devote his time to climbing, he couldn't have imagined what fate had in store for him. After six days pinned by a boulder in the bottom of a hidden canyon in Utah, the young rock climber resorted to the unthinkable in order to save his own life.

Aron Lee Ralston was a solo climber. Now 27 years old, he had graduated six years earlier from Carnegie-Mellon University with a bachelor's degree in mechanical engineering, a double major in French and a minor in piano performance. In addition to finishing first in his class academically, he had become a serious mountaineer while in college. In fact, climbing was so important to him that in 2002 he had left a high-paying corporate job to climb all of Colorado's "fourteeners" (the name given to the peaks over 14,000 feet [4,267 m] high).

After a winter of solo climbing, Ralston decided to spend a warm and dry Saturday canyoneering. After choosing the beautiful and remote Blue John Canyon (near Moab, Utah), the outdoorsman packed his gear and his bike into a truck and drove to the park entrance. Then he left the vehicle by the park's welcome sign and biked several miles into the canyon, finally stopping about a mile southeast of

ATTENTION BLUE JOHN HIKERS!!

Bluejohn canyon is NOT in Canyonlands National Park. It is on BLM land in a Wilderness Study Area. There are no marked trails. The canyon is NOT patrolled. YOU ARE ON YOUR OWN when you hike Bluejohn Canyon. This is a hike requiring TECHNICAL knowledge, and you should BE PREPARED FOR SELF RESCUE.

The complete loop hike (exiting at the Horseshoe Canyon parking area) takes longer for most people than what is stated in some guidebooks. Hikers have been getting in trouble because they think they can start the hike at noon and be out before dark. This is NOT the case. You should plan on a minimum of 8 hours for the hike. This does not include shuttle time. More time is required if the canyon has recently flooded. Please plan your trip accordingly so it does not turn into an unpleasant ordeal. And remember, this is a slot canyon — you should not enter if rain is predicted!

Take heed: The trail advisory notice for Blue John Canyon.

Iconic scenery: Blue John Canyon is near Moab, Utah, which draws tourists to the Arches and Canyonlands National Parks. John Huston filmed his classic movie *Stagecoach* in the inspiring sandstone landscape. Cougars are regular visitors to sandstone rainwater pools.

Burr Pass. From there he continued alone on foot, enjoying the natural world all around him.

For Aron Ralston, this truly would be a walk in the park; a time to relax, he thought. Unfortunately, he was not carrying a satellite phone. Nor had he told anyone where he was going or when he would be back. He was alone. Dangerously alone.

> **It took some good calm thinking in order to get myself to calm down and stop throwing myself against the boulder.**
>
> Aron Ralston

Stuck

At midday Ralston was downclimbing in a deep and narrow slot canyon when a chockstone above him came loose and fell. The boulder smashed his left hand against the south wall, then crushed his right hand and ensnared his right arm at the wrist, palm in, fingers extended, before the rock slid another foot down the wall with his arm in tow, tearing the skin off the lateral side of his forearm.

Feeling the shock and pain, the stunned climber tried to move his trapped arm by pushing the rock and shifting his position. The physics were not in his favor: his wedged hand was not just stuck, it was actually holding the boulder off the wall.

Beautiful but deadly: In the depths of Blue John Canyon. Apart from the hazards of falling rocks, a sudden downpour can turn a slot canyon into a raging torrent. Rain was one hazard that Ralston managed to avoid.

After drinking five ounces of water from his plastic bottle, it dawned on him that he had only 22 ounces left. Soon he realized that he was now irreversibly stuck — imprisoned at the bottom of a dimly lit canyon, unable to move more than a few inches in any direction. He was in one of the most remote areas of the park, exposed to the elements. Nobody knew where he was. He had very little food or water within reach. The chances of a rescue were now extremely poor. His pinned arm was numb and the visible part of his right fingers were already turning a sickly gray. Aron Ralston was truly caught between a rock and a hard place.

The only items within reach included some empty chocolate bar wrappers with crumbs of the chocolate muffin he had eaten; two small bean burritos, consisting of about 500 calories total; a CD player with CDs, extra AA batteries; his mini digital video camcorder; his small multi-use tool; a three-LED headlamp and some rappelling equipment. He would have to tightly ration his food and water.

True grit: Aron Ralston with his father Larry at his first public appearance at St. Mary's Hospital, Grand Junction, Colorado, May 8, 2003.

Recording a message

Come nightfall the hot temperatures of the canyon plummeted to the mid-50s (10°C), making it chilly and even more uncomfortable. He expended considerable energy chipping at the rock and trying to stay warm, telling himself that he should not go to sleep or he might not wake up. Given the lack of water and the cold, he reckoned that he probably could not survive under such conditions past Monday night.

In weighing his options, the last resort would be to try to cut off his arm in order to get free. But in doing so, he figured that he would probably bleed to death and not be able to climb out of his hole and walk the eight miles (12.9 km) back to his car. Turning on his camcorder, he recorded his first video message.

"It's 3:05 p.m. on Sunday, April 27, 2003," he said. "This marks my 24-hour mark of being stuck in Blue John Canyon. My name is Aron Ralston. My parents are Donna and Larry Ralston, of Englewood, Colorado. Whoever finds this, please make an attempt to get this to them. Be sure of it. I would appreciate it."

Probing his arm

The more he thought about it, the more he realized that time was running out. By Sunday night, he calculated he probably couldn't last to Tuesday. Yet it probably wouldn't be until Thursday or Friday that anyone would start searching for him. Meanwhile, he was finding it harder to stay awake. After 48 hours, he had only five ounces of water left. Although his mind was playing games, he knew he had to act or he was doomed.

Using some of his tubing insulation, he made a tourniquet around his forearm, knotted it twice and clipped it secure. Taking his small multi-use tool, he chose the shorter of the two knives and grasped the handle with his fist, then aimed it at a spot on his arm and jammed the inch-and-a-half blade to the hilt into the meat of his forearm. He barely felt anything.

He kept probing with the knife, digging at the flesh, tapping at the bone. But as hard as he tried, he could not break through the forearm bones. He had cut through the skin and fatty tissue and maybe severed a tendon, but he had not severed an artery.

Dehydration

Now he was out of water and out of food. Eventually, he resorted to drinking urine. He already had lost about 20 pounds from his lean frame. Sometimes he carved words into the rock, making notches like Robinson Crusoe. He wrote his name and expected time of death.

By the fourth day, suffering from extreme dehydration and insomnia, he passed in and out of a trance. At 2 p.m. on the fifth day, Wednesday afternoon, he videotaped some last requests to his loved ones, specifying whom he wished to serve as pallbearer.

Although he couldn't know it at the time, some of his relatives and friends already had swung into action, looking into his email messages and any other clues that would help them determine where he had gone. They also went to the authorities to get them to initiate a search.

Grip, squeeze, twist and tear

Ralston hadn't slept for 120 hours and sometimes he wasn't sure if he was dead or alive.

After five days of trying to lift and break the boulder, Ralston fought through his delirium to do the only thing left: he proceeded to cut off his already dead arm. He could smell foul gases coming from the wound.

By levering the arm against a chockstone, he snapped the radius and ulna bones. Using the dull blade on his multi-use tool, he cut the soft tissue around the break. Then he used the tool's pliers to tear at the tougher tendons. Grip, squeeze, twist and tear. Grip, squeeze, twist and tear.

Then he was tightening his tourniquet, attacking the arteries. Cutting and ripping, pulling and tearing, pushing with all of his might.

On Thursday, May 1, at 11:30 a.m., his body broke away and he was free of the boulder. But now he had to get out of his hole and make it to safety.

He gathered his gear and took only the barest essentials. He put the arm in his bag. Then, through sheer force of will and expert climbing, Ralston pulled himself together and climbed out of the rock coffin he had occupied for the last six days. After completing a series of difficult climbing maneuvers, including rappelling down a 65-foot (20 m) steep wall, he made it out of the rocks and onto the path.

There was nobody to help him but he did find a puddle and he frantically drank five liters of the syrupy water, keeping more of it in his bottle for the eight-mile (12.9 km) walk that lay ahead. After six-and-a-half miles (10.5 km), he encountered three figures on the distant trail. "Help!" he cried. "I need help!"

It was a Dutch couple with their young son. The woman ran to get help. By then the police had found his truck and dispatched a helicopter. It landed and took him away; Ralston was struggling to stay awake and alive. They made it to intensive care and he was nursed back to life and put through a series of surgical operations and rehab.

> **Judging by my degradation in the last 24 hours, I'll be surprised if I make it to Tuesday.**
>
> Aron Ralston

Inspiring others

In 2004 Ralston published a book, *Between a Rock and a Hard Place*, and his ordeal became the subject of countless articles, television interviews and at least one computer game. Fitted with a prosthetic limb, he resumed mountain climbing and planned to tackle Mount Everest with polar explorer Eric Larsen in order to raise public awareness on climate change. His story of survival and escape ranks among the most harrowing episodes ever recorded.

Ralston also travels the world lecture circuit as a much-in-demand inspirational speaker sharing his love for the outdoors and his passion for life. He has had to confront the impact of the poor decision he made of hiking alone in the canyon that fateful day. He also continues to struggle with the meaning of his near-death ordeal, facing such questions as what can others learn from his dilemma, and how a simple "accident" can become the dominant force of your existence.

Ralston's story has also brought additional fame to Utah's beautiful and equally treacherous, Blue John Canyon. Ironically, the place takes its name from a notorious nineteenth-century outlaw (Blue John Griffith) who vanished there. Today, hikers from across the globe flock to the slots and boulders that Ralston tested.

The ghost train

SHENTH RAVINDRA   **December 26, 2004**

While on holiday from Britain to visit his relatives in Sri Lanka, Shenth Ravindra's train carriage was upturned by a freak wave. Little did he know that he would soon be facing the wrath of the Asian Tsunami — one of the deadliest natural disasters ever recorded.

British tourist Shenth Ravindra was vacationing in Sri Lanka, hoping to visit his relatives and enjoy some of the ocean resorts. The *Queen of the Sea* passenger train he was riding was crammed with 1,500 happy and excited people celebrating Poya Day, a Buddhist bank holiday. Although the cars were noisy with rambunctious children and chattering vendors selling tea and treats, the 25-year-old Ravindra was enjoying the festive atmosphere.

At 9 a.m. the train had just left Ambalangoda station, the last stop before his destination, and the young tourist was busy getting his stuff together for the arrival at Hikkaduwa. But then something happened. The train jerked to a stop and he started hearing screams and shouts.

At first, he thought, "Oh, no, we're going to be stuck for a couple of minutes. I just want to get off this train."

Looking out the window, Ravindra saw women running away from the coast. He was just beginning to notice the look of terror on their faces and to hear the sound of rushing water when suddenly he felt the train being jolted off its tracks as the flood began rushing into the passenger car. Then his car became detached from the other carriages, tilting so wildly that he ended up in one of the doorways, up to his neck in seawater.

Climbing out

As thoughts of a bomb attack flashed through his mind, his first instinct was to climb out of the car onto

Rail disaster: The carriages of the train as they lay after being hit by the earthquake-induced tsunami of December 26, 2004.

Unimaginable force: The rail line follows the coast between Sri Lanka's capital Colombo in the north and the city of Galle towards the southern tip of the island. The tsunami wave hit the line square on, twisting it out of recognition.

the roof, which he proceeded to do along with many others. Parents were lifting their children up through gaps to outstretched hands. All around him people were screaming and shouting. He was glad not to be hurt.

Up on the roof the pandemonium gradually diminished and people regained their composure. Ravindra and some of his fellow tourists speculated about the "freak wave" that had endangered everyone, and one person took snapshots to show the folks back home.

Looking down from the roof Ravindra saw other parts of the train that appeared to be have been spared from the disaster: many passengers were still waiting patiently for the repair crews to come so they could continue on their way. At first, Ravindra and his acquaintances up on the rooftop thought they had been the unlucky ones, whereas the ones in the other untouched cars had gotten off dry and unruffled. The roof of the train was crowded with frightened children who were hugging the adults for protection.

"A cliff face of water"

A half hour had passed since the flooding without any rescue assistance and some travelers were becoming frustrated. Then, as Ravindra and his newfound friends were basking in the bright sunshine and starting to think about finding some shade, he first began to notice that colors were fading and the daylight was dimming; everything was suddenly and oddly turning gray and dark. He also noticed that the water level was receding fast, as if by magic. Turning toward the sun, he found the sky

> **❝I just saw this wall of water coming towards us and then the screaming and the shouting.❞**
>
> Shenth Ravindra

Last resting place: The train had stopped at signals in the village of Telwatta, 15 miles (24 km) from Colombo, when the tsunami picked it up "like a toy train."

cars. Then it all disappeared beneath the choppy surface and he knew that hundreds of trapped passengers had been drowned.

Ravindra couldn't tell how long his crumbling house would last. The water was tearing its foundation and an uprooted coconut tree had severed the roof, leaving them and several other stranded victims holding on in terror. But luckily, it endured.

Bodies everywhere

Even after the force of the water eased a bit, many still feared another wave would come and end their lives. All around them the raging currents carried the tumbling bodies of women, children, men and animals along with household goods and cars.

Hours later Ravindra was wading among the bodies, trying to reach dry land.

After making his way to the British Embassy, he called home to let his mother know that he had survived with a cut on his leg. He was one of the few survivors of one of the greatest rail disasters in history, a victim of the great Asian Tsunami that had taken more than 230,000 lives in a dozen countries in the deadliest natural disaster of modern times.

blocked by a giant cliff face of water that took up about 85 percent of the horizon. He heard the roar. The massive tsunami was charging toward them, devouring houses and trees in its path.

As Ravindra stood paralyzed with fear, several children started clinging to his legs and hugging him tight, nearly causing him to topple over.

The rushing water pushed the train car along like a water toy without tipping it over, so when the swirling torrent pinned their bobbing carriage against a tall house, Ravindra weighed his chances. Just as he jumped with one of the children onto the house roof for better protection, the train spun around in the maelstrom, revealing a large woman in a pink sari trapped inside one of the

The saddest epitaph: Brigadier Daya Ratnayake of the Sri Lankan army reported that 802 bodies were recovered from the train. Of those, 204 remained unclaimed and were buried in a mass grave.

Moments after devastation: This is the satellite view on December 26, 2004, just after the tsunami has inundated the coastal stretch between Colombo and Galle and the flood waters are sucked back out to sea.

Six days later: Matching up is the view taken on January 1, 2005, which shows the same stretch of coastline. With the flood water receded, the rail track and its proximity to the coast becomes very clear.

Force of the killer wave

The catastrophe of December 26, 2004 began with radical shakeups of the Earth's crust beneath the Indian Ocean. The earthquake's epicenter was 155 miles (249.4 km) from the west end of the Indonesian island of Sumatra, but it tore a rupture about 745 miles (1,199 km) long, shoving the continental plate out over the oceanic plate by about 30 to 70 feet (9–21 m) with incredible force that sent shock waves for hundreds of miles across the globe. The earthquake continued for about four minutes and measured a magnitude of 9.3 on the Richter scale, making it the second most violent earthquake ever measured on a seismograph.

Because the quake was so shallow — only about 19 miles (30.5 km) deep — it released as much energy as 23,000 Hiroshima-sized bombs, initiating a tsunami, or giant wave, that raced toward Sumatra at 500 miles per hour (805 kph). As it approached land, the wave slowed to 400, 300 and 200 miles an hour (644, 483 and 322 kph), but the back of the wave was still moving at 500 miles an hour (805 kph), so the back eventually caught up with the front to cause a bigger buildup of water.

In some locations the killer wave rose to 100 feet (30 m). Most victims were caught entirely by surprise, giving many little chance of escape.

Satellite images show the great tsunami striking Galle, Sri Lanka on December 26 — but they cannot convey the horrors posed for those at sea level. These images (see above) show the size and turbulence of the killer wave looking like a hurricane on a weather map.

Shark attack!

VIC CALANDRA & JOEY EVERETT | July 22, 2007

While racing paddleboards off Malibu, Vic Calandra and Joey Everett were confronted by a determined great white shark. And they only had their paddles and fists to defend themselves.

Sunday morning started as a great day to be paddleboarding in the ocean off Malibu. The sky was slightly overcast, there was little or no wind, and the waves were running in small, gentle swells that seemed to offer ideal conditions for the 10-mile (16 km) Tommy Zahn Paddleboard Race.

At age 47, Vic Calandra was holding his own, staying in third place among 20-plus contestants and moving along the surface at a good clip. His nearest competitor was about 300 yards (274 m) away. Having just gone around Point Dume, he was headed straight for Surfrider and had almost reached the incline where Malibu Road starts, putting him about a mile and a quarter (2 km) or so off Corral Beach.

As he stood on his 18-foot (5.5 m) paddleboard, using his oar to propel the heavy board, he heard something cutting through the water behind him. Thinking it might be a dolphin, he turned to look and saw something riding in his wake, about 90 feet (27.4 m) away. To his surprise the fin kept rising out of the water until it was fully 18 to 24 inches (46–61 cm) high and headed right for him. As it approached to within 10 feet (3 m), he began to make out its form through the waves and realized it was a large shark.

Great white shark

Although Calandra was an experienced surfer and paddle boarder, he had never encountered anything like this before and the terror immediately unleashed a tremendous surge of adrenalin, prompting him to act instinctively. As the huge shark brushed against his paddleboard, almost knocking him into the water, Calandra immediately started wielding the side of his paddle to slap at it with as much force as he could muster just as it was turning on its side beneath him.

It was a great white shark, swimming less than two feet (60 cm) below, and as it passed by he shuddered to think that it was only a few feet shorter than his board; the creature's enormous girth extended to about 3.5 feet (1 m) on each side of the dorsal fin. Such size would make it a young great white — one that was just old enough to be acquiring a taste for mammals.

The monster kept coming back at him, acting very agitated and aggressive. Each time it returned, the lonely paddler tried to maneuver his board to avoid being struck and he swung his paddle at the killer shark, smacking the water to try to scare him away. Each time the shark

Jaws: Though great white sharks can launch themselves in surprise attacks, they don't like to break their teeth, often adopting a strategy of "bump and bite" where the victim is evaluated first.

grazed his board, it bumped and tilted Calandra's perch so that he sometimes had to crouch and hold on to avoid being capsized.

Warning others

After this interplay had gone on for several minutes, Calandra noticed three other racers approaching and he shouted loud enough for them to hear, "Shark! Shark!"

The first paddler to detect his cries of distress was Joey Everett, who also happened to be a Los Angeles County firefighter and lifeguard. He responded as a professional, trying to quickly assess the emergency situation. Based on his training, the intrepid lifesaver believed that the best way to deal with an aggressive shark was to act aggressively in response. Everett also knew that white sharks have sensors called ampullae in their snouts and jaws, which they use to hone in on vibrations; moreover these ampullae receptors are very sensitive and therefore constitute a vulnerable spot.

Punching his snout

Everett paddled close and aimed the tip of his board directly at the shark's head. Then, incredibly, he started punching its snout with his fists, trying to divert the ferocious animal.

Calandra was also flailing away with his paddle and screaming at the beast in hopes of scaring it away. Each time the shark banged against Calandra's board, the beleaguered paddler had to gyrate like a circus performer struggling to keep his balance.

Shark tales: The much-relieved Joey Everett (left) and Vic Calandra (right) posing with the paddleboards they were piloting during their encounter with a great white shark.

> **❝ It came up and brushed the back of my board, then came up on the side of me and showed its underbelly. ❞**
>
> Vic Calandra

In order to form a more perfect union, the men positioned their boards close together so each could look in a different direction, guarding against a future sneak attack. Great whites had been known to leap out of the water.

The pair's aggression seemed to be working as the shark retreated. When the two men saw a fishing boat about 200 yards (183 m) away, Everett paddled to it and climbed aboard, calling an end to his racing for the day. As he was radioing Baywatch to ask for assistance, Calandra remained on his board to warn the other racers and continue.

Soon lifeguards on jet skis were crisscrossing the area to warn away the other racers. Calandra ended up taking fourth place and emerged from the water shaking but still in one piece.

In the grip of the "Savage Mountain"

WILCO VAN ROOIJEN | **August 2008**

When Dutch climber Wilco van Rooijen led his expedition team to the forbidding summit of K2 he was elated. His triumph was short-lived, though. A treacherous descent into whiteout conditions left van Rooijen stranded at 26,250 feet (8,001 m), with only enough oxygen to last him 24 hours.

Making it to the top

In late July 2008, when weather conditions appeared to be just right, 17 climbers from eight different countries, including some of the world's most serious mountaineers, set out in three separate expeditions toward the 28,251-foot (8,611 m) peak of K2.

The team that had made the most progress was part of the Norit K2 Expedition organized by Jasmine Tours. Its members included oil-company executive Gerard McDonnell of Ireland, Gyalje Sherpa of Pakistan, Cas van de Gevel of Holland, and his countryman, the team leader Wilco van Rooijen. The 40-year-old van Rooijen was an accomplished climber, having scaled Everest and attempted K2 on two occasions. On Friday, August 1, he had succeeded in leading them to the summit with clear skies and a new moon overhead. He was in good spirits, having achieved the first part of his goal. Now all he had to do was get down.

From triumph to nightmare

However, it was already 7 p.m. — much too late in the evening, and darkness and whiteouts hindered their progress down the slope. As a result, they couldn't find C4 (the highest camp), where they had planned to spend the night. They were lost.

Tougher than Everest: A climbing expedition makes camp in the foothills of Pakistan while the ultimate goal of K2 lies beyond them.

K2 — "the holy grail of mountains"

It looks like a giant rock salt crystal covered with snow, rising to a height of 28,251 feet (8,611 m). K2 is the second highest elevation on Earth. The pyramid-shaped mountain, located on the border between Pakistan's northern territories and Xinjiang, China, is named K2 because it is the second peak of the Karakoram Range of the Himalayas.

Known for its steep rock slopes that are absolutely treacherous to climb from all approaches, and weather that is unpredictable and often unrelenting, climbers call it the "Savage Mountain" because it is much more difficult to ascend than even Mount Everest. It kills, on average, one in every four climbers who try to reach its forbidding summit. As of August 2008, only 299 people had reached the top, compared with about 2,600 individuals who had conquered Everest. K2, which many regard as "the holy grail of mountains," has claimed at least 77 lives.

The mountain's severe weather conditions have typically limited any climbing attempts to a window in June, July or August, with a targeted ascent based on weather forecasts. But conditions can change in a flash. In 1902 the first climbing expedition spent 68 days on the mountain, only eight of them clear days.

Avalanche: An avalanche crashes through the Savoia Pass on the northwest side of K2 — van Rooijen's climbing group were struck in darkness with devastating consequences.

each other in the dense mists and clouds shrouding the mountain. He had radio contact with his climbing partners in the nearest camp (C4), but he still couldn't find it.

Van Rooijen learned he was on the wrong side of the mountain. People at base camp had seen him go over the wrong side of the ridge and they radioed climbers in C4. But he had to sit out a whiteout because he couldn't see anything and he knew he couldn't go down any further. So he waited for a few hours until he could see better through an opening in the clouds.

Finding that they were stranded, a few of the climbers from the other parties panicked. People were scattering. Some of the climbers ran blindly down the slope without knowing where they were. Although van Rooijen screamed at them to work together, some of the others resorted to an every-person-for-him- or herself response, even trying to take away van Rooijen's gas and rope. Some fell down the gorge to their deaths.

Van Rooijen tried to head down the slope with caution. The saddest scene that he witnessed involved three exhausted South Korean climbers who had elected to remain there to await rescue. One sat dazed in the snow while another held a rope from which the third man was suspended at the other end, hanging upside down. All three were just trying to survive in the frigid, oxygen-starved air. But they were too high up to be rescued. Helicopters were not designed to fly at such a high altitude and the whiteout conditions would have made it even more dangerous; and besides, the mountainous terrain would not allow any chopper to land successfully.

Making matters much worse, that night a giant serac (a sheaf of ice), hundreds of feet long and wide and weighing thousands of pounds, broke off from the rock face and plummeted down the slope, crushing at least three climbers and throwing the others into a frenzy. The collapse also severed the fixed ropes used mostly for descending the near-vertical portions of slopes called The Bottleneck, thereby leaving van Rooijen and his party as well as several others cut off at an oxygen-thin elevation known as the "Dead Zone."

At that height their ability to survive without additional oxygen was extremely limited and now that they were trapped above the gorge without their security ropes and needing supplies, the prospects of escape looked bleak indeed. Overnight, van Rooijen's historic triumph had turned to a nightmare.

> **" People were running down but didn't know where to go, so a lot of people were lost on the mountain. "**
>
> Wilco van Rooijen

Chaos

After a sleepless night without food or water, van Rooijen and his party began descending, but they lost track of

Safe: Experienced Italian climber Marco Confortola was the last man to be rescued from K2 alive. He had to hobble down to base camp on blackened, frost-bitten feet.

hopeful that when the clouds disappeared he could reach the easier slopes. And he did. He had gone a long time without eating or drinking. His tongue and lips were blistered; it was like hell. He was drinking snow. There was only one focus: going down. Often he thought he saw another climber and thought he heard voices, but he knew there couldn't be anyone there. It was a scary moment when he realized he was reaching his limits. He kept thinking, no one knows where I am and they will not be coming back.

Rescue

Finally, snow-blinded and nearly delirious, without knowing where he was, he crawled into C3 at an altitude of 23,950 feet (7,300 m), and rescuers started giving him oxygen and melted snow to drink. On Monday, after three days and three nights on the peak, the rescuers took him down to the base camp at an altitude of 17,060 feet (5,200 m), where he and the other Dutchman (Cas van de Gevel) were removed by Pakistani army helicopter to the hospital.

Their Italian team member, Marco Confortola, was also later brought down by rescuers. He was suffering from extreme frostbite and other injuries. McDonnell the Irishman was dead.

When the final count was made, 11 men — three South Koreans, two Nepalis and two Pakistanis, a Serbian, an Irishman, a Norwegian and a Frenchman — were officially confirmed dead, making it the worst accident in more than 20 years on the giant peak. Once again, escape from the Savage Mountain had not come easily.

Sadly, Van Rooijen had to leave the doomed Koreans behind.

Down below, some mountaineers were scanning the cloud-shrouded peak and GPS readings for clues to what was happening. They were also trying to exchange messages via radio and satellite telephone, but time was quickly running out.

Once a climber reached 26,250 feet (8,000 m), the chances were that he or she could not survive for more than 24 to 48 hours without supplementary oxygen. And Rooijen had been up there for too long without it.

Then, through the clouds, he saw an easier slope. To reach it he had to employ all of his strength and skill without using a rope, and for a long time he was pingponging between hope and failure. Finally, he was

Expedition leader: After his ordeal Wilco van Rooijen shows journalists in Islamabad some of the promotional material published for the expedition.

Racing the volcano

RAY BUCHHEIT & CHRIS FORD | **August 7, 2008**

In August 2008 two federal biologists were undertaking a field trip to the remote Alaskan island of Kasatochi when they started to feel tremors. One of the Pacific's "Ring of Fire" volcanoes, Kasatochi had lain dormant for over a century, until that moment.

In May of 2008 two federal biologists from the Alaska Maritime National Wildlife Refuge, Ray Buchheit and Chris Ford, unloaded their supplies from their agency's 120-foot (36.6 m) vessel, M/V *Tiglax*, and stepped onto one of the greatest bird sanctuaries in that part of the world. Located in the central Aleutians, 1,100 miles (1,770 km) southwest of Anchorage, Kasatochi Island was a wonder in its own right, with 700 lush green acres and a magnificent blue lake in a deep caldera at the island's center.

But what attracted them seemed even more enticing; the island served as a refuge for 100,000 chattering, flitting and flying auklets, stormy petrels and puffins, making it a paradise for bird study.

The two were scheduled to live among the seabirds in a sturdy trapper's cabin that had been built in the 1920s. They would be the island's only human inhabitants, with their nearest colleague 50 miles (80 km) away. As other biologists before them had done for the last 13 years, the plan was for them to remain on site until late August, a span of nearly four idyllic months, when the support vessel would return to pick them up.

The place seemed so peaceful they almost forgot

Kasatochi Island: A support boat from the Alaska Maritime National Wildlife Refuge vessel M/V *Tiglax* delivers scientists to Kasatochi Island in the Aleutian chain.

what it was and how it had been formed: Kasatochi represented the summit of a predominantly submarine volcano. Although it had not erupted in modern times, it was still part of the Pacific's "Ring of Fire" volcanoes.

More specifically, it was a "strato"-type, so called because it was formed with one layer on top of another layer on top of another layer and so on; a kind that didn't leak out a lot of lava. Some volcano watchers liked to say that when a strato finally awoke, it could explode.

Volcanic activity

Volcanoes turned out to become more of a concern in the Aleutians that summer of 2008. On July 12 Okmok Caldera Volcano had begun erupting unexpectedly and explosively, followed nine days later by the eruption of Mt. Cleveland Volcano, just 100 miles (161 km) away. Each eruption had sent ash plumes skyrocketing and caused commercial airline flights to be diverted or cancelled as far away as Anchorage and Seattle. Their activity was visible from outer space.

None of the vulcanologists, however, ever suspected that little and long-dormant Kasatochi was apt to cause a problem like the others. So when the two bird watchers felt the island quiver and shake, they initially chalked it up to normal island activity.

Following days of more serious tremors, however, they

Crater edge: The verdant edge of Kasatochi's huge caldera prior to the explosion in 2008. The many ledges and slopes were a haven for seabirds such as auklets, puffins and stormy petrels.

Monitoring the situation: Alaskan scientists record the horizon-blackening effect of the Okmok eruption on July 13, 2008. The explosion sent plumes of ash over six miles (10 km) into the sky. Dutch Harbor, a settlement 65 miles (104 km) away, experienced a light ash fall.

> **Kasatochi went from a quiet volcano to an explosive eruption within 24 hours and with very little warning.**
>
> AVO scientist Marianne Guffanti

began to grow more anxious. Knowing that other scientists were working around the clock to monitor the volcanoes and keep the public and emergency responders informed, on August 5, Buchheit and Ford radioed their concerns to their nearest colleague, Lisa Spitler, who was stationed on Adak Island 50 miles (80.4 km) away.

Spitler in turn checked the Alaska Volcano Observatory (AVO) monitoring website, but saw no indication posted of any trouble brewing. Just to be sure, she called the AVO to hear that Kasatochi was considered "dormant" with no historically recorded eruptions. However, she then learned that the AVO had no monitoring instruments on Kasatochi, so she realized that no one truly knew what was going on. Meanwhile, word from her two worried colleagues was that the tremors were getting stronger.

AVO scientists discovered that the existing seismic networks on other nearby volcanoes were picking up activity at Kasatochi, indicating that it appeared to have entered the first stage of a major eruption. By August 6, everyone concurred that the island should be evacuated. Spitler began to arrange it.

How to escape?

Spitler found this was easier said than done. The M/V *Tiglax* was 24 hours away. So was the nearest Coast Guard ship. And there were no fishing boats in the area. The Coast Guard helicopter had become disabled and wouldn't be available for at least another day. Eventually, a local fisherman, Al Giddings, agreed to sail at dawn from Adak in his 32-foot (9.8 m) boat, *Homeward Bound*, to retrieve the stranded men.

But as August 7 dawned on Kasatochi, the two bleary-eyed biologists reported the island was experiencing increasing tremors and they had become aware of a strong sulfur smell, which vulcanologists warned was a sign of imminent volcanic activity. By 10 a.m. a nine-minute earthquake and falling rocks convinced Buchheit and Ford to retreat to the beach, hoping that their vessel would arrive before it was too late.

Surveying the sea they could tell that the surf was too rough for them to try to use their own tiny launch to reach the nearest island, 20 miles (32 km) away. Besides, they needed to meet up with their rescuer who was already on the way. But they couldn't reach him by radio.

Finally, his voice came on to say he was seven miles (11.3 km) away and heading there fast. At last he arrived and the two scientists hurried to climb aboard the aptly named *Homeward Bound*, leaving all of their gear and computers behind in their rush to make it away before it was too late.

Two hours later, as the boat rode over the waves, they heard a loud explosion and saw a gigantic mushroom cloud rising 35,000 feet (10,668 m) into the sky.

Kasatochi had awakened. "If they had been there, they certainly could have died," said Stephanie Prejean, U.S. Geological Survey seismologist with the AVO.

Return to Kasatochi

Two weeks after their escape, Buchheit returned to Kasatochi by helicopter with a team of scientists. He couldn't believe his eyes. What had been a verdant island pulsating with animal life had changed to a barren landscape covered in a uniform shade of gray. All of the birds were gone. Hundreds of yards of new coastline had appeared. And the refuge cabin had disappeared, buried under 100 feet (30.5 m) of ash.

Hoping to walk closer to find it, he found the ground too hot. All greenery and animal life had disappeared except for a few sea lion pups. The sky was overcast and the frantic clamor of seabird colonies was replaced with the lone sound of the waves roaring and crashing on the empty beach.

White water nightmare

DAVID WILSON | **September 2008**

A weekend away with friends kayaking in the Kiewa River in southeast Australia turned into more than a thrilling adventure for father-of-two, David Wilson. Trapped underwater in the cold rapids, he was forced to make a snap decision to save his life.

In southeast Australia the Kiewa River's long, violent rapids, steep drops and swirling currents made it a popular destination for experienced white-water kayakers and rafters. But it was not a spot to be taken lightly. Just getting to and from its raging waters could be arduous, as it required a six-mile (9.7 km) hike through dense bush with gear.

Yet for David Wilson, a 38-year-old auto worker and married father of two, the excitement was worth it. Kayaking the Kiewa was one of his favorite pastimes. He had paddled it several times before and now he was glad to be back.

The previous day he and his friends had paddled the even more hazardous East Kiewa River, and now the four veteran outdoorsmen were off to enjoy a fun-filled Sunday on the West Kiewa with all of its rugged beauty and treacherous rapids. Experience had taught them to exercise due caution and before entering the water they walked along the shore of each stretch in order to scout its potential hazards and high points.

The sharp bend

The group got underway, and everything was going well. By about 3 p.m. they were near Mount Beauty and entering the last 20 minutes of the course. One man after the other approached a sharp bend in the river that would require the paddler to shoot the rapids into an area he could not see in advance — a thrilling blind spot that added to the challenge — yet one that they had navigated before and headed into a relatively straightforward rapid. One after the other, the three paddlers disappeared around the bend.

Wilson was in fourth position, trailing the others through the racing currents and spray. As he turned the corner, however, the river surprised him as two-thirds of the course was blocked by a large tree, three feet (0.9 m) thick, that had fallen into the water and lodged there at an angle. His friends had safely made it around, but Wilson's speed and angle made it too difficult for him to try.

White-water kayaking is full of split-second decisions and Wilson knew what to do. He certainly didn't want to hit the log head-on and didn't have time to completely avoid contact, so he tried to drop in beside the obstruction and slide along it until he was free and clear.

Trapped

But the raging current did not cooperate. The force of the

Rapid reaction: Experienced kayaker David Wilson in action on the Kiewa River in Victoria, Australia.

water immediately flipped him over and pinned him to the bottom of the river with the water surging over him from behind, forcing his chest onto the kayak's front deck. With a huge effort he pushed up and was able to make a small air pocket but he could not sustain it. Although he immediately tried to break free, he could feel he was stuck. Wilson knew there was no hope of any rescue; he would have to free himself, or drown in the ice-cold water.

He popped the spraydeck, flooding the boat, and made a big push against the water to get his legs backwards and out of the kayak. Once he started to come up and out of the kayak the water pushed him forward and up, trapping his shins against the cockpit rim and wedging his feet on the bottom of the boat.

Kayaks are designed so the legs are held extended under the cockpit of a boat. If they become trapped, it is impossible to free them. His knee was acting as the jamming agent.

Snapping his leg

As soon as it became clear that he was not coming out, Wilson thought to himself, "This is probably where it ends." The avalanche of water was ending his life. He couldn't hold his breath much longer. Quickly, he figured he had only one option left. The only thing he could do was push his upper body up to get the maximum force of water against it and exert leverage on his legs, hoping that they would break. Only by breaking one or both knees might his legs come loose, enabling him to roll out of the boat. All he could do was try to use the huge force of the water to his advantage.

Wilson levered himself partly out of the submerged kayak against the cascading water pounding against his body in a furious attempt to deliberately break his leg against the rim of the kayak. After much strenuous exertion, he felt his leg crunch as it bent the wrong way and he rolled forward out of the boat, into the swirling water.

His twisted body bobbed like a rag doll through the rapids. Finally, he came to the surface, gasping for air, and swam to an eddy at the end of the log, to await help from his friends.

Rescue

The others came to his aid and pulled him to shore, but that would not be the end of his ordeal. Nightfall was near and the paddlers were six miles (9.7 km) into the bush. The air was cold and Wilson was in pain.

Two of his companions hiked back to get help while the third, a physician, stayed behind to tend to his injuries. It would take his buddies more than two hours to contact emergency services, but due to the darkness and the terrain, a rescue would have to be put off until dawn. In the meantime, a local constable and emergency services volunteer hiked back into the bush to administer treatment.

In the morning a helicopter arrived and carried him to the hospital, just before a storm set in.

Wilson's wife was relieved to learn her husband was safe. "I must admit he was incredibly magnificent under intense pressure." As for him continuing with the sport, she said she had no concerns. "I'd hate to see him stop doing something he loves so much," she said. After the surgery, he was good as new.

> ❝ I must admit he was incredibly magnificent under intense pressure. ❞
>
> David Wilson's wife

Experience essential: The West Kiewa River in spate provides a wide variety of challenges for the experienced kayaker. And it almost provided one too many for David Wilson.

2
Kidnappers

Rescue from Entebbe

An Air France flight from Tel Aviv to Paris became the focus of media attention when it was hijacked by armed terrorists. A week-long stand-off ensued, but while negotiators were buying time with the hijackers, planeloads of Israeli commandos were on their way to Entebbe.

At 12:30 p.m. on June 27, 1976, Air France Flight 139, an Airbus A300 originating from Tel Aviv and bound for Paris, took off from Athens. The plane was carrying a crew of 12 and 238 passengers from several countries, many of them Jewish tourists traveling from Israel.

Everything seemed normal until about an hour into the flight, when a commotion broke out as four tense-looking passengers started moving about the aisles and cockpit waving guns. "This is the Che Guevara Brigade of the Popular Front for the Liberation of Palestine," one of them announced. "I am your new commandant. This

Some are safe: Fourteen French hostages and 12 crew members of the Air France jet arrive in Paris after they were released early by the Entebbe hijackers.

plane is renamed 'Haifa.' You are our prisoners."

Memories of the Munich massacre four years earlier added to the terror as everyone realized they had become pawns in a life-or-death international political drama.

The hijackers' apparent leader was an intense blonde man in his mid-20s who was accompanied by a young woman wearing blue jeans. Both were German radicals, suggesting that they might be from the infamous Baader-Meinhof Gang. Two young Arab men followed their lead. They all appeared to be well trained and no one referred to another accomplice by name, using numbers instead.

The hijackers kept their terrified prisoners in line with terse instructions and threats that they occasionally laced with political statements. The most talkative one — the German man — told them a French aircraft had been targeted because "France is the foremost enemy of the Arabs," and it had sold Mirage fighters and nuclear technology to Israel. He also proclaimed that the Popular Front was part of a worldwide revolutionary movement aimed against the United States, Japan, France and West Germany.

Media briefing: Major Dan Shomron, commander of the Israeli raid at Entebbe, briefs the press about the mission that killed 45 Ugandans and all seven hijackers.

Libya to Uganda

As the passengers quaked in their seats, wondering what would happen next, the plane landed in Benghazi, Libya, where it was refueled as the hostage-takers engaged in secret communications. As everyone waited, a female hostage, who claimed to be pregnant and having a miscarriage, was allowed to leave and she was escorted away.

After seven uncomfortable hours on the ground in Benghazi, the plane took off again and flew to another location, which turned out to be Entebbe Airport in

Real-life drama: Released the same year, the movie *Victory at Entebbe* recreated the drama of the long-distance raid. Anthony Hopkins starred as Yitzhak Rabin with Burt Lancaster as Shimon Peres. The hero of the raid, Yonatan Netanyahu, was played by Richard Dreyfuss.

Uganda, where the passengers and crew were herded into a dingy transit terminal, directly adjacent to the runway. Four more armed terrorists joined the hijackers.

It appeared the hostage-takers had a whole state complete with its armed forces standing behind them.

Uganda was known to be under the iron grip of President Idi Amin, who was lately attracting notice as one of the world's worst despots and a murderer in his own right, and who was, along with his friend and fellow strongman, Muammar al-Gaddafi of Libya, an outspoken foe of Israel.

Soon it became apparent that Amin himself was helping the hijackers, allowing them to keep the hostages in his military airfield terminal. The jovial dictator visited the hostages on a number of occasions, acting very jolly

> **❝ I am your new commandant. This plane is renamed 'Haifa.' You are our prisoners. ❞**
>
> Hijacker's announcement

and telling them he had been appointed by God and was their friend. Their release, he said, would depend on the Israeli government's ability to be reasonable and release 53 imprisoned Palestinian "freedom fighters." Each time he left them, Amin said, "Shalom."

Jews to the left

Panic spread when the hijackers proceeded to sort their hostages into two groups — Jews and Gentiles — stirring thoughts of what the Nazis had done in the Holocaust. A defiant older passenger responded by pulling back his sleeve, exposing a concentration camp registration number tattooed on his arm — to which the German terrorist responded, "I'm no Nazi! . . . I am an idealist." But the hostages' fears only deepened.

As the ordeal continued, Michel Cojot, a 38-year-old

French Jew whose father had been murdered in Auschwitz, emerged as a translator and spokesman for the passengers, and he attempted to reason with the leader. In one exchange, after the German ringleader had railed against colonialism and fascism, Cojot gently wondered if his captor wasn't being a bit hypocritical; after all, wasn't he a European from a country with a long history of colonialism who seemed to be ordering around Arabs, and weren't there here some parallels to how the Nazis had treated the Jews? But again the German insisted, "We are behaving in a humane manner. We are being very correct with you."

When the hijackers announced that the airline crew and non-Jewish passengers would be released and put on another Air France plane that had been brought to Entebbe for that purpose, the French flight captain, Michel Bacos, told the hijackers that all passengers, including the remaining ones, were his responsibility and he refused to leave them behind. Bacos's entire crew followed suit. A French nun also refused to leave, offering to take the place of one of the remaining hostages, but Ugandan soldiers forced her onto the other Air France plane. The soldiers also removed an elderly Jewish passenger, Dora Bloch, who had fallen ill, saying she would be brought to the hospital.

When all was said and done, 105 Israelis and French Jews, along with the crew, remained captive at the airport. The hijackers said if their demands weren't met, at 14:00 hours on July 1 they would begin killing hostages.

Although the deadline passed without incident, apparently due to ongoing negotiations involving the Israeli government, many of the hostages wondered how long they could hold out. Their ordeal had gone on for a full week but it seemed an eternity.

"Get down!"

Soon they got their answer. At about 11:30 p.m. on the night of July 3, most of the hostages were asleep on the terminal floor. A few of them were sitting up, playing card games or daydreaming. Suddenly they saw flashes outside the window and heard shooting.

Hostage Arye Brodsky threw himself on his six-year-old and 10-year-old daughters and held his wife's head down to protect her from harm.

A stranger burst into the terminal shouting in Hebrew and English through a megaphone, "Stay down! Stay down! We are Israeli soldiers."

In the chaos a 19-year-old French Jewish hostage, Jean-Jacques Maimoni, stood up and was riddled with bullets. Another hostage, Pasco Cohen, 52, manager of an Israeli medical insurance fund, was also fatally wounded by gunfire and 56-year-old Ida Borochovitch, a Russian Jew who had emigrated to Israel, was also shot to death. (All apparently died from friendly fire.)

An Israeli commando called out in Hebrew, apparently referring to the hijackers, "Where are the rest of them?" A few seconds earlier, three or four of the terrorists had been sitting just outside the main door, talking with some Ugandans, so some of the hostages pointed there and the commandos immediately threw several hand grenades in that direction. Instantly after the explosions they entered the room and shot dead the three remaining hijackers.

"You are going home"

"It is OK now," one of the commandos barked. "Get ready to move to the door. You are going home."

Only the Ugandans were shooting back. But they were no match for the elite Israeli soldiers.

Many of the hostages were only partially dressed and not wearing any shoes. But the Israeli soldiers began

The wrong Mercedes: Israeli special forces shipped in a stretched Mercedes similar to the one used by Idi Amin to create the impression of a government delegation and allow them to get close to the terminal building. However, in the weeks before the raid, Amin had switched his Mercedes from a black car to a white car.

ushering them into the darkness, toward a Hercules C-130 troop transport plane that was starting up its engines, as other commandos ringed the tarmac.

In the exchange of gunfire between the Israelis and Ugandan soldiers, a sniper positioned in the control tower fatally wounded the Israeli commander, Yonatan Netanyahu. Five Israeli commandos were also wounded, and one of them would remain paralyzed for life.

An officer counted heads as the hostages boarded the air transport. Of the 105 hostages, only three were dead and 10 more were wounded.

All of the hostage-takers and 45 Ugandans lay dead. The Israelis had also destroyed 11 MiG-17 fighter planes that were parked at the airport in order to prevent the Ugandans from later using them to mount a counterattack.

Joyous homecoming: Foreign minister Yigal Allon, with his back to camera, greets the hostages as they disembark from an Israeli Airforce C-135 transport aircraft at Ben Gurion airport, Tel Aviv. To the left is the captain of the Air France airbus.

Aftermath

The entire assault lasted for less than half an hour. The rescued hostages were flown via Nairobi to Tel Aviv, where an excited crowd welcomed them back with shrieks of joy. People flung their arms around each other, and swayed in weeping embraces. Israel was seen to have scored an electrifying victory.

But the raid had other negative consequences too. Dora Bloch, the 75-year-old hostage who had been taken away to the hospital, was later found to have been murdered by two Ugandan Army officers, who had also killed some of her doctors and nurses for trying to intervene.

The incident created an international uproar, with a few leaders condemning Israel for its response. But most world opinion favored the Israel Defense Forces (IDF) for pulling off the greatest hostage rescue in modern history. Soon the Entebbe raid was the subject of several dramatic books and films, among them *Victory at Entebbe*, starring Anthony Hopkins and Elizabeth Taylor, and *Raid on Entebbe* starring Peter Finch and Horst Buchholz. They too contributed to the legend.

> " It is OK now. Get ready to move to the door. You are going home. "
>
> Israeli commandos to hostages

Hero's welcome: July 4th, 1976. While the rest of the world watches the American bicentennial celebrations, the crowd in Tel Aviv give a hero's welcome to the squadron leader of the rescue planes.

Operation Thunderball

The planning and execution of the Entebbe raid involved many extraordinary tactical and logistical obstacles that were addressed at breakneck speed. And Israel used everything it could to its advantage.

Although Uganda's airport was situated 2,300 miles (3,701.5 km) from Tel Aviv, the terminal was built by Israeli contractors, who later provided the crucial blueprints to aid the commandos. In addition, some of the hostages whom the terrorists had freed also supplied remarkably detailed intelligence about the hijackers and their defenses, the role and positioning of the Ugandans and other key variables.

Israel's bold approach was built on deception — as diplomats professed to be conducting negotiations with the terrorists, the military forces were mounting their surprise assault.

Although several rescue plans were considered, the one selected — "Operation Thunderball" — proposed to transport a large military force with 29 elite commandos and equipment in four airplanes. An initial team would reach the terminal in a Mercedes escorted by two Land Rovers that had been disguised to look like Idi Amin's official entourage. The soldiers would drive to the terminal, confuse and surprise the terrorists and free the hostages. Later, a backup force would arrive to help.

The incoming flight route was plotted over Sharm al-Sheikh and down the international flight path over the Red Sea, flying at a height of no more than 100 feet (30 m) to avoid radar detection by Egyptian, Sudanese and Saudi Arabian forces. Near the south outlet of the Red Sea, the C-130s turned right and headed to a point northeast of Nairobi, then turned west and continued over Lake Victoria. They were followed by two Boeing 707s equipped with medical facilities that were directed to Nairobi's international airport.

Upon arriving in Entebbe, however, the plan hit a snag. It turned out that Amin had recently replaced his black Mercedes with a white one, and two alert Ugandan sentries became suspicious. Before they could sound the alarm, Israeli commandos killed them, thereby forcing the assault team to begin their attack. They carried it out with lightning speed.

Left: The now-derelict control tower at Entebbe airport, with a plaque at its base that commemorates the daring raid.
Above left: A Hercules C-135 plane of the Israeli airforce. **Above right:** The shell of the Air France airbus abandoned at the airport.

Who dares wins — the Iranian Embassy siege

April–May 1980

A six-day siege at the Iranian Embassy in London resulted in the murder of one captive by Iraqi militants and prompted a British SAS squad to unleash a rapid strike on the building. A widely televised hostage rescue operation followed as the world held its breath.

Wednesday, April 30, 1980 started out as just another spring day at the Iranian Embassy in Princes Gate, a highly desirable part of West London looking out across Hyde Park. It was a world away from the situation at the American Embassy in Tehran, where Iranian revolutionaries were into their sixth highly publicized month of holding 52 Americans hostage. Or so it seemed.

Police Constable Trevor Lock of the London Metropolitan police was performing diplomatic protection duty at the building. Just before 11:30 a.m. the uniformed officer was sipping thick Iranian coffee

Failed rescue: The portents for success of the rescue mission weren't good. Just days before the siege in London, President Jimmy Carter had sanctioned an ill-fated raid to try and rescue the hostages taken from the American Embassy in Tehran.

In full view: The London rescue by the SAS (Special Air Service) was made more dramatic in that it was carried out in full view of the world's media. Five SAS men equipped with stun grenades and breathing equipment await their moment to go in.

with the embassy concierge when he saw a young man's face through the door. The man pulled out a machine pistol and started firing. Bits of glass struck Lock in the face, causing him to bleed and fall stunned to the floor.

Within minutes, six revolutionaries of the Democratic Revolutionary Movement for the Liberation of Arabistan (DRMLA), armed with automatic weapons and grenades, had seized the embassy and taken 26 people hostage, including PC Lock. The gunmen were members of an Iraqi-backed, anti-Khomeni organization, the said goal of which was regional autonomy for Arabistan, an oil-rich province in southwest Iran known as Khuzestan. Their leader, Oan, also demanded the release of 91 Arab prisoners in Arabistan.

SAS alerted

Unbeknownst to the terrorists, PC Lock had activated a hidden alarm device on his lapel that alerted the Metropolitan Police. Soon the department's C13 Antiterrorist Squad arrived at the scene, along with

electronic intelligence specialists from C7 (Scotland Yard's Technical Support Branch) and other personnel. Police snipers took up positions around the site. An elite special-forces team was also sent from the 22 Special Air Service Regiment (SAS) headquarters. Within hours the SAS specialists were assembling explosive devices and building a scale model of the embassy.

The terrorists released a female Iranian hostage and a BBC sound technician, both of whom had taken ill. But the British government refused to give in to the terrorists' demands. The previous year Prime Minister Margaret Thatcher had lost her close friend, Airey Neave, as well as Lord Mountbatten and 18 paratroopers — victims of the Irish National Liberation Army, and she did not want to appear as weak as President Jimmy Carter looked in the Tehran hostage crisis.

A tough situation

The London embassy posed a major challenge for any Entebbe-style military rescue. The C7 specialists installed

By day six, the hostage-takers were frustrated by the lack of negotiations and they threatened to kill a hostage if their demands weren't met. The Iranians' young press attaché, Abbas Lavasani, offered himself up as a martyr for the Islamic revolution and he was shot dead. When his lifeless body was dumped out the front door, Prime Minister Thatcher secretly ordered the SAS to intervene and the message was conveyed not to spare any of the hostage-takers.

The assault plan called for two four-man teams to rappel down from the roof while another team would cross from an adjoining balcony. Each SAS man was dressed all in black with hooded suit, body armor, and full-face gas mask, and armed with awesome firepower. To disorient the terrorists they were to use stun grenades and CS gas before killing their prey. Operation Nimrod was about to begin.

Operation Nimrod

Twenty-three minutes after the dead hostage's body was displayed, the assault was begun with the detonation of explosive charges at several locations. The building's electrical power was suddenly cut and special forces commandos began rappelling down from the roof. However, one of the ropes became tangled, leaving Fijian

> **We didn't want them to surrender. We wanted them to stay there so we could go in and hit them.**
>
> Robin Horsfall, SAS commander

Staff Sergeant "Tak" Takavesi stranded precariously outside one of the second-story windows, and this caused a temporary delay with some of the explosives.

Oan had already reacted to sounds of the commandos above, but before he could shoot, PC Lock tackled him and the two men began struggling. To the terrorist's surprise, Lock pulled a handgun he had hidden in his jacket and now held it to Oan's head. "It's your fault, you bastard," Lock said. "You caused all this. I f****ing told you!" Just then a trooper broke into the room and stitched the terrorist leader with bullets from his eye to his chest.

After the fire: The interior of the Iranian Embassy at Princes Gate after the fires had been extinguished and the building made safe.

covert fiber-optic surveillance devices and microphones through adjoining walls and chimneys that enabled them to monitor the movements of terrorists and hostages alike, actually watching them on live video or overhearing their conversations. The police could see that they would require extraordinary planning and execution in order to storm the 50-room complex and kill the terrorists before they carried out a massacre.

News teams had also encircled the embassy and the British news organization ITN was maintaining a viewpoint of the embassy that SAS commanders feared might tip off the terrorists of any impending raid. Oan, the terrorist leader, wanted his demands broadcast on national television and he tried to shape the news that was being reported about the takeover.

Simultaneously, commandos were crashing into other key rooms. One of the terrorists opened fire, killing a hostage and injuring two. But after realizing that they were going to be overpowered, he and his fellow terrorists — Shai and Makki — then threw down their weapons and shouted in Farsi, "We surrender!" diving onto the floor. An instant later a trooper jumped into the room and asked, "Who are the terrorists?" When one of the hostages pointed them out, the trooper lined them up against the wall and shot them dead.

Another terrorist with a grenade was knocked down the stairs and he also died in a hail of bullets; another was killed hiding in a closet.

The only remaining terrorist — Fowzi Nejad — who was guarding the four female hostages threw his weapon down and attempted to hide among his hostages, but he was dragged out of the building in front of the TV cameras. Otherwise he would have been shot as well. He was the only terrorist to survive the assault.

Eleven minutes after it began, the siege was over. All of the hostages but one had escaped death and five of the six gunmen were killed.

Aftermath

The widely televised operation sent a message to terrorists worldwide that Great Britain would not be intimidated by, or tolerate, terrorism perpetrated against its citizens.

Although it was not yet known that Iraq had trained and armed the terrorists to embarrass Iran, the episode was followed four months later by the bloody Iran–Iraq War.

Despite some controversy in Great Britain over some of the killings, a coroner's inquest later cleared the SAS officers of any unlawful conduct. Fowzi Nejad was convicted and sentenced to life imprisonment for his part in the siege. In November 2008 he was released.

Princes Gate went down in history as one of the most successful hostage rescues of the twentieth century.

Hostage: BBC sound recordist Sim Harris (left) and journalist Chris Cramer (right) wrote about their experiences at Princes Gate after the event. Cramer went on to become one of the leading figures in the rise of news broadcaster CNN.

Escaping from "Satan himself"

| **Tracy Edwards** | **July 22, 1991** |

When Tracy Edwards accepted Jeffrey Dahmer's offer of a drink, he thought Dahmer was a "normal, everyday, average person." That soon changed. Drugged, handcuffed and locked in Dahmer's apartment, the chances of Edwards' survival looked slim.

While in high school in Ohio, Jeffrey Dahmer began showing an inordinate interest in dead animals. At age 18 he picked up a hitchhiker and took him home to his father's house for sex; then he bludgeoned the youth to death with a barbell and buried the body in the backyard. Heavy drinking contributed to his dropping out of college and the Army. Eventually he landed work in a chocolate factory.

During the early 1980s, while living with his grandmother in Wisconsin, the troubled Dahmer was

> **His violent compulsions became habitual and his actions more ghoulish. Now he was a serial killer.**

arrested several times on charges of drunk and disorderly conduct and indecent exposure involving young boys. After getting away with sexually assaulting and killing another young man in 1987, his violent compulsions became habitual and his actions turned more and more ghoulish. Now he was a serial killer.

In September 1988, Dahmer was arrested for drugging and sexually fondling a 13-year-old boy in Milwaukee, for which he was sentenced to five years probation and one year in a work-release camp, and

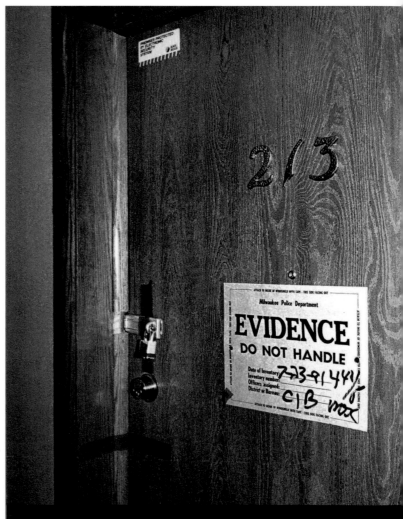

Home of a killer: Dahmer's lair, No. 213, Oxford Apartments. Unlike a normal living space it had multiple locks on the inner doors.

required to register as a sex offender. But he kept committing murders — all of them undetected. By 1990 he had kidnapped, tortured and killed at least 12 young men.

Police don't respond

In the early morning hours of May 30, 1991, Milwaukee police responded to a 911 call from two women who had discovered a naked boy, drugged and wandering in the street. Coincidentally, he was the 14-year-old brother of the youth Dahmer had been convicted of molesting two years earlier.

When police officers took the boy to Dahmer's apartment and asked him about it, Dahmer insisted the youth was his 19-year-old boyfriend and they had been drinking and having a lovers' spat.

The homophobic cops failed to conduct a background check; nor did they investigate the strange odor they smelled coming from Dahmer's apartment, which would have led them to the decomposing body of an earlier victim. Instead, they laughed over the police radio about reuniting the gay "lovers," and left the terrified victim in Dahmer's hands.

Shortly after the police officers had gone, Dahmer dismembered the youngster and saved his skull as a souvenir.

Following this police blunder, Dahmer went on to torture and kill four more young males.

"I'll eat your heart"

On July 22, 1991 Dahmer lured another man into his apartment to drink beer. Tracy Edwards, 31, was new in

Suburban horror story: The Oxford Apartments at 924 N. 25th Street, Milwaukee, pictured in July 1991. Following the grisly revelations of the case, the entire block was demolished in 1992.

town but he recognized Dahmer from his brother's neighborhood and thought him just another "normal, everyday, average person." Dahmer seemed to have a

girlfriend and appeared to be someone he might like to know. He agreed to stop by Dahmer's place.

Upon arriving at the apartment building, Edwards immediately noticed a foul smell, which Dahmer casually attributed to "sewer problems." Edwards suggested, "Let's grab a beer and get out of here."

After the pair went inside apartment 213 and Dahmer locked the door, his guest found the stench almost overpowering; yet at first he didn't notice anything odd about the living quarters.

They began to talk and Dahmer gave him a drink, which Edwards later realized had been spiked. However, it didn't immobilize him and he only pretended to be drunk, hoping to gain some trust from his bigger and stronger captor. As the hours passed, Edwards witnessed his once-charming host transform himself from Mr. Right to Satan himself.

Dahmer chanted as the two watched a video of *The Exorcist* and then he laid his head on Edwards' chest to listen to his heartbeat, saying he was going to eat his heart. As the two men struggled, Dahmer snapped one of his guest's wrists into a pair of handcuffs but he wasn't yet able to secure the other hand.

Wielding a large butcher knife, he made his victim look into his

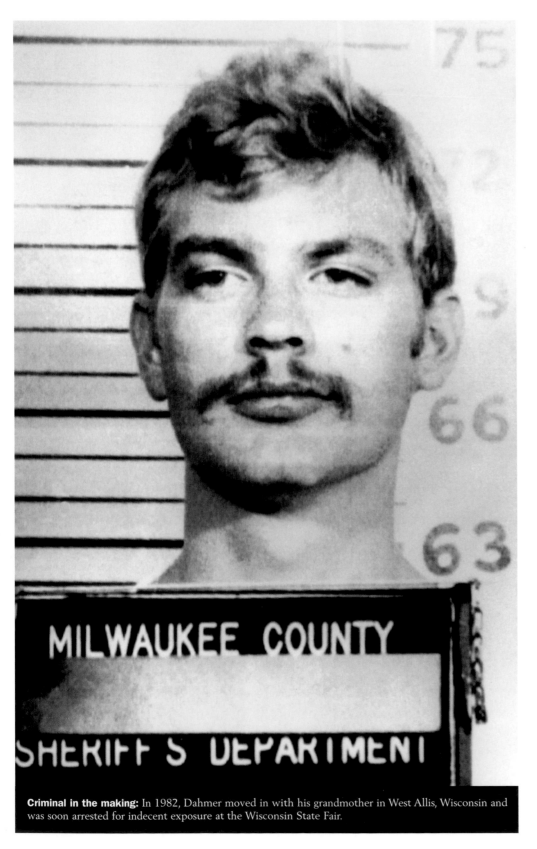

Criminal in the making: In 1982, Dahmer moved in with his grandmother in West Allis, Wisconsin and was soon arrested for indecent exposure at the Wisconsin State Fair.

Prosecution: Brought to trial in January 1992, Dahmer's plea of insanity was rejected by the court. Such was the public revulsion at his crimes that the courtroom had to be searched for explosives by sniffer dogs for fear that Dahmer would be murdered before justice could be done.

refrigerator so he would see that it contained a human head. Now Edwards was fighting for his life. As the killer dragged him into the bedroom, Edwards saw strewn all around shocking photographs of mangled bodies, severed heads and sexual organs, and he was struck by a horrid smell coming from a large blue barrel standing in an open closet.

In a split second when Dahmer took his eyes off him, Edwards punched him in the face, kicked him in the groin and ran for the door. Dahmer was in no shape to follow, so his prisoner was able to bolt out of the apartment building into the night. Now he would need to convince the police.

> He laid his head on Edwards' chest to listen to his heartbeat, saying he was going to eat his heart.

"Weird dude"

It was just about midnight when two Milwaukee police officers that were driving around the neighborhood spotted a wiry man stumbling along with a handcuff dangling from his wrist. Suspecting he may have escaped from police custody, they confronted him on the street and asked him what he was doing. After Edwards began pouring out a story about the "weird dude" who had held him captive nearby, they decided to check out his claims and had him take them to 924 North 25th Street, apartment 213.

The young, blond man who opened the door seemed calm and rational at first and he even offered to get his key to unlock the handcuffs. But something didn't add up and the police decided to do what their predecessors had not done: they investigated further. One of them asked to see the knife in the kitchen that he had allegedly used to threaten this other individual, Mr. Edwards.

Finding out

Soon one of the officers came across a large collection of gruesome Polaroid pictures and called for his partner to arrest Dahmer. While one policeman subdued him, the other searched the kitchen and discovered the human head in the refrigerator. They took Dahmer away for booking and interrogation and called in a forensic team.

What the investigators discovered shocked and repulsed them beyond belief. Body parts stuffed into dresser drawers, photos of torture sessions, abundant supplies of chloroform and formaldehyde, bloodstained cutting tools and pieces of corpses soaking in acid-filled vats. In his confession, Dahmer admitted having committed the most depraved acts a human being could commit, including necrophilia and cannibalism.

Indicted for 17 murders, Dahmer became the focus of worldwide media coverage and incredulity.

Trial and sentence: Dahmer in the courtroom in Milwaukee. The serial killer chose to wear a shirt belonging to one of his 17 victims.

JUDGE L. C. GRAM. JR.
PRESIDING

Trial and sentence

Dahmer's super-sensational case went to trial on January 30, 1992. There was never any question that he was guilty of hideous mass murders. But could any sane person have acted in such a manner? Facing certain conviction, Dahmer's lawyers attempted to plead him not guilty by reason of insanity. The whole world had been shocked by the crazy nature of his horrendous acts, particularly his cannibalism and necrophilia. But prosecutors insisted that he knew what he was doing was wrong and against the law. So, incredibly, despite the extraordinarily perverted and bizarre nature of his acts, the court found him sane, and he was convicted of killing and dismembering 15 young men. The outcome demonstrated how difficult it had become in a high-profile case in America to be found insane and not criminally responsible.

Put before the judge for sentencing, he expressed remorse for his crimes and said he wished he was dead. He was sentenced to 15 life terms totaling 957 years in prison. He also later pleaded guilty to a 1978 murder in Ohio.

Wrecking crews tore down Dahmer's former apartment and the entire apartment complex at 924 North 25th Street, but the stain did not go away. In 1994 another inmate, Christopher Scarver, beat Dahmer to death with a metal bar at the Columbia Correctional Institution in Portage, Wisconsin. Had one of his victims not escaped from the butcher's block and convinced authorities to inquire within, Dahmer's toll might have been even greater.

A life or death decision

Dr. Mary Quin

December 1998

While on vacation in the Yemeni desert, Dr. Mary Quin was taken hostage by radical Islamists. When she became a human shield in a gun battle between the Islamic Army and Yemeni troops, she knew she had to make a run for it. But first she needed to wrestle an AK-47 out of her captor's hands.

Tourist trap: The Dar al-Hajar (Rock Palace) perched on a rock pinnacle. Despite the inherent risks, tourists are drawn to Yemen by some of the most stunning architecture in the world.

At 11a.m. on December 28, 1998, a caravan of five Toyota Land Cruisers was winding its way along a harsh desert road in Yemen's Abyan province, headed toward Aden. The group was on a two-week tour organized by a travel agency. Among the 21 persons in the vehicles were 16 Western tourists — 12 Britons, two Australians and two Americans — most of them in their 40s or 50s, who were enjoying a Christmas vacation. One of them — Mary Quin, a woman in her mid-40s who held joint citizenship from the United States and New Zealand — was a successful corporate executive for Xerox with a taste for exotic places; some of the others were not such experienced travelers.

Suddenly a white pickup truck full of men blocked their path. Their faces were covered with khafiyas and they were all heavily armed. The men quickly surrounded the convoy and motioned at the drivers to put down their weapons. The ambush appeared to involve at least 18 gunmen, some of whom were toting automatic weapons and rocket-propelled grenade-launchers, so the drivers grudgingly complied.

Quin and her companions realized they had been kidnapped — the latest in more than 100 kidnappings of foreigners that had occurred in Yemen over the last few years. In most instances, the hostages had been released unharmed after some ransom was paid.

Human shields

In this case, however, what the hostages didn't know yet was that their captors were members of the radical

Weapons galore: Violence and kidnapping are a way of life in Yemen. Here customers haggle with an illegal arms dealer over the price of a machine gun. It is estimated that there are 50 million guns held by a population of 18 million people.

Islamic Army of Aden (IAA), an affiliate group of Al-Qaeda, which then was engaged in an ongoing jihad against Western interests and the Yemeni government. The group's leader, Zein al-Abidine Almihdhar, had ordered the hostages to be taken in exchange for the release of six IAA operatives who had been arrested a few days earlier, and he also was demanding the release of more militant prisoners, an end to the U.S.-led bombing of Iraq and a change of government in Yemen. Almihdhar said if his demands weren't met, the hostages would be executed.

Quin and her fellow hostages tried to size up their captors, but they were at a serious disadvantage. The Yemeni drivers had been separated from the group, leaving their group with no Arabic-speaker to translate what the kidnappers were communicating. From time to time the kidnappers told them some things in English, assuring them not to worry. But Quin and the others were not so sure.

The kidnappers were dressed in typical Yemeni style, wearing shabby suit jackets and wraparound futas. They kept their khafiyas wrapped over their faces, leaving the hostages to search their body movements and eyes for signs of danger. In an effort to keep them straight, Quin took to identifying each by his clothing: one was Purple Shirt, another was Yellow Pants or Gray Shirt. And one, who kept holding an ominous block of explosive, she called Grenade.

Stuck in the middle

The kidnappers kept moving them from place to place; on one occasion they simply barreled through a military

As shells started exploding overhead, the kidnappers herded them behind a low dirt berm in the middle of the field and told them to immediately line up against the wall with their hands in the air. Shots from Yemeni troops were landing all around them. Quin realized the terrorists intended to carry out a mass execution.

Grabbing the gun

As they moved toward the wall, Quin felt the butt of her guard's AK-47 sticking in her back and as soon as it went away, she turned to face him. It was then that she saw that Purple Shirt was shot and preparing to shoot her. Ahead the troops were also firing, putting her in the middle of a crossfire.

At first she started to run, but then in an effort to prevent him from shooting her in the back, she reached back and grabbed his gun barrel. He had hold of the stock and they were locked in a tug of war for control of the weapon, screaming and fighting for their lives. Finally she used her foot to hold down his head and wrested away the Kalashnikov. Then she raced off. Bullets were flying.

As this was happening, one of the other gunmen had grabbed a young woman hostage and was pushing her forward when she was struck and killed by a bullet that ripped through the chest. Suddenly Gray Shirt started executing hostages from left to right. A high-velocity bullet struck Dr. Peter Rowe in the chest, killing him instantly. His wife Claire was shot in the right hip; a second bullet slammed through her right shoulder blade and exited in front of her arm; a third clipped her fingertip. In their horror, the remaining hostages jumped down from the dirt wall and tried to take shelter in front of it. One woman was hit in the left thigh. Another

> **❝I put my foot down on his head and it gave me enough leverage to get the gun out of his arms and make a run for it. ❞**
>
> **Dr. Mary Quin**

woman spun around to see Gray Shirt leveling the gun at her chest. She looked him straight in the eye long enough for him to hesitate and she curled up in a ball on the ground. The gunman swung his aim at a male hostage

Fighting back: Dr. Mary Quin realized that she would not survive if she didn't take fate into her own hands.

checkpoint. Clearly, the authorities knew where they were and a confrontation was looming. But so far there hadn't been any major showdown.

At 10:57 a.m. on the morning of their second day of captivity, Quin heard gunshots nearby. Having read that 79 percent of all hostage fatalities occurred during a rescue attempt, she worried that one was going on and this could result in their death. Her fears grew as the kidnappers became more tense and ordered the hostages to congregate. She and ten of her companions were seated on the ground and the other prisoners were walking ahead, under armed escort.

Quin kept watching Grenade, who was stationed nearby, nervously holding his block of explosives. For more than 20 minutes the distant sound of gunfire and automatic weapons continued. Some of the hostages were becoming very agitated.

who also faced him, yelling, "No! No! No!" Gray Shirt seemed unable to shoot them face-to-face. He turned and ran after the other kidnappers who were fleeing into the desert, leaving some of the hostages to try to tend to the wounded. Quin had made it to safety behind a rock, 90 feet (27 m) away.

Outcome

Three of the kidnappers were dead, three (including Almihdhar) were captured and the others got away.

The dead Britons were Peter Rowe, aged 60, a math lecturer at Durham University; Margaret Whitehouse, aged 53, a teacher from Hook, Hampshire; and Ruth Williamson, aged 34, from Edinburgh. Andrew Thirsk, aged 35, of Sydney, Australia, also died. Dr. Rowe's wife, Claire Marston, aged 43, was severely wounded as was the American woman who had been shot in the pelvis.

Quin faulted the Yemeni army for a botched rescue attempt, saying the government seemed more concerned with defeating the rebels than safeguarding the hostages. She later wrote a book, *Kidnapped in Yemen: One Woman's Amazing Escape from Terrorists* (2005), about the experience.

Yemeni officials identified one of the kidnappers who died as an Egyptian extremist known as Osama al-Masri, who was known to have belonged to the Islamic Jihad. The government also later reported that Almihdhar had been tried and executed.

A few months later, the Army of Aden was credited with carrying out the deadly attack on the American warship, USS *Cole*; and two years after that one of Almihdhar's distant relatives, Khalid Almihdhar, was one of the hijackers who flew the airliner into the Pentagon on September 11, 2001. Luck and quick thinking had enabled Quin to escape death in an extremely dangerous situation.

Attacks linked: Terrorists involved in the kidnap of Mary Quin were also responsible for the bombing of the USS *Cole*. Seventeen sailors were killed in 2000 when the American warship was attacked in the port of Aden in Yemen.

On the edge of a precipice

After setting out on a rock climbing adventure in the formidable mountains of Kyrgyzstan, four young Americans were taken hostage by murderous Islamic terrorists. In a desperate attempt to escape from their captors, they were faced with committing an act they never thought they would have to do.

Dangerous beauty: Nomadic goat herders litter the mountain landscape in the foothills of the towering Pamir-Alai mountain range, the location of the challenging "Yellow Wall."

In the summer of 2000, four young and adventurous American alpinists traveled all the way to Kyrgyzstan in Central Asia to experience some of the most spectacular big-wall climbing in the world.

Jason "Singer" Smith, a 22-year-old Californian, had organized the trip with his friends: John Dickey, aged 25, from Colorado; Tommy Caldwell, 22 years old, from Utah; and his girlfriend, Beth Rodden, aged 20, of Davis, California, using sponsorship from North Face.

Situated near the border of Tajikistan, close to Afghanistan, Pakistan and China, Kyrgyzstan is a nomadic land of incredible natural beauty that received its independence in 1991 after the collapse of the Soviet Union. The four Americans were drawn to the Pamir-Alai mountain range of Kyrgyzstan, revered for its towering peaks, magnificent canyons and glaciers, and particularly its great Yellow Wall.

Despite their tender years, and the fact that Rodden weighed less than 100 pounds (45 kg), the quartet were considered some of America's best and up-and-coming young rock climbers on the international circuit, and they wanted to test their skills in new and exciting ways. But they could not have anticipated how dangerous a test it would prove to be.

Stopped for the night: The group made camp against the sheer face of the Yellow Wall using the climbing device known as a portaledge.

Taken prisoner

Just before dawn on August 12, the four climbers were sleeping strapped inside their portaledges (portable ledges) 1,000 feet (304 m) up the Yellow Wall, when they were awakened by the sound of bullets ricocheting just a few feet away and the echoes of gunshots reverberating through the canyon of the Kara Su River.

Looking down through his camera lenses, Dickey could see two armed men on the canyon floor, motioning him to come down. Being the oldest, he rappelled down first to investigate.

The full-bearded men were dressed like *mujahidin*, toting automatic weapons, grenades and knives. They did not speak English. Although they shook hands and acted friendly at first, they made it clear to Dickey that they wanted all of his companions to join them. The youths feared they were going to be robbed, but they did not see any hope in resisting, so they did what they were told.

> **" There were three men in army fatigues, they had full beards, and rifles and grenades and handguns and knives. "**
>
> Beth Rodden

When all four were assembled, the two gunmen — identified as Abdul and Obid — took them to the climbers' nearby camp, where two more gunmen were waiting with a captive Kyrgyzstani soldier.

Islamic militants

Sergeant Turtabek Osmanov of the Kyrgyz army (Turat for short) tried to communicate with his fellow prisoners by charade-type hand movements. He seemed to be saying that their captors were Islamic militants who had already killed several of his fellow soldiers. He indicated he had been spared only because they thought he might be useful to help guide them through the mountains. But he knew they would eventually kill him. The youths were terrified when Turat made the universal throat-cutting motion, particularly since they didn't know if that meant they would be doomed as well.

Soon it became apparent that the terrorists, who were

barely out of their teens, intended to use their hostages as human shields for ransom as they moved across Kyrgyzstan.

The climbers knew virtually nothing about the political situation they had entered. Nor had they paid much attention to travel warnings from the U.S. State Department. But now they were getting an education in geopolitics and international terrorism. For in fact, their captors were members of the radical Islamic Movement of Uzbekistan (IMU), linked to Osama bin Laden's Al-Qaeda network that operated out of secret bases in Tajikistan and Afghanistan. In recent weeks, dozens of heavily armed IMU militants had been staging a violent invasion into the country, murdering Kyrgyz soldiers, terrorizing local

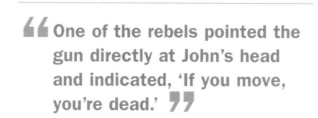

One of the rebels pointed the gun directly at John's head and indicated, 'If you move, you're dead.'

Tommy Caldwell

Climbing superstar: Beth Rodden has gone on to become one of the sport's best-known female stars.

shepherds, and kidnapping foreigners for ransom. Now the four Americans were also caught up in their jihad.

Soldiers killed

The *mujahidin* prodded them along through the rocky terrain. But after they crossed a river and started heading up the side of the valley, Kyrgyz soldiers appeared and a gun battle broke out. The rebels shot several Kyrgyz soldiers as the youths tried to stay out of the line of fire.

Abdul, the rebel leader, took Sergeant Osmanov out of sight and shot him twice in the head. Then the gunmen forced the Americans to rest near the corpse as the killer knelt on his prayer mat and prayed to Allah even as bullets whizzed by. Eventually, the gunfight ended and they resumed their trek, aware that they were still being hunted. From time to time a Mi8 helicopter approached and their captors forced them to hide under rocks or bushes. One rebel pointed the gun directly at Dickey's head, indicating, "If you move, you're dead."

In another instance, two of the hostages were herded into a tiny cave to lie for 17 hours in the teeth-chattering cold as the others hid nearby. At night they were marched through the freezing, treacherous mountains, receiving very little food and no fresh water, living in constant dread of execution.

"What have I done?"

From time to time the four climbers discussed a possible escape attempt, but they ruled it out as too risky. Abdul was simply too overpowering.

Finally, however, Abdul ran out of batteries for the walkie-talkies that he and his men used to communicate with their comrades, and he decided to leave — ostensibly to go back to the climbers' camp to get more batteries. This left the four youths in the custody of only one armed captor, who was supposed to escort them to another location. Their guard, Stu, was even younger than they and he seemed rather dull-witted. The youths waited for the right opportunity to make their move.

Edging along the 2,000-foot (608 m) cliff together in darkness, the expert rock climbers waited until Stu was in a most precarious position. Then Tommy Caldwell

Army checkpoint: Kyrgyz soldiers carry out passport and identity checks on civilians at Kara Su Bridge on the Uzbekistan and Kyrgyzstan border in a bid to stem the flow of militants. When the climbers finally reached Kara Su they were mistaken for terrorists.

grabbed him by his dangling rifle and Stu lost his balance. The other three climbers watched as the militant fell 30 feet (9 m) onto a ledge, where he landed flat on his back, then rolled off into the inky night, bouncing off the wall to what must have been a certain death.

The three observers were relieved that their friend had saved their lives. But Caldwell was stricken, saying, "What have I done?" Stu had done bad things, but he was a human being, and now Caldwell had to come to terms with the fact he had committed an act he never would have thought possible: he had killed someone.

Rescued

The four climbers were now fleeing for their lives, desperate to get away before Abdul or some other killer could hunt them down. After running for 18 hours, they reached the west side of the Kara Su, only to see three armed figures appear in the distance. Bullets started landing all around them. Kyrgyz soldiers, thinking they were *mujahidin*, were shooting at them from all sides.

Minutes later, the sprinting youths ran inside a hut

containing a reporter and several soldiers. At last they were safe. A helicopter flew them to the U.S. embassy in Bishkek and Kyrgyzstan's president, Askar Akayev, hosted them at a reception where they were honored as heroes for killing a terrorist. They later learned that the soldiers had killed the ringleader Sabir Abdul and his two other companions.

At home they tried to get over the trauma of their ordeal. But Caldwell continued to feel guilty that he had been forced to kill Stu. However, the story of the killing took another turn when it was revealed that Stu (aka Ravshan Sharipov) was actually alive in a Russian jail. The 20-year-old *mujahidin* from Tajikistan had miraculously escaped from his fall off the cliff with only cuts and bruises and no broken bones. But Stu wasn't rejoicing. Soon he was going to be put to death for his terrorist activities.

The climbers' story was later told in Greg Child's gripping book, *Over the Edge: The True Story of Four American Climbers' Kidnap and Escape in the Mountains of Central Asia* (2002).

A gap year to remember

MATTHEW SCOTT | September 2003

In September 2003, Matthew Scott was making the most of his gap year on an organized trek through the Sierra Nevada mountains. When he and his fellow companions became prisoners of armed guerrilas, the student made a courageous bid for freedom, which he knew might cost him his life.

The backpackers were of different countries and backgrounds. Two were British, one was Dutch, one German, one Spanish, and there were six Israelis — it was an interesting group of persons, mostly in their late 20s or 30s.

The highlight of their journey was expected to be seeing the spectacular remains of the 2,500-year-old "Lost City" that the Indians had abandoned after the invasion of the Spanish Conquistadors. But in the course of their exotic summer adventure of trekking through the mist-shrouded Sierra Nevada mountains near Colombia's Caribbean coast, the tourists found they shared many things in common besides their interest in ancient ruins.

After two glorious days of strenuous hiking and an evening of bonding under the stars, they had fallen asleep to the sounds of crickets, frogs and water rushing down the lush tropical mountainside — delights that seemed too good to be true.

At age 19, Matthew Scott was the youngest of the group, a gap year student of engineering from Oxford University, and an avid outdoorsman. He was a meticulous planner, but nothing could have prepared him for the surprise that greeted him when he was awakened shortly before dawn the next morning, September 12.

"Get up!"

Colombian soldiers or paramilitaries in camouflage uniforms were ordering everyone to get up, prodding the tourists with assault rifles. As Scott saw some of them roughly searching through everyone's bags, he began to

Ciudad Perdida: The backpackers were on their way to the "Lost City," hoping to see the pre-Colombian settlement built by Tayrona Indians. It is only accessible via a three-day hike.

Manhunt: A soldier patrols near the area where the backpackers disappeared. The Colombian Army carried out extensive search operations thinking that the tourists had been kidnapped by the Revolutionary Armed Forces of Colombia (FARC).

suspect it was a robbery. Then he saw the soldiers tying up the porter and the guide and making them lie down. The groggy prisoners were motioned down the hillside to a camp where more armed men had congregated. The sight of their machine guns startled Scott and his fellow captives.

The soldiers tried to determine the travelers' nationalities. Then they lined up all the foreigners and selected the fittest ones, among them Scott and eight others. Now it became apparent that some of them were being kidnapped. Kidnaps for ransom were a rather common occurrence in Colombia at that time — the country had already experienced more

> **❝ I heard the river on the right and I followed the sound. I jumped off a cliff very quickly. ❞**
>
> **Matthew Scott**

than 1,000 in that year alone — but certainly kidnapping was not anything to which any of the tourists were accustomed.

The hostage-takers split them into two groups and proceeded to march them through the jungle at gunpoint. This continued for several hours. Along the way some of the soldiers communicated via hand-held radios and the worried captives whispered among themselves as they trudged through the thick vegetation up and down the mountainous terrain. At times they had to grab vines or plants to avoid slipping down the muddy paths, careful not to tangle with any poisonous snakes.

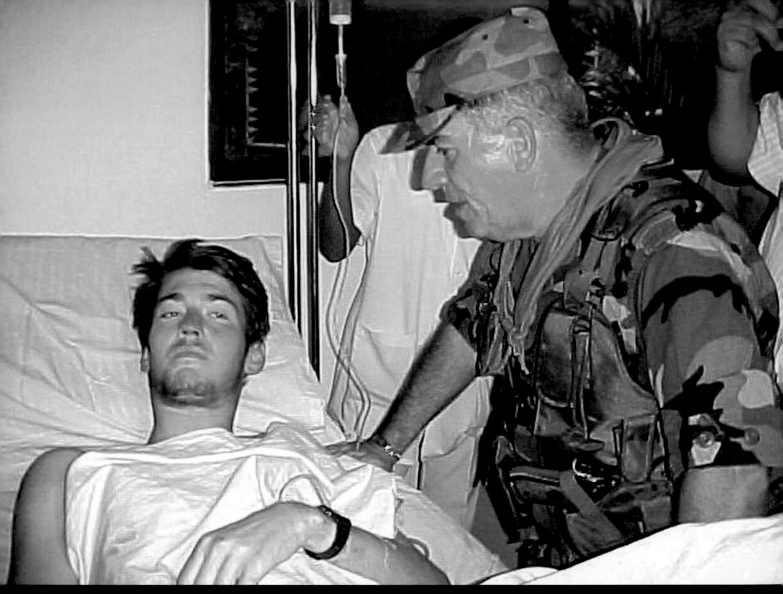

Photo opportunity: Hospitalized but safe, a weak Matthew Scott is visited in hospital in Santa Marta by General Leonel Gomez of the Colombian Army, September 24, 2003.

Decision to escape

The hostages thought they were being held by Revolutionary Armed Forces of Colombia (FARC) rebels or cocaine traffickers. Later it appeared the kidnappers were from *El Ejército de Liberación Nacional* (National Liberation Army or ELN), a Marxist insurgent group, but the soldiers would not explain their intentions.

The only food their kidnappers gave them was a slice of processed cheese and several chunks of panella — a honey-soaked disc with bees stuck in it. Scott stuffed some of it into his water bottle, thinking that he might later need it. The first day of captivity turned into the second and they were still hiking through the rain forest, heading farther from the Lost City.

Whenever they could, Scott and the others surreptitiously discussed their options, including the prospect of trying to escape. But all of the older hostages were opposed, fearing they would get shot or lost in the jungle. One of Scott's friends advised him that somebody's escape attempt might also prompt their captors to take out their anger on the others.

But Scott was persistent. He didn't want his parents to be extorted for ransom on his account; he had plans for his life and he didn't want those dreams to become ruined. Upon hearing the river running nearby on their right hand side, he said he thought he could follow the rivers to Santa Marta. He had made up his mind to flee. Now he had to wait for the right chance.

Escape

Visibility was poor due to the rain and mist. He hoped it would work in his favor. Seizing a moment when the guards were distracted, he bolted into the forest and plunged down the slippery precipice to the swollen river rushing below.

When he crawled ashore, he was alone and exposed. All he could do was keep to the course of the river that he hoped would take him to Santa Marta. It would be a struggle to survive. Day turned into night and night into day. His only food was the crumbs of panella floating in his water bottle. He slept amid the rocks and bushes, alert for people or animals that might cause him harm. He was famished and tired, assaulted by insects and plants. Soon he became worried that he might never reach safety.

Two-month wait: Marxist rebels finally handed over the remaining hostages, starting in November with Asier Huegen (left) from Spain and Reinhilt Weigel (right) from Germany.

Home again: A relieved Matthew Scott talks about his ordeal in the Colombian jungle at a press conference held at Heathrow Airport on September 26, 2003.

Finally, after 12 days of arduous wandering along the meandering river, most of it without any food and only river water to drink, the exhausted teenager came upon a tiny village in the jungle. The inhabitants turned out to be Arahuaco Indians, who took him in. The Indians gave him some soup and beans with a little salt and three oranges, which he wolfed down. He stayed with them until a government patrol came by.

The troops took him to the hospital in Santa Marta for treatment. But although Scott gradually recovered, he remained worried about his fellow hostages. Were they still alive? Might they have suffered on his account?

Afterward

In the months that followed, the rebels released the German woman and the male Spaniard. Finally, 102 days after the group had been taken hostage, the others were also freed. The rebels said they had kidnapped the party to publicize the persecution of Indian villagers by right wing paramilitaries, and not for a ransom.

> ❝It was very risky ... he could have broken his arms or legs or he could have been shot.❞
>
> Matthew Scott's father

The girl they gave up for dead

When Natascha Kampusch disappeared on her way to school in March 1998 a nationwide missing persons campaign was launched. Years went by without news and everyone assumed the worst. But in 2006, Kampusch made a bold dash for freedom from the man who had held her captive.

Natascha's prison: The house in Strasshof, Austria, where Natascha Kampusch was held captive for eight years. Police were able to confirm her identity by matching a scar she had picked up as a ten-year-old.

A 71-year-old resident of the Lower Austrian town of Strasshof an der Nordbahn heard some rapid knocking on the glass pane and looked out to see the ghostlike figure of a young woman, standing in front of her kitchen window, panicking, white in the face and shaking with fear. Upon hearing her say, "I am Natascha Kampusch," the lady called the police, thus beginning one of Europe's most sensational recent crime dramas.

The girl was six inches taller than the missing girl had been, but she weighed about the same as she had eight years earlier. Could it really be her?

Based on a scar and other telltale signs, and her family's identification, the police determined that it was true — their eight-year-long manhunt for the kidnapped girl they had long ago considered dead had suddenly ended. And soon their pursuit of the suspect she identified as her abductor — Wolfgang Priklopil — culminated in the discovery of his abandoned BMW 850i outside a station. He had just thrown himself in front of an oncoming train.

At the morgue, a sympathetic police woman noted that the traumatized girl lit a candle for her former captor — and she wondered if as a result of her ordeal Natascha was exhibiting "Stockholm Syndrome," a psychological response in which a former hostage identifies with and shows signs of loyalty to the hostage-taker, regardless of what they have suffered.

Twisted: Passport photo of Natascha's captor, Wolfgang Priklopil. Priklopil killed himself on the day Natascha broke free, but the rumors still persist that he could not have acted entirely alone.

"A white minivan"

More than eight years earlier, on March 2, 1998, the region had been rocked by the reported abduction of a 10-year-old girl as she walked to school.

Natascha was raised by her mother Brigitta Sirny (née Kampusch) and her biological father Ludwig Koch, in Vienna, although the unmarried couple had separated after a few years. Natascha lived with her mother and her mother's new boyfriend but spent weekends with her father in Hungary, from whom she had returned just the day before the kidnapping. Her extended family included two adult sisters, and five nieces and nephews.

A 12-year-old witness reported having seen her being dragged into a white minivan. The witness described the

> **❝ I wanted to scream, but nothing came out. I just thought he was going to kill me. ❞**
>
> Natascha Kampusch

abductors as two men. She said as the girl walked past, a man aged between 20 and 40 jumped out and bundled her in the back, while a second man, whom the witness did not get a good look at, drove the van away. She thought the vehicle bore a Gänserndorf district license plate. Other evidence seemed to confirm at least parts of her account.

The police conducted a massive dragnet. More than 700 minivan owners were questioned, including Priklopil, but police ruled him out as a suspect after he claimed to have been using his minivan to transport construction debris. Eventually the probe came up empty, fueling speculation that the attractive girl had been taken by a serial killer or stolen for sexual slavery or organ theft. For all practical purposes, she was considered lost.

The tiny prison

Natascha later described the day she was kidnapped, but said she had no knowledge of a second man. "He grabbed me," she said. "I wanted to scream, but nothing came out. I just thought he was going to kill me."

Within hours of her kidnapping, she added, "I was already conscious of the fact that there was something wrong with this man, something missing, a deficiency." Over time she came to believe he was lacking in self-confidence.

He took her to a small cellar underneath his garage in the commuter town of Strasshof, located about 15 miles (24 km) outside Vienna. The entrance was concealed behind a cupboard. The room was dark. The cellar only had 54 square feet (5 m²) of space and when she arrived it was so low she could barely stand upright. Sealed by a steel door, it had no windows and was soundproof.

Nevertheless, she attempted to summon help by throwing plastic water bottles against the walls and banging them with her fists. All she wanted to do was escape.

Priklopil warned her that the doors and windows of the house were booby-trapped with high explosives. He said he carried a gun and threatened that if she roused the neighbors, first he would kill all of them, then her and then himself. And she believed him.

To make her obey, Priklopil beat her so badly she could hardly walk. Then he would photograph her. Sometimes she fantasized about chopping his head off with an axe.

Total control

For the first six months or so of her captivity, Natascha was not allowed to leave the

Basement cell: The small box room that confined Natascha Kampusch for almost all her teenage years; lacking a window or a wardrobe, but equipped with TV.

Initial hunt: The original poster that was distributed hoping for information on Natascha's abduction.

chamber at any time. Afterwards, she was sometimes allowed to go upstairs to perform chores, but each night and while Priklopil was at work, she was sent back to the claustrophobic chamber to sleep. He adhered to a rigid schedule, controlling every facet of her life.

He also used psychological manipulation, telling her that he had called her parents but they had refused to pay anything to get her back. He claimed they had written her off as worthless.

Establishing himself as a sort of father figure, he gave her geography and history lessons, and read her children's stories during which she asked him normal girl's questions about foreign countries and animals. To pass the time, she taught herself to knit. And to better herself, she read as much as she could and built an impressive vocabulary.

After two years, he permitted her to start listening to classical music on the radio and she could read parts of the newspaper that he had scrutinized. But he often fed her horror stories about life outside her cell, pointing out the reports about alcoholics and drug addicts. "Look," he said, "I've been protecting you from all these terrible things."

Then he would bring her Easter eggs, a birthday gift and Christmas presents. "I think he had a very guilty conscience," Natascha later said.

Longing to break free

After years had gone by, he began to occasionally take her into the outside world on brief errands, but he always made her walk in front of him so he could keep his eyes on her. Once in a hardware store a worker asked her if she needed any help. But her kidnapper quickly pulled her away. The girl feared he would kill them if she spoke up.

Natascha devised a silent strategy to attract attention to herself when they went out, thinking that if she showed the same smile as the missing girl in the wanted poster, somebody would recognize her and call the police. But the prolonged darkness in her tiny pen had made her eyes sensitive to light. And it was hard to smile.

Back in her den of torment, she kept a secret diary that ran to hundreds of pages. Often hungry, she developed circulation problems and had trouble concentrating.

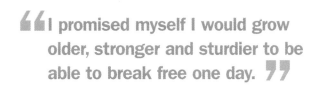

> **I promised myself I would grow older, stronger and sturdier to be able to break free one day.**
>
> Natascha Kampusch

Secret entrance: Natascha's bedroom was accessed via the trapdoor to the left in this picture that was released by Austrian police. For the first six months of her captivity she was not allowed into the rest of the house.

Mystery solved: Investigators protect Natascha from the lenses of the press as she is taken back to the house in Strasshof to help confirm details about her captivity. Her escape solved one of the country's longest-running mysteries.

"I always felt like a poor chicken in a hen house," Natascha later said.

But thoughts of freedom sustained her. At age 15 or so, she later said, "I promised myself I would grow older, stronger and sturdier to be able to break free one day."

The escape

Then it happened. One day she was in the garden, washing and vacuuming his car. At 12:53 p.m. someone called Priklopil on his mobile phone, and he turned away from the vacuuming noise. "I knew at that moment that if I didn't do it then I might never have the chance again," Natascha recalled. She seized her opportunity and bolted 200 yards (183 m) through gardens and a street, jumping fences, and asking passersby to call the police.

Then she approached Inge T's window and banged on the glass. The 71-year-old neighbor took her in and called the police, who arrived at 1:04 p.m. Kampusch was later taken to the police station in the town of Deutsch Wagram. After more than eight years, her ordeal was finally over.

> **❝ I knew at that moment that if I didn't do it then I might never have the chance again. ❞**
>
> Natascha Kampusch

Media frenzy

Natascha's story attracted a media feeding frenzy. Hundreds of outlets requested an interview and some offered vast sums of money. The tabloids screamed every kind of prurient story they could gather around the question of whether or not the girl had been sexually abused or turned into a sex slave. A heavyweight media advisor and agent was hired to help her navigate the shoals of celebrity. Finally, only five days after her rescue, she issued a statement: "Dear reporters, dear journalists, dear world, I want to make it clear that I will not answer now nor at any time, any intimate questions about my life with Priklopil." But the media would not relent. Soon, the former hostage was thrust in front of TV cameras, reliving her ordeal for millions of viewers. What followed was a series of lucrative deals with TV, magazines, newspapers, and motion picture studios from around the world. Some outlets offered her hundreds of thousands of euros, making her and her family well-to-do almost overnight. Months later, she had her own website documenting her meteoric escape into the public limelight. In June 2008 she started hosting her own TV show on Austria TV station PULS 4. Natascha has lost her pale pallor and now has access to computers and cell phones, limousines and jet planes.

3 Regimes

The great slave disguise

WILLIAM AND ELLEN CRAFT	December 1848

William and Ellen Craft, a married couple, had been born into slavery in Georgia. They knew that any attempt to escape would be fraught with obstacles and would take an extraordinary feat to accomplish. However, in 1848 they devised an outlandish plan they hoped would set them on the road to freedom.

By 1848 the northern states of the United States had abolished slavery, but the South remained determined to defend it to the death. Blacks were condemned to perpetual bondage, passed on from one generation to the next. And for most, particularly in the Deep South, there was no escape.

William and Ellen Craft had been born into slavery in Georgia and fallen in love. Although their masters had allowed them to marry, the constant threat of separation was more than the couple could bear. "It is true; our condition as slaves was not by any means the worst," William later acknowledged, "but the mere idea that we were held as chattels, and deprived of all legal rights — the thought that we had to give up our hard earnings to a tyrant, to enable him to live in idleness and luxury — the thought that we could not call the bones and sinews that God gave us our own: but above all, the fact that another man had the power to tear from our cradle the new-born babe and sell it in the shambles like a brute, and then scourge us if we dared to lift a finger to save it from such a fate, haunted us for years."

Concluding that their future was dim, they decided to attempt the unthinkable — they would flee. If caught, they would suffer a horrible punishment — never being allowed to see each other again. Yet it was a risk they had to take.

Ingenious plan

The couple faced enormous obstacles. They had little connection with any underground that might assist them and therefore would have to make it on their own. They had no travel passes, little money, and had never previously ventured far from home. Worst of all, an entire society with all of its customs and legal apparatus was conditioned to prevent any black person from escaping.

Nevertheless they had one thing going for them: Ellen was so light-colored she could probably pass for white. This gave them the idea for a daring plan. They would try to escape during the busy Christmas season. They knew that her passing for white would not be sufficient. Despite her light color, it wasn't socially acceptable for slave mistresses in the South to travel alone with a male slave. Therefore, they decided that she would also pose as a man. The white-looking woman would disguise herself in men's clothes as a young male planter who was traveling north with her black man-servant in tow.

Fearing that Ellen would be betrayed by her feminine-sounding voice, they also devised another ruse: they

Ellen Craft: Dressed as a man, Ellen was able to escort her husband to freedom. But new slavery laws made them fearful and they moved to England until after the Civil War.

fashioned a bandage around her jaw to give the impression she was injured and unable to speak. Ellen had her hair cut and donned spectacles and a gentleman's fine clothes, complete with a master's top hat and suit. Cultural mores of race, class, gender and cross-dressing would all be turned on their head.

The long divide

In order to escape to a "free state," they would have to travel more than 1,000 miles (1,609 km), proceeding by train to Savannah, Georgia, then by steamer to Charleston, South Carolina, and Wilmington, North Carolina, and finally by train to Philadelphia. Such travel meant that William would often have to remain in separate quarters reserved for blacks whereas Ellen would ride with whites.

Donning a disguise was one thing, but carrying it off was another. For in order to succeed, she would have to take on a radically new persona.

Along the way they had several close calls. On one occasion, Ellen had to engage in a conversation with a white slave trader who wished to purchase William.

Another crisis occurred when they hit the crucial Baltimore to Philadelphia leg of the journey that would take them across the "Mason and Dixon line" from slave state to free state. Ellen had just stepped aboard her fine train carriage and William was about to enter the baggage car when an officer suddenly appeared and tapped him on the shoulder.

"Where are you going, boy?" the low-born officer with a Yankee twang demanded.

"To Philadelphia, sir," William humbly replied.

"Well, what are you going there for?"

"I am traveling with my master, who is in the next carriage, sir," he answered, careful not to reveal his master's true gender.

"You had better get him out; and be mighty quick about it, because the train will soon be starting. It is against my rules to let any man take a slave past here, unless he can satisfy them in the office that he has a right to take him along.'"

The confrontation forced Ellen to go to the dreaded office to seek their necessary clearance.

> **The mere idea that we were chattels, and deprived of our legal rights ... haunted us for years.**
>
> William Craft

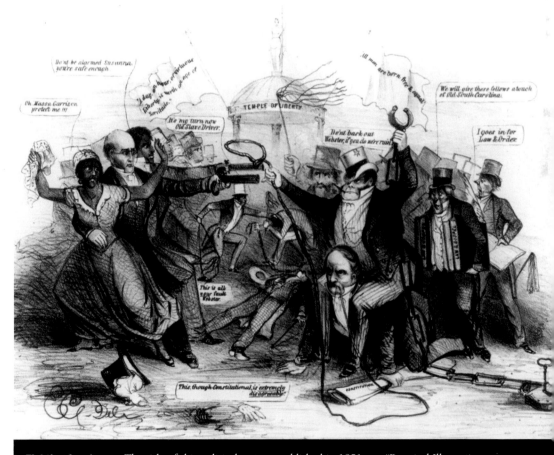

Fighting for change: The title of this political cartoon published in 1851 was "Practical Illustration of the Fugitive Slave Law." It was a satire on the antagonism between northern abolitionists, represented by the pistol-wielding William Lloyd Garrison on the left, and U.S. Secretary of State, Daniel Webster (kneeling) and other supporters of the Fugitive Slave Law. The slave catcher wielding a noose and manacles is expensively dressed and is thought to represent the federal marshals authorized by the act.

"Do you wish to see me, sir?" she asked, struggling to sound as masculine and masterly as possible.

The eagle-eyed officer looked over his latest applicant. "Yes," he said. "It is against our rules, sir, to allow any person to take a slave out of Baltimore into Philadelphia, unless he can satisfy us that he has a right to take him along."

"Why is that?" Ellen asked, with haughty firmness.

"Because, sir," the man continued, in a voice and manner that almost chilled their blood, "if we should suffer any gentleman to take a slave past here into Philadelphia; and should the gentleman with whom the slave might be traveling turn out not to be his rightful owner, and should the proper master come and prove

> ❝ It is against our rules, sir, to allow any person to take a slave out of Baltimore into Philadelphia. ❞
>
> Train officer

that his slave escaped on our road, we shall have him to pay for; and, therefore, we cannot let any slave pass here without receiving security to show, and to satisfy us, that it is all right."

Luckily for the Crafts, their predicament attracted sympathy from several other white travelers who assumed this master must be the rightful owner and was now being subjected to an obnoxious inconvenience, and some of them spoke up in support. Finally, as the train was about to depart, the harried officer relented and let them pass, thereby enabling them to resume the last leg of their trip.

On Christmas day, they reached Philadelphia and got off the train. At the end of their perilous journey, after they had left the Philadelphia station, William later recalled, "On leaving the station my master — or rather, my wife, so I may now say — who had from the commencement of the journey borne up in a manner that much surprised us both, grasped me by the hand, and said, 'Thank God, William, we are safe!' then burst into tears, leant upon me, and wept like a child."

Heroes

When abolitionists learned of the Crafts' achievement, they encouraged the couple to tell their story. But this time they were subject to the cultural mores of the day. In many instances, William would speak on stage to spellbound audiences, while his wife would have to remain demurely silent. And when their hair-raising narrative of escape was published, it was written in William's voice.

Embarrassed by news of their triumph, Southern lawmakers responded by demanding stricter laws aimed at curbing slave escapes. But the ingenuity and resolve of these fugitive slaves could not be denied.

Abolitionist: William Lloyd Garrison was a staunch abolitionist and publisher of Boston newspaper, the *Liberator*. In 1850, the paper ran a story of an abortive attempt by slaveholder agents to recapture the Crafts and return them to Georgia.

Harriet Tubman

From the period of the 1790s to the eve of the Civil War in 1860, many fugitive slaves attempted to escape from bondage to freedom. Eventually an organized system and network arose to aid them in getting away and assist them as refugees. By the 1840s it came to be known as the "Underground Railroad" (UGRR).

Comprised of blacks and whites working together, the UGRR clearly violated the state and federal laws upholding slavery. But its participants held they were following a "higher law."

Historians may disagree over the number of fugitives who were smuggled north to other states or Canada via its clandestine stations. Today, however, the most reliable estimates of the number of fleeing slaves who were assisted range from 50,000 to 100,000 persons. Ironically, the greatest volume occurred after Congress enacted the Fugitive Slave Law in 1850, which contained harsh new procedures and criminal penalties for anyone anywhere in the United States (including the "free states") who assisted a runaway slave — because abolitionists used the measure as a recruiting tool. The mounting sectional conflict over slavery led to the secession of the Southern states from the Union and the outbreak of the Civil War.

Harriet Tubman (c. 1820–1913), is shown here after she escaped from the slavery into which she was born. After she found refuge in Philadelphia in 1849, she returned to Maryland to save her family. Tubman went back to the South on 13 missions in order to help others on the road to freedom. Using a network of anti-slavery activists and safe houses along the Underground Railroad, Tubman managed to rescue more than 70 slaves

Shipping himself to freedom

| HENRY "BOX" BROWN | March 1849 |

Born into slavery in 1815, Henry Brown went to work in a tobacco factory in Richmond. When his wife and three children were sold to another slave owner, Brown was determined to escape. In 1849 he hatched an astonishing plan to freight himself to freedom.

Henry Brown was born into slavery in 1815 in Virginia. At age 15 his master died and was sent to Richmond to work in a tobacco factory. For a while, his lot was relatively good: he wasn't whipped or starved and he was able to marry another slave, Nancy, who belonged to a different master. Over the years the couple had three children.

But that was fated to change. When his wife's master threatened to sell her and the children, Brown offered to purchase their freedom. But the master refused, so in 1848, his loved ones were sold to a slave trader and sent to North Carolina in a coffle gang. As he watched them being led away, Brown was powerless to prevent it and, smoldering with resentment, he vowed to run away.

With encouragement from a free black friend from the African Baptist Church of Richmond, Brown conceived the idea to have himself shipped to a free state in a box, via railway express, as if he were a container of dry goods.

A white merchant, Samuel Smith, agreed to help him. Brown paid $88 (out of his life savings of $166) to Samuel Smith, who contacted Philadelphia Vigilance Committee at the Pennsylvania Anti-Slavery Society Office and asked if they would be willing to receive such a box. They were reluctant to do so, saying

Henry "Box" Brown emerges: The popular engraving that publicized Henry Brown's escape into free society. He was later joined in the North by James "Boxer" Smith, the free black who boxed him in.

that Brown might die in transit. However, Smith told them Brown was determined to escape, and they eventually accepted.

Shipped express

On March 23, 1849, Brown met with two accomplices in Smith's office. At about five foot eight inches (173 cm) tall and weighing 200 pounds (91 kg), he would not have much room in the pine box that one of his black carpenter friends had built. It measured only three feet one inch (94 cm) wide, two feet six inches (76 cm) high, and two feet (61 cm) wide. The only ventilation would

> ❝ When they heard that I was alive they soon managed to break open the box, and then came my resurrection from the grave of slavery. ❞
>
> Henry "Box" Brown

come from three tiny gimlet holes bored into the side opposite from where his face was supposed to be.

The slave said his goodbyes and climbed into the canvas-lined box, equipped only with a cow's bladder filled with water, a few crackers to stave off hunger, and a sharp tool with which to poke air holes. Then his friend nailed shut the lid. On the side of the box, Smith had scrawled THIS SIDE UP to keep its handlers from turning Brown on his head. Then they took the crate to the shipping office where it began its journey.

No sooner had he been delivered to the train depot than he felt himself being turned upside down, where he would have remained, except that during some rough handling the box fell down and became upright again.

The box continued by railroad, steamboat, wagon, railroad, ferry, railroad and finally delivery wagon, until it was eventually brought to its destination. Twenty-seven uncomfortable hours had elapsed. Had he suffocated?

"Is all right within?"

Members of the Vigilance Committee urgently gathered around the box as their leader, J. Miller McKim, rapped on the container and said, "Is all right within?" A faint voice replied, "All right."

The abolitionists pried off the lid to see a dazed black man with veins on his head that were as thick as pencils, struggling to arise from his tomb. After briefly fainting and regaining consciousness, his first words to them were, "How do you do, gentlemen?" Then he broke into a musical version of Psalm 40, singing, "I waited patiently for the Lord."

Brown soon became a popular celebrity speaker for the Anti-Slavery Society, using the name of Henry "Box" Brown. He published two versions of his autobiography and became famous throughout the United States and Europe as one of America's most intrepid and ingenious fugitive slaves.

In May 1849, after assisting other slaves who were trying to follow Brown's example, Samuel Smith was caught and imprisoned for six-and-a-half years.

The legend of Box Brown lived on as one of the greatest escape stories in Underground Railroad history.

CORN EXCHANGE, WOLVERHAMPTON.
THE AMERICAN KOSSUTH!!!
For Six Nights!!! On the Evenings of Monday, Tuesday, Wednesday, Thursday, Friday, and Saturday, the 15th, 16th, 17th, 18th, 19th, and 20th of March, 1852.

MR. HENRY BOX BROWN, the celebrated American Fugitive Slave, who escaped from Slavery, packed as luggage, in a box 3 feet 1 inch long, 2 feet wide, and 2 feet 6 inches high, traveling a distance of 350 miles! from Richmond, Virginia, to Philadelphia, Pennsylvania, the journey occupying 27 hours, will OPEN FOR PUBLIC EXHIBITION, in the CORN EXCHANGE ROOM, his unrivaled PANORAMA of AFRICAN and AMERICAN SLAVERY!!

Mr. Henry Box Brown is traveling under the patronage of the Ministers, Superintendents, and Magisterial authorities of Lancashire, Yorkshire, Cheshire, and Staffordshire, endeavouring to raise the sympathies of the people of England in behalf of three millions and a half of his race, in a state of degradation and slavery in America!

The Panorama is painted on 50,000 feet of canvass, by Wolcott, Rose, and Johnson, of Boston, U.S. and has been exhibited to three hundred and sixty-five thousand persons since its arrival in this country!

The scenes will be accompanied by the celebrated ITALIAN HARPISTS. The celebrated Italian Minstrels will introduce several Italian Duets, &c.

Admission. — Front Seats, 1s.; Second Seats, 6d.; Back Seats, 4d.

"Box" on tour: Anti-slavery campaigners in America sponsored Brown on a tour of England, trying to raise sympathies for their cause. James "Boxer" Smith joined him, but the two men quarreled after Smith claimed that Brown was not sufficiently pious or serious in his efforts to buy his wife and children out of slavery. The sober men who directed the movement withdrew their funding.

The rabbit-proof fence

MOLLY CRAIG	1931

Separated from their family for racial reasons, three Aboriginal girls decided to run away and trek 1,500 miles (2,414 km) home through barren bush, all the while trying to evade their pursuers. Their only guide home was a fence designed to keep rabbits out of Western Australia.

Like the colonial powers' treatment of Native Americans, Australia's treatment of its Aboriginal population was a great human rights abuse. By the early twentieth century it had gone on for more than a century, sometimes couched in terms of scientific racism and eugenics as official policy to control the "inferior race." In time Aborigines were treated as wards of the state to be protected from themselves and others "for

Rabbit-proof fence: Pictured in 1926, the State Barrier Fence of Western Australia was actually one of three fences and known as Fence No.1. It stretches from the south coast of Australia at Jerdacuttup, to the north coast at Wallal Downs. The girls mostly followed Fence No.2.

Protector of Aborigines: In the film of Doris Pilkington Garimara's book, Kenneth Branagh plays A.O. Neville, Protector of Aborigines, and the man responsible for the welfare of children separated from their parents by the state.

their own good." Besides removing the Aborigines from their land and consigning them to restricted tracts, the white powers-that-be enacted laws to separate the races

> ❝ We'll find Rabbit-Proof Fence, and follow it all the way home. We're gonna walk all the way. ❞
>
> From Doris Pilkington Garimara's
> *Follow the Rabbit-Proof Fence*

and prevent the assimilation of mixed-race persons into white society.

Between 1920 and 1930 as many as 50,000 to 100,000 mixed-race children were taken from their mothers and sent to remand homes to be trained for their proper role in the white-dominated society — supposedly for their "best interests." The children were later absorbed into foster homes. Some Australians called them the "stolen generation."

In August 1931 a government official ordered three such children — Molly Craig, aged 14; her half-sister Daisy Kadibil; and their eight-year-old cousin, Gracie Fields — to be forcibly removed from their mother among their "mob" (community) at Jigalong in Western Australia's northern interior. They were sent to a residential school at the Moore River Native Settlement, 1,500 miles (2,414 km) to the southwest. A.O. Neville, the Protector of Aborigines in Western Australia, was the official responsible for carrying out the displacement of "half-caste" children.

As the government agent was taking them away and the girls were disappearing through the river gums, their agonized relatives let out anguished cries and banged their heads with stones in an expression of sorrow.

Determined to escape

Molly, Daisy and Gracie were transported far from their homeland to the distant region near Perth. After arriving

Head north: Some critics of the film have maintained that the portrayal of the children as being chased by police with dogs is unfair and that in reality they were sought by concerned adults fearful for the three girls' safety.

at the school, the girls were placed in regimented dormitories with barred windows and rule infractions were punished by solitary confinement and flogging — almost as if they were in prison.

The girls missed their loved ones and wanted to return home. On the second day, Molly led her two relatives in walking out of the settlement and they were determined to trudge home on foot.

One of their greatest obstacles was how to find their way back. They had no maps or money. They had no shoes, equipment or supplies. Their destination was far away, through a barren and arid landscape. Moreover, they knew a skilled Aboriginal tracker would be assigned to hunt them down.

> ❝ **[The trek] had taken months to complete and nothing or nobody could take this moment of happiness and satisfaction from them.** ❞
>
> From Doris Pilkington Garimara's
> *Follow the Rabbit-Proof Fence*

Rabbit-proof fence

The girls had an idea. They knew that their community and the Moore settlement as well were located along the long "rabbit-proof fence" that separated the country. Built from 1901 to 1907, the fence had been erected to keep obnoxious rabbits, an imported species, from invading the countryside and becoming a pest. The barrier extended for a total of 2,023 miles (3,256 km), making it the longest fence in the world. The main spur, known as the State-Barrier Fence of Western Australia ran a total of 1,139 miles (1,833 km) from Wallal to Jerdacuttup. They decided to follow the long fence until they reached home.

The girls left shortly before a rainstorm, hoping it would wash away their footprints; they also waded through streams and ran through the bush to try to stay ahead of their pursuer. Their Aboriginal culture had taught them something about how to survive in the bush and how to track. They used every trick they could think of to try to conceal their trail and confuse their tracker. They knew how to scavenge. And they also were adept at calling upon other sympathetic Aborigines for assistance in sneaking them food and clothing.

Although the authorities issued notices for their capture and repeatedly organized traps to try to catch them along the route, the girls proceeded cautiously and avoided getting apprehended. The hours and days of their escape turned into weeks.

Daughter and "mother": Molly's daughter, author Doris Pilkington Garimara (left), with the girl who played her mother, Molly, in the film, actress Everlyn Sampi.

Happy ending: With Gracie gone, the girls were able to cover ground far quicker than before. By October they were home, by which time their families had moved to ensure they weren't taken back by the government.

In the third week of September Gracie was too exhausted to continue and upon learning that her mother had moved to another Aboriginal settlement at Wiluna, she wanted to leave her companions in order to join her. While waiting at the train station, she was captured.

The other two continued on without her. Stories about their exploits appeared in newspapers and their flight attracted considerable support, particularly among the Aborigines, to the authorities' considerable embarrassment.

Finally, in early October, after a journey of nine weeks, they reached Jigalong, where they were reunited with their mother.

Afterward

Rabbit-Proof Fence is a 2002 Australian film based on the award-winning book, *Follow the Rabbit-Proof Fence*, written by Molly's daughter, Doris Pilkington Garimara. The author wrote it as the second book in a trilogy documenting her family's stories. The film follows the girls as they trek while being pursued by their white "protector" and an Aboriginal tracker. The highly praised film generated a degree of controversy after some Australians persisted in denying the legacy of the "stolen generation" and tried to claim that the girls' story had been distorted. But historians have generally supported the book's account and sided with the movie-makers.

Leaving Tibet

THE DALAI LAMA	March 1959

The Dalai Lama was under intense pressure from the Chinese army who had already occupied Tibet for eight years. As his countrymen started to agitate against the Chinese occupation, he sensed it would not be long before he would be made an example and arrested. His only escape was across the Himalayas.

The Chinese communists invaded Tibet in 1951, claiming it as Chinese land. However, Tibetans were opposed to the occupation from the beginning and they mounted an insurgency that eventually spread to the capital, Lhasa (meaning "sacred place").

In early 1959, armed rebels roamed the streets of Lhasa as the city prepared for a religious celebration in March that Tibet's spiritual leader, the Dalai Lama, was scheduled to attend. Then 23 years old, the Dalai Lama had been recognized at age two as the reincarnation of the 13th Dalai Lama, Thubten Gyatso. Shy and studious, he was fourteenth in a line of god-kings who had ruled Tibet for about 600 years. Some of his other titles included the All-Embracing Lama, the Holder of the Thunderbolt, the Presence, the Precious Protector and the Inmost One, although he liked to think of himself as a Buddhist monk.

But a Chinese official demanded that the Dalai Lama instead attend a "theatrical performance" in a Chinese Army camp, two miles (3.2 km) away — alone. Many lamas feared he was going to be arrested.

On March 10, 1959 the crisis deepened. For many Tibetans, the thought that

Closing the border: Chinese soldiers guard the border between Tibet and India in 1959 to prevent Tibetan nationals from leaving the country.

Magnificent prison: The Norbulingka Palace in Lhasa, Tibet, was the summer residence of the Dalai Lama. When Chinese officials insisted that the man Tibetans revere as a god attend a function at a Chinese Army camp, his supporters surrounded the palace in his defense.

the godless Chinese might take away their spiritual leader — whom they saw as the incarnation of the Buddha — was the last straw. Crowds of his followers, some armed, surrounded Norbulingka Palace where the Dalai Lama had gone as always to spend the summer.

"The Chinese must go! Leave Tibet to the Tibetans!" the protesters chanted.

Disguised as a soldier

On March 17, inside the palace the Dalai Lama's aides heard three mortar rounds and the young ruler was confronted with a decision. "If I did escape from Lhasa," he would later write, "where was I to go, and how could I reach asylum? Everything was uncertain. Our minds were overwhelmed by such

> **If I did escape from Lhasa, where was I to go, and how could I reach asylum?**
>
> The Dalai Lama

unanswerable questions. We could not tell where the journey would lead or how it would end."

Amid the panic and confusion, the Dalai Lama calmly weighed the situation. "It was I who had to find the answer and make the decision," he said; "but with my inexperience in the affairs of the world it was not easy."

At 10 p.m., the Dalai Lama removed his maroon monastic robes and put on the clothes of a common soldier, donned a fur cap, and slung a rifle over his shoulder. Then he walked out of the palace into the crowded grounds. A dust storm helped provide more cover as he casually made his way past the Chinese troops and headed for the prearranged rendezvous point.

Several of his aides and close associates also escaped from the palace and together they rode out of the city on horses to join his family and begin a harried trek to seek a safe haven in the mountains.

Norbulingka bombed

The night he left Lhasa, the entourage crossed the Kyichu River and into the protection of Khampa guerrillas, who, with U.S. support, had been battling Chinese troops in eastern Tibet for years. However, their escape appears to have remained a Tibetan operation — contrary to what some would later claim, it was not carried out by the Central Intelligence Agency, although American officials may have assisted the Tibetans in communicating diplomatically with Indian officials.

Behind them the city erupted in violence. Thousands of Tibetans were killed as Chinese forces smashed the rebellion. By the time they took control of the palace on March 20 and discovered the Dalai Lama was gone, he and his party already had a two-day head start.

While in flight he received news that Norbulingka had been bombed, and he decided to leave Tibet altogether and cross into exile.

Chinese soldiers tossed the Tibetan corpses into funeral pyres and continued their search for the fugitive Dalai Lama.

Arduous trek

The Dalai Lama and his 37-strong entourage had to travel at night to avoid Chinese troops. They also had to endure the harsh climate and extreme heights as they climbed over the Himalayas and then cross a 1,640-foot (500 m) wide stretch of the deep Brahmaputra River.

After a difficult 13-day journey, on March 30 the exhausted fugitives finally crossed into India at the Khenzimana Pass and were greeted by Indian troops, who

Mountain trail: This Himalayan caravan follows the same route in 1959 used by the Dalai Lama to elude his Chinese "captors." The 23-year-old spiritual leader was trekking with his mother, younger brother, two sisters and 12 members of the Tibetan cabinet.

Safe arrival: The "living Buddha" arrives in Tezpur, India, courtesy of an Indian army jeep.

allowed them entry. They then proceeded to the seventeenth-century Tawang Monastery, 50 miles (80.5 km) inside the border, where the Dalai Lama rested among his fellow monks before undertaking the week-long trek from 10,827 feet (3,300 m) down to the town of Tezpur on the north bank of the Brahmaputra River, in Assam.

Word of his escape flashed over the news wires. India's Prime Minister Jawaharlal Nehru offered the Dalai Lama political asylum in India and in due course he settled into exile in Dharamsala. He was followed by about 80,000 Tibetans, most of whom settled in the same area of northern India, which has since become known as "Little Lhasa" and is home to the Tibetan government-in-exile.

A world symbol of peaceful resistance to oppression, the Dalai Lama was awarded the Nobel Peace Prize in 1989. At home and abroad, the Tibetans continue to demand autonomy from the Chinese and to restore their Lama to the Norbulingka Palace.

Spiritual meets political: The Dalai Lama meets Indian prime minister Jawaharlal Nehru at New Delhi Airport in September 1959. Nehru granted the Dalai Lama political asylum in Dharamsala where he has remained ever since.

Fleeing from a mass suicide

It was a settlement named after their charismatic leader, the Reverend Jim Jones. But the cult he had established in the jungle of Guyana was in serious trouble. The tipping point came during a visit by Congressman Leo Ryan. In the frenzy that followed, 33 members of the cult fled for their lives.

By mid-November 1978, 21-year-old Leslie Wagner-Wilson had been involved with the People's Temple Disciples of Christ for eight years. Leslie's mother had introduced her and her sister to the disciples when they were in the United States. The family eventually moved to Guyana to live in a commune under the church's charismatic and mercurial leader, Rev. Jim Jones.

A self-appointed minister from a small town in the Midwest, Jones had first led his flock to the South American location saying they would establish a "pure" communist state, and most of his followers went along. They gave him all of their belongings.

Over the last year or so, however, Jones's mental health had seriously deteriorated and he had become extremely paranoid. The members' living conditions were nightmarish. Those trying to escape were hunted down by gun-wielding guards, put in the punishment box, forced to work on chain gangs or heavily sedated. Jones brought in Indians from the rain forest to teach his followers how to survive in the wild and how to evade pursuers. At least once a week Jones declared a "white night," or state of emergency, when the entire population would be awakened by blaring sirens and required to arm themselves in preparation for a coming invasion. There was constant talk about death. Once or twice a month he required them to participate in "suicide drills" in which they drank fake poison. Now many residents feared for

Cult leader: Jim Jones, wearing trademark sunglasses and a straw hat. FBI officers recovered a cult member's photo album from the site, which revealed his rock star obsession with wearing sunglasses, even while giving sermons indoors.

Saved: Survivors of the Jonestown massacre, photographed in October 1979 outside the former People's Temple on Geary Boulevard, San Francisco. From left to right: Julius Evans, Sandra Evans, Leslie Wagner-Wilson, Richard Clark and Diane Louie.

their lives, but they were too scared to cross their insane leader. Physically and psychologically, Jones's hold on his followers was almost complete.

Congressman Ryan intervenes

After receiving many dire complaints from his constituents about the Jonestown "cult," U.S. Rep. Leo Ryan of California arrived on an investigative mission, bringing along a TV camera crew and various reporters.

Although Jones tried to have his followers put on a contented facade, it wasn't long before Congressman Ryan detected that many residents had been brainwashed

> **" The ones that they capture, they're gonna just let them grow up and be dummies. "**
>
> Rev. Jim Jones on Congressman Ryan's visit

into maintaining blind submission to their mentally deranged leader. Jim Jones realized his Utopian experiment had reached the end of the line.

Although she knew it might be fatal to resist, Leslie Wagner-Wilson longed to get out with her three-year-old son Jakari. So, along with ten others (four of them small children), she fled into the jungle, hoping to make it to safety about 30 miles (48 km) away. Meanwhile, 15 other residents begged Congressman Ryan to be taken back to the United States — a plea that he agreed to.

As Ryan's party arrived at the airstrip, however, a gang of gunmen opened fire on them, murdering the

Beginning of the end: Bodies lie on the Port Kaituma airstrip. Congressman Leo Ryan, who was investigating intimidation claims from relatives of the Jonestown congregation, was gunned down with four other Americans. At this point, Jones realized his mission was over.

congressman, an NBC correspondent and his cameraman, a newspaper photographer and one of the fleeing family members.

Ryan's 14 remaining passengers scattered into the jungle to hide. One of them was a 17-year-old boy who had been shot in the leg.

Flight through the jungle
Meanwhile, the leader of Leslie's tiny group, Richard Clark, had already placed markers in the jungle to help guide them, but in the rush to escape they were unable to stay on the trail.

Leslie carried her son, but she was so frightened she had trouble keeping her footing and gave him Kool-Aid

> " You can go down in history saying you chose your own way to go. "
>
> Rev. Jim Jones

laced with Valium so he wouldn't cry out — especially when they were near the compound's heavily guarded front gate. Her husband was a gung-ho security guard and she knew if he saw them he would shoot them all.

The escapees knew they had to move fast or they would be caught and killed. To throw off their pursuers they used every trick the Indians had taught them, leading their trackers in big circles and crossbacks and wading through streams to cover their scent. Slowed by wounds and weak from hunger and dehydration, they struggled to reach safety 30 miles (48 km) away.

While making their way over the railroad tracks, Leslie and the others heard a loud rumbling and realized a train was coming. As the train slowed, the curious conductor asked them if they needed a ride. But he was headed in the wrong direction and they told him no, leaving him with a puzzled look on his face. He couldn't understand why they were hurrying away from Jonestown.

They kept running. After four or five hours had passed, they had to cross a high railroad bridge spanning the river. Leslie was afraid of heights and it was all she could do to have one of the others carry her son while she crawled on her hands and knees to get across.

At dark, the train returned and they tried to hide but they were spotted. After it screeched to a stop, they expected to be shot as defectors, but the conductor asked them if they wanted a ride. This time the train was headed in the right direction and they accepted.

Upon reaching the town of Matthews Ridge, they were arrested. It was not until a police captain began to

Hard to bear: Victims of the tragedy lie where they fell after drinking Kool-Aid laced with a cocktail of poisons. The coordinated mass suicide was testament to the mind control that Jones exercised over his "community."

Nature takes over: Thirty years later and the site in the jungle has been cleared and nature left to reclaim the space. Little remains to remind visitors of the horrifying events that occurred.

Throne room: The quote above Jim Jones's sermonizing seat is borrowed from American philosopher George Santayana.

question them about shootings at Port Kaituma that Leslie and her companions began to learn of the bloodshed that had followed their escape. Luckily for them, the conductor vouched for them, saying he had seen them earlier, so they could not have been involved in the shootings.

When Jones learned that Congressman Ryan had been shot dead he knew it would destroy the way of life he had created for his settlement in Guyana.

Rather than face being brought back to the United States, Jones gave his followers the only alternative — suicide. He told them that their church could only survive if they were to make this ultimate sacrifice. Jones convinced his followers that their deaths would be a form of "revolutionary" suicide: "You can go down in history saying you chose your own way to go, and it is your commitment to refuse capitalism and in support of socialism." His brainwashed devotees took a lethal mixture of Kool-Aid combined with doses of cyanide, sedatives and tranquilizers. The poison caused death within minutes.

In total, 909 people died in the mass suicide at Jonestown. The Rev. Jim Jones died of a self-inflicted gun wound to the head. What has become known as the "Jonestown massacre" was the worst case of non-natural loss of American civilian life on record, until the events of September 11, 2001.

The fate of others

Within hours, Leslie Wagner-Wilson and her fellow escapees learned that 909 persons had died at Jonestown, most of them by drinking Kool-Aid laced with cyanide. One-third of the victims were children. Jones was also dead from a self-inflicted gunshot to the head. Leslie had lost her husband, her mother, a brother, sister, niece and nephew, as well as hundreds of friends.

In all, besides the 25 persons who had gained safety in the jungle, eight others from Jonestown had also survived the slaughter.

Three of those survivors claimed they had been given an assignment by Maria Katsaris, a top lieutenant of Jones, which had enabled them to escape. Of those, two brothers, Tim and Mike Carter (30 and 20 years old respectively), and Mike Prokes (aged 31, pictured at left above) were given luggage containing $500,000 and a document, which they were told to deliver to Guyana's Soviet Embassy in Georgetown. They soon ditched most of the money and were apprehended heading for the Temple boat (Cudjo) at Kaituma.

Larry Layton, aged 32, also claimed to have been a defector, but other survivors identified him as one of the gunmen and he was convicted in the United States and paroled from prison in 2002.

Four persons who were supposed to be poisoned somehow managed to survive the mass suicides and murders. These included 25-year-old Stanley Clayton, a kitchen worker and cousin of Huey Newton, who tricked security guards and ran into the jungle; Grover Davis, a hearing-impaired man of 79 who missed the announcement on the loudspeaker to assemble and had laid down in a ditch and pretended to be dead; Odell Rhodes, 36, a Jonestown teacher and craftsman who volunteered to fetch a stethoscope and hid under a building; and 76-year-old Hyacinth Thrash, who hid under her bed when nurses were going through her dormitory with cups of poison.

Today Jonestown remains infamous, not for its escapees, but for those who stayed.

Over the wall by balloon

Peter Strelzyk, Güenter Wetzel	September 15–16, 1979

Two East German families decided to risk their lives to cross the border into West Germany in a homemade hot-air balloon. But would the authorities spot them and shoot them down before they reached their destination, and would the balloon even make it?

By 1979 the Soviet Union had ruled East Germany with a tight grip for more than 34 years. Inside the Iron Curtain, the city of Berlin was partitioned in two: one section was communist-controlled and the other section governed by democratic West Germany.

On August 13, 1961, the Soviets resorted to erecting the infamous Berlin Wall to stem the rising flow of refugees seeking freedom in the West. The Wall was a barrier of barbed wire walls, security devices, automated explosives and armed guards that was rimmed by a No Man's Land of exposed ground known as "The Death Strip."

The East German border guards (Grepos) were ordered to shoot dead any person who attempted to cross it. According to one directive issued to the guards: "Do not hesitate to use your firearm, not even when the border is breached in the company of women and children, which is a tactic the traitors have often used."

Previous escape attempts

Hundreds of residents were shot down as they attempted to flee. In one especially notorious case, an 18-year-old boy who had tried to breach the wall, Peter Fechter, was wounded and left to bleed to death in full view of Western news media as a lesson to would-be escapers.

Nevertheless, thousands of East Germans persisted in trying; constantly devising new methods to defeat the authoritarians.

Some of them tried to climb over, tunnel out, or stow away in crossing trucks or cars to get past the checkpoints. In one instance, an East Berlin engineer who was piloting a glider on an authorized flight suddenly altered his course and rode the currents over to the West; in another, a Dresden family stole a plane, and although none of them had ever flown before, they boldly took off and steered the craft across the border before safely crash landing on the other side.

Success story: September 20, 1965, Stanislaus Gefroerer lies in the back of a lorry as his accomplices move to cover him up. Gefroerer had escaped over the Berlin Wall by ladder.

Wall repairs: April 1963, East German policemen, to the left of the wall, carry out hasty repairs. This section of the wall was damaged when Wolfgang Engels, 19, rammed an East German armored car into the wall and escaped into West Berlin. He was shot but recovered in hospital.

But besides the wall itself, the Soviets had also created a fearsome secret police force — the Stasi — to carry out rampant spying. In size it was three times larger than the Gestapo that Hitler had used to spy on a population that was about a quarter as big as Nazi Germany's. Its agents monitored all communications, watched every move, and turned many East Germans into secret informers against their customers, neighbors and co-workers. Paranoia reigned.

Strelzyk and Wetzel

Hans Peter Strelzyk was a former aircraft mechanic who longed to escape with his family. One day he viewed a program on East German television that presented some of the history of hot-air ballooning. It piqued his interest

enough for him to study the principles established by France's pioneering Montgolfier brothers in the 1780s and gave him an idea. After a neighbor's teenage son was shot to death trying to flee the country, Strelzyk decided to seek the help of a trusted friend, Güenter Wetzel, a bricklayer who also possessed some building skills. Together they decided to try to construct their own balloon that would carry them and their families south to freedom in West Germany.

The pair and their wives secretly collaborated on the project, working at night in their basements. The men wanted to create a flamethrower and gas burner powerful enough to propel their craft, and instead of building a heavy gondola, they gradually put together a cast-iron platform with posts at the corners for handholds and rope anchors. After fastening four propane cooking-gas cylinders to the center, they had the first part.

Meanwhile, their wives purchased nylon and other light cloth in small enough amounts to avert suspicion, on one occasion narrowly escaping a watchful store clerk who had called the police. Finally they had cobbled together 60 different pieces of canvas, bed sheets, and random scraps to form a large balloon, 65 feet (19.8 m) wide and 75 feet (22.9 m) high. Now they had the second part.

First attempt

On July 4, 1979 the Wetzels declined to accompany the four Strelzyks on the balloon's first escape ascent. Their chosen launch spot was a vacant meadow 25 miles (40.2 km) from the border. The craft became airborne and flew for 25 minutes, rising to a peak altitude of 6,235 feet (1,900 m). But the winds were wrong and the gas supply proved too small; as the balloon became weighed down from cloud moisture they ended up descending and fell just 655 feet (200 m) short of The Death Strip.

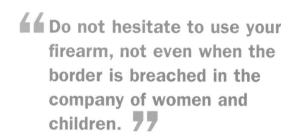

" Do not hesitate to use your firearm, not even when the border is breached in the company of women and children. "

Directive issued to East German border guards

Fortunately, they were not apprehended and their success convinced the Wetzels to join them on another attempt. After restudying the matter, using books and crude calculations, they elected to build a bigger balloon, 92 feet (28 m) high and 66 feet (20 m) wide, that would accommodate both families.

Second attempt

Two months later they were ready for the second try. On the night of September 15, noting that the wind and other weather conditions seemed to favor their launch, the two married couples and their four young children climbed into the gondola and fired up the burner.

In the darkness, the crazy-quilt balloon filled with hot air and rose to a peak of 8,200 feet (2,499 m), riding a good wind. But it began to descend to 6,000 feet (1,829 m) as they approached what they thought was the border.

Floating along at a gentle speed of only 10 to 15 knots, they were lucky not to be caught in the cross fires of the menacing searchlights that swept through the sky. But after descending to a height of only 15 feet (4.6 m), their propane ran out and they plummeted into bushes.

Their flight was over, but they didn't know where they were. They noted some nearby farm machinery that looked more modern than anything available at home, but then became startled when police officers appeared. Strelzyk asked if they were in West Germany. And one of the officers said, "Of course."

They had landed in the Bavarian town of Naila. Although only 14 miles (22.5 km) and 28 minutes away from lift off, the Strelzyks and Wetzels were a whole world away.

Museum piece: Peter Strelzyk with his wife Doris and their two sons stand in front of a painting depicting their escape in the Berlin Wall Museum. A part of the original balloon hangs behind them.

The car with a secret

Klaus Jacobi (right) and Manfred Koster stand behind the BMW Isetta, a popular post-war car, in which Koster successfully escaped through the Berlin Wall on November 5, 1963. Using a special hidden compartment built into the tiny three-wheeler by Jacobi, Koster passed under the noses of border guards without detection. In total, this type of car made possible eight such escapes until the ninth failed as guards discovered the extra passenger.

Authorities in the eastern German city of Magdeburg recently discovered a 1973 document of the former East German internal security agency, the Stasi, giving guards at border posts the order to shoot anyone trying to flee the country, even women and children. The document confirms that shooting escapees was an official policy of the former East German government, something former East German politicians have long denied. More than a thousand East Germans died while attempting to escape East Germany for the West. East German officials and Allied forces often used Glienicker Bridge, which stands at the former border between East Germany and West Berlin, to exchange refugees and captured spies during the Cold War.

The killing fields

Dith Pran, a courageous Cambodian translator and photojournalist, survived Pol Pot's bone-chilling killing fields, only to set off on an arduous odyssey of escape through the jungle to Thailand. Sydney Schanberg, his anguished former colleague, was left to search for signs of his whereabouts.

By early 1975 Sydney Schanberg had spent several years covering the war in Southeast Asia as a correspondent for *The New York Times*. Since coming to Phnom Penh, Cambodia in 1972, he had often worked with an educated, middle-class Cambodian translator and photojournalist, Dith Pran, and the two had become close friends. The American had come to rely on his colleague as much as any correspondent could. Now that bond would be sorely tested.

With the American retreat from Vietnam, the communist Khmer Rouge were about to take over Cambodia, prompting Dith to hurriedly send away his wife and four children on a U.S. military truck while he remained to help Schanberg report the story of the country's fall to the communists. The American Embassy was evacuated on April 12.

On April 17, guerillas led by Pol Pot seized Phnom Penh, thirsting to exact their revenge for years of corrupt colonial rule. The Khmer Rouge quickly began to show some of their brutal intentions, looting shops and wantonly slaughtering civilians in the streets. When Schanberg and Dith went with other reporters to a city hospital to ascertain details about the violence, thuggish soldiers put them under arrest and looked ready to kill them. But Dith used his remarkable verbal skills to beg and cajole them, eventually winning their release.

The Killing Fields: Sam Wannamaker played Sydney Schanberg in the 1984 film *The Killing Fields*, while Hang S. Nor won an Oscar playing Dith Pran.

The depths of horror: Pran had to deny his former occupation as the Khmer Rouge sought to rid the country of any traces of Western culture or dangerous intellectualism. When the invading Vietnamese discovered he had worked as a translator his days were numbered.

Cambodia looked to be sinking into an abyss

Schanberg and other foreign reporters were forced to leave the country. However, the Khmer told Pran he must remain behind. As the two parted, Schanberg feared that his friend, the man who had saved his life, would soon become another victim of the murderous new regime. He slipped Dith $2,600 in bribe money and threw his arms around him in a final embrace. Then he left. For the next four years the anguished correspondent would remain wracked with guilt over Dith's unknown fate — and Schanberg was determined to find out if he was still alive.

> " For God's sake, get inside ... if you go on arguing, they'll shoot you down in the street. "
>
> Schanberg to Pran, from his book
> *The Death and Life of Dith Pran*

Under Pol Pot

The Khmer Rouge renamed Cambodia *Kampuchéa* and imposed the most extreme measures to rid the country of Western influence. They banned hospitals, newspapers, churches and temples, and took children away from their parents for indoctrination. The soldiers were ordered to execute anyone who wore sunglasses or makeup. City dwellers were forced into rural labor camps. During Pol Pot's terrifying rule, which lasted three years, eight months and 20 days, an estimated 2 million Cambodians — or about 30 percent of the country's population — died by starvation, torture or execution in one of the worst genocides in modern history.

Dith, meanwhile, tried to survive through it all. After a few days in the French Embassy, he headed north as part of the mass exodus from the city, noticing that the communists were bent on treating the populace like livestock. Weighing his options, he threw away the money, donned dirty peasant clothes, and changed his appearance to look like a humble taxi driver, hoping to divert suspicion. The ruse convinced his interrogators well enough to save him from summary execution.

Bitter homecoming: Dith Pran returned to Cambodia in 1989 and visited his home village of Siem Reap. This was the scene that greeted him in the abandoned schoolhouse. Pran set up the Dith Pran Holocaust Awareness Project in 1994. It has been estimated that 25 percent of the Cambodian population died under the Khmer Rouge.

The years went by. The pace of the killings continued to increase.

In December 1978, Vietnamese communist troops mounted a massive blitzkrieg against the Khmer Rouge and on January 7, 1979 Vietnamese forces took Phnom Penh. In the months that followed, the world was confronted with grisly evidence of some of Pol Pot's crimes against humanity, his torture prisons and insane purges, the mass graves.

Dith, meanwhile, was made a commune chief in the village of Bat Dangkor, but conditions remained intolerable. When the Vietnamese found out that he had worked as a translator for Western media, he knew his days were numbered.

He decided to attempt his escape.

Thailand

On July 29, 1979 he slipped out of Siem Reap and headed for another place 40 miles (64 km) to the northwest. Once there, he made contact with people

All around him others were being murdered for the slightest infraction, such as a boy and girl who were holding hands. Famine was also claiming many more.

Dith traveled back to his home village, only to learn that 50 members of his family, including his father and three of his brothers, had died. Wells were filled with skulls and bones, and the grassland covered many unmarked graves. He called them the "killing fields." In another village, the hunger was so bad that some starving victims were said to be digging up freshly buried human bodies in order to cook and eat the flesh.

Consigned to endless labor, Dith suffered from gnawing hunger and beatings, but he somehow survived.

who could help him and they prepared for a dash out of the country.

In mid-September, Dith and 11 other men set out on a perilous hike, braving landmines and roving killers from the Vietnamese and Khmer forces. Although their objective was 35 miles (56 km) away, the journey took them 60 harrowing miles (97 km) through jungle terrain that was laced with deadly pungi traps (sharpened bamboo stakes that were arranged under camouflaged pits) and other hazards. An exploding mine killed two of his companions. After separating from the rest of his party, on October 3, 1979 he finally crossed the border into Thailand and he entered a refugee camp.

Pran and Schanberg are reunited

After passing a message to Schanberg, the two old comrades were reunited. Schanberg helped him enter the United States and rejoin his family.

Hired by *The New York Times* as a reporter, he became a U.S. citizen in 1986 and devoted the rest of his life to helping fellow Cambodians who had suffered under the Khmer Rouge.

Schanberg had earned a Pulitzer Prize for his Cambodia coverage and later published a famous magazine article about his and Pran's deep human relationship. In 1984 it was made into a critically acclaimed Hollywood movie, *The Killing Fields*, starring Sam Waterson as Schanberg and Haing S. Ngor as his courageous friend. (Ngor's portrayal won an Oscar but he was later murdered in the United States.)

Thanks in part to Pran's and Schanberg's reporting, the horrors of the killing fields were condemned as one of the century's worst genocides, and Cambodia awakened from its long nightmare.

The world-renowned human rights champion Dith Pran died of pancreatic cancer in 2008

The runner

When the simmering ethnic tension between the Hutu and Tutsi tribes exploded in Burundi, villages were split down the middle as schools, churches and even sports clubs divided on tribal lines. Escape seemed impossible when Gilbert Tuhabonye was herded into a burning slaughterhouse.

Gilbert Tuhabonye had accomplished much in his young life. Considered the golden child of his high school, the Lycée Kibimba, he was a top student who at age 17 had already become Burundi's national running champion in the 400 meters and 800 meters and was known as the fastest and strongest boy in his age group. His high status made him stand out.

The road to destruction: Refugees in Burundi flee from the ethnic violence between Hutus and Tutsis after President Ndadaye was assassinated in an abortive army coup.

Living with his family and other members of his clan in a cluster of huts in beautiful surroundings, he thought he was in paradise.

However, the history of Burundi had long been marred by acrimony and civil war between its main rival tribes, the Tutsis and Hutus. The Tutsis were the cattle-owning elite who held more political power, while the more numerous Hutus were mostly farmers. It was said that Tutsis were often taller and thinner, with slimmer noses, while the Hutus tended to be smaller and stockier, though in fact this had probably changed due to inter-marriage.

Tuhabonye was a Tutsi, but many of his neighbors, schoolmates and friends were Hutu, and relations between the two groups seemed to have improved in his region. But after some Tutsis overthrew and assassinated Melchior Ndadaye, a Hutu and Burundi's first elected president, the Hutus exploded in rage and many demanded revenge.

The slaughterhouse

On October 21, 1993, a Hutu mob that included some of Tuhabonye's classmates and fellow relay team members invaded his high school and threatened every Tutsi they could find, including him. Just the previous day, many of the same Hutus had been his friends. He had trained with them on the drumming team and the running team and even shared track shoes with one of them, his Hutu friend Severin. But now Severin was part of the mob, chanting for revenge, demanding blood.

Kibimba's Tutsi pupils had fled to their Hutu headmaster, begging for help. Tuhabonye was his star pupil. But now that shining star watched the foaming spittle of hatred form on the headmaster's bottom lip as he snarled, "You are now going to see what Jesus saw on the cross."

> **"You are now going to see what Jesus saw on the cross."**
>
> Tuhabonye's headmaster

The machete-wielding mob tied them together and took them to an empty building that was due to become a gas station. They were told to go inside or they would be killed. Tutsis were beaten and some of the screaming victims were stabbed with spears or hacked with blades, falling down in a growing pile all around him. The carnage was sickening. People he knew were dying beside him, while on the other side, people he knew were doing the killing.

The remaining Tutsis were herded into the building,

Grisly remains: Many from Gilbert Tuhabonye's village were killed by being burned alive. Those that escaped were inevitably hacked to death with machetes. Tuhabonye escaped.

Survivor's story: After winning a track scholarship to the U.S., Tuhabonye settled in Texas. He now runs a successful athletics club, Gilbert's Gazelles.

the fire. Yet living was more than he could bear. After a long time inside the burning building, finding he was the only survivor, he climbed up on to a concrete partition and threw himself to the ground, meaning to end his own life by breaking his neck. But at the last second he instinctively tucked his head round and landed on his shoulder instead.

The futility made him cry with fear and frustration. Unable to endure it any more, he picked up a burning femur, scorching his own flesh, then swung it like a hammer, smashing one of the glass windowpanes. Prepared to sacrifice himself to the mob, he climbed out of the opening and jumped into the smoky night, straight into the middle of the hysterical crowd. Miraculously, they did not see him at first, although his back was on fire and what was left of his clothes were smoldering. Although he was badly burned, dehydrated, and traumatized with terror, he started running away. He had always been such a good runner, but now he was running for his life.

Some of the Hutus let him go, yelling that they would get him in the morning, but one pursuer remained on his tail, chasing him through the black night. The rain was stinging his back. Exhausted, Tuhabonye approached a fresh hole that must have been dug there for the Hutus' victims — to hide the evidence — and he jumped into it and waited. As his pursuer ran past, he jumped out and knocked him to the ground, then snapped the Hutu's neck just as he had seen in Sylvester Stallone and Chuck Norris movies. He heard a "satisfying pop," and felt the body crumple dead.

Then he got up and ran to the hospital, where Tutsi soldiers provided protection. As the doctors treated him for his injuries, he learned that the mob had murdered his father in a separate attack.

while the Hutus began pouring in petrol and throwing burning eucalyptus branches through the windows to ignite the chemicals. The hot air was thick with smoke and the smell of blood, fear, urine, burning flesh and singed hair. Curled up in a small alcove off the main room, Tuhabonye watched as the skin shriveled, burned, blistered, then simply disappeared to expose sinew and bone. The drums beat on, accompanied by singing and exultant chants of "We did it! We did it! We did it!"

Anyone who tried to escape through the windows was butchered on the spot. Tuhabonye did not want to die in

> He had always been such a good runner, but now he was running for his life.

Recovery

Tuhabonye spent three months recuperating in hospital, where his cousin helped care for him. At first, his doctors told him that he would never run again. However, after a long rehabilitation he went on to win the NCAA All-American honor six times, authored a best-selling autobiography, and carried the Olympic torch in 1996. His strength as a runner has served him well.

A genocide survivor's story

Tuhabonye spent three months recuperating in hospital, then eventually left the country to attend college in the United States on a track scholarship. He was named NCAA All-American runner six times at Abilene Christian University in Texas, where he also received his bachelor's degree. He later authored a best-selling book entitled, *This Voice in My Heart: A Runner's Memoir of Genocide, Faith, and Forgiveness.* In addition to competing for Burundi in various international track competitions, despite the scars from his injuries, he carried the Olympic torch in Birmingham, Alabama en route to the 1996 Atlanta Games. His strength as a runner had served him well. He currently lives with his wife and two daughters in Austin, Texas, where he coaches Gilbert's Gazelles, an award-winning track club. Tuhabonye is considered one of the most inspirational figures on the running scene today.

4
Prison and the law

Papillon

It took nine attempts over a period of nine agonizing years for the French convict known as Papillon to escape from the world's most infamous penal colony. Henri Charrière's account of his amazing adventures went on to captivate millions. But were they too amazing to be real?

Henri Charrière was a French safecracker and career criminal wrongly charged with murdering a Paris pimp. Despite his strenuous claims that he hadn't committed the crime in question, on October 26, 1931, Charrière was quickly tried, convicted and sentenced to hard labor for life, forcing him to bid a final adieu to his pregnant wife and daughter.

He had begun his descent into hell. Now he would be known to his fellow convicts as "Papillon" for the tattoo of a butterfly he wore on his chest.

Heading for misery: Prisoners line up for a barge that will take them to the cargo boat *Martinere* and on to Devil's Island, the most notorious of the *Iles du Salut*, in French Guiana. The penal colony had a formidable reputation for disease and suffering.

Devil's Island: The main detention center with solitary confinement cells. Buildings in the complex dated to 1852 when the penal colony was first established. Napoleon III, asked by whom the convicts would be guarded, replied "by worse crooks than they are."

After a two-year stint in the Beaulieu transit prison in Caen in northern France, Papillon was put aboard a transport vessel and taken to Saint Laurent prison on the Maroni river in French Guiana, east of Venezuela, South America.

"Le bagne"

By the time Papillon arrived there, French Guiana was already the world's most infamous penal colony.

French rulers had spent centuries trying to colonize Guiana. But each attempt had ended with the colonists' deaths from tropical diseases, Indian attacks and starvation. One motley group had sought refuge on the *Iles du Salut* ("Islands of Salvation") — an archipelago of three tiny islands located eight miles (13 km) from the South American coastline — hoping to escape the disease-spreading mosquitoes and jungle predators that had plagued their mainland efforts. The French called the largest island *Isle Royale* after the king; and named another St. Joseph for divine protection. The third and smallest, and also the least inhabitable, was called *Isle du Diable* ("Devil's Island") because of its lethal turbulence and forbidding topography.

In 1852, Louis Napoleon tried to utilize Guiana as a penal colony, shipping over the first 354 French convicts to the mainland. But that too consumed many lives: of 7,000 convicts sent there in 1856, 2,500 perished in the first year alone. This high casualty rate failed to trouble the French authorities, however, and by 1867 the nation had sent off about 18,000 convicts to its hell on earth, which it called "le bagne." Many were never heard from again.

On location: Charrière's story was made into a film starring Steve McQueen as Henri Charrière and Dustin Hoffman as his friend, the fraudster Louis Dega.

prompting many dark rumors back in Europe. But it wasn't until the famous Alfred Dreyfus legal case of 1895–1899 that the place became a national scandal. Despite the bad publicity, the French government continued in using the area as a penal colony.

First escape

Papillon first landed at St. Laurent on November 2, 1933 and quickly decided it was not for him. But if escaping from prison custody wasn't hard enough, the most difficult thing would be to survive the jungle or the shark-infested waters to make it to freedom and live to tell the tale.

Four weeks later, Papillon bribed his way into the prison hospital and tried to escape with two other convicts. The plan was simple: his friend Joanes Clousiot the forger and an 18-year-old homosexual named Maturette would club their Arab guards, enabling them all to scale the prison wall and make their exit. Then, aided by a well-connected convict wheeler-dealer named Jésus, they would gain access to the dugout boat that would carry them away.

From the start, however, things did not go according to plan. Clousiot hurt his foot landing from the wall, and the dugout they had purchased turned out to be rotten. But Papillon was determined to continue and he led them to a nearby leper colony on Pigeon Island where they obtained a better boat.

The convicts called Devil's Island "The Rock" and referred to the jungle-based outposts of *le bagne* as the "Dry Guillotine."

Conditions on the mainland and neighboring islands remained horrendous through the 1880s and 90s,

It took them all the way to Trinidad, a journey of more than 1,000 miles (1,610 km), where they met up with three other French fugitives and made their way to the island of Curaçao in the southern Caribbean sea. From there they hoped to sail to Honduras in Central America.

Reimprisoned

They were later recaptured and reimprisoned in Colombia. Papillon escaped again with the aid of a fellow convict and they later parted ways, leaving him to go on alone to Guarjira, where he spent several months living among Indian pearl divers. There he formed a rapturous love relationship with two young women who bore his children. But he eventually left and continued heading westward in hopes of gaining his freedom.

Recaptured once again, he was taken to the "Black Hole" at Santa Marta and later transferred to Barranquilla where he again encountered Clousiot and Maturette. In the course of repeatedly trying to escape again, he broke both of his heels, permanently injuring himself, and the three were extradited back to French Guiana.

As punishment for their previous escape, Papillon and his two comrades were sentenced to two years of solitary confinement on St. Joseph in the place the convicts called the "Devourer of Men." As a result of being locked away in such a tiny cell with poisonous centipedes and forced to maintain absolute silence, most convicts went mad. But Papillon barely held onto his sanity and survived. Shortly after their release on June 26, 1936, Clousiot died and Papillon was transferred to the island of Royale — seemingly, a broken man.

By now a hardened convict, Papillon murdered a fellow prisoner who was foiling his next plan to escape via a raft, for which he was sentenced to another eight years in solitary confinement. But after only 19 months, he rescued a drowning girl in shark-infested waters and was rewarded with a release from his solitary punishment sentence.

Next, he feigned insanity in order to escape from the island's asylum. There, he and an Italian convict plotted to make their ocean escape on barrels they had lashed together. But the Italian perished on the rocks.

In the end, Papillon made his ninth attempt by building a raft from coconuts, which he and another convict deployed into the rough seas and used to transport themselves toward the mainland. His companion died on the journey, but Papillon reached the coast, where he connected with Chinese smugglers who

Papillon: The reason why Charrière got his butterfly nickname is revealed by McQueen in the film. There was to be a bizarre twist to the story of the tattoo in 2005.

helped him get to Georgetown in British Guiana. It was October 1941 and France was at war with Britain in World War II, so this time he evaded arrest and extradition.

The rest of his journey went perfectly well.

In 1945, Charrière settled in Venezuela, where he married a local woman and started another family. He became a successful businessman, opening a restaurant and hotels in Caracas and Maracaibo and achieving some celebrity as a chef. Twenty years later he wrote a book about his experiences that made him rich and famous.

Fact or fiction?

Charrière's 1969 autobiography, *Papillon*, sold more than one million copies in France and went on to become a big international bestseller, with an English version translated by the novelist Patrick O'Brian. It inspired the hugely successful movie, also called *Papillon*, starring Steve McQueen and Dustin Hoffman, which probably remains the best prison escape and adventure film ever made. (At this writing, Hollywood is undertaking an expensive remake.)

Controversy: Charrière died in 1973 before the release of the film of his life story, but from the moment it was published there were doubts over its authenticity. Many believe it to be an aggregation of other prisoners' stories. In 2005 Charles Brunier came forward and revealed his own butterfly tattoo. The 104-year-old had been incarcerated with Charrière.

After the book came out, some critics chided the author for "factual errors" and charged that he had

> **" I should never have believed or imagined that a country like mine, a country like France, the mother of freedom throughout the world, a country that had brought forth the Rights of Man and of the citizen, could possibly possess an establishment of such barbarous repressions as the St. Joseph solitary confinement prison. "**
>
> Henri Charrière, *Papillon*

padded his memoir with material from other former convicts' accounts. Somebody said Papillon had only tried to escape twice, not nine times as he claimed. Journalists also said they had dug into old police records to examine Charrière's claim he had never murdered the Paris pimp in question, and reported that the documents seemed to show there was little doubt about his guilt.

But Charrière stuck by his story, saying his account was as accurate as he could make it, adding that he hadn't gone into "that hell" with a typewriter. He also later appeared in a documentary film, *Magnificent Rebel*, which purported to tell the true facts behind his life and the making of the Hollywood movie.

In 1973 he died in Madrid from throat cancer. But 32 years after his reported passing, Charrière continued to spark controversy when reports from Venezuela claimed he was still alive and on the voter rolls as voter number 1,728,629. Another elderly French ex-convict also came forward to insist he was the real Papillon and that Charrière had simply stolen his identity. Charles Brunier, aged 104, even rolled back his shirt to reveal an aged tattoo of a butterfly on his wrinkled skin. Records showed that he had been imprisoned with Charrière in the Isles du Salut.

Devil's Island today

After using French Guiana as a penal colony for nearly a century, France ended sending convicts there in 1938 and started closing down some of its penal colonies at the conclusion of World War II. In 1965, the French government transferred the responsibility of most of the islands to the newly founded Guiana Space Centre. The French space agency, in association with other agencies, has since had some of the historical sites on the islands restored. Tourism facilities were added; the islands now welcome more than 50,000 tourists each year.

Today, the Iles du Salut are a popular tourist attraction. The island of Royale attracts ferries laden with vacationers on a highpriced getaway to one of the equatorial Atlantic's more exotic spots. The island is owned by the French National Space Agency as a monitoring site for Ariane rockets and satellites launched from nearby Kourou. Nearby Saint-Joseph (site of the infamous reclusion prison) and tiny Ile du Diable (Devil's Island) are also accessible by boat and feature several restored historical sites and museums. Getting off the islands today is much easier than it was for Papillon and his fellow convicts.

Prison escape artist

He was the gentleman bankrobber. Willie Sutton was America's top career criminal and a consummate prison escape artist. But when he was sent to the historic, "escape-proof" Eastern State Penitentiary in Philadelphia, his criminal ingenuity faced its greatest challenge.

Brooklyn's storied Irish mobster William "Willie" Sutton — aka "Slick Willie" or "Willie the Actor" — was famous as a gentlemanly bank robber who was always immaculately dressed and never robbed a bank when a woman screamed or a baby cried. Although he had usually carried a pistol or a Thompson submachine gun, explaining, "You can't rob a bank on charm and personality," he later said such weapons hadn't really been loaded because "somebody might get hurt." A brilliant strategist and meticulous planner, he may have been one of the most ingenious criminals who had ever lived, and by the 1940s he was also renowned for his elaborate prison escapes, having busted out of some of the country's toughest joints.

Since being founded in the 1830s, Philadelphia's castle-like Eastern State Penitentiary had always been one of the world's best known and most "escape-proof" prisons. This jail was an architectural wonder of classic beauty and impregnable strength that had defeated many generations of rebellious captives.

So when Sutton was sent there, carrying a 25–50-year sentence for one of his most brazen bank robberies, Eastern's warden, "Hard-Boiled" Smith, immediately issued a stern warning. As long as he'd been in charge of the institution, he said,

Sing Sing: Sutton escaped from New York's notorious prison in 1932 by finding his way past seven locked doors, three barred gates and deploying a makeshift ladder.

Charismatic: Sutton was ever the gentleman, witty and non-violent. Many mafia inmates he was locked up with sought his company, even though their criminal worlds were miles apart. Pictured here at the time of his final arrest in 1952, he is thought to have robbed 100 banks in his career.

"Nobody has escaped on me yet . . . All the guards have been notified to be on the alert." One false move and they would blow Sutton's head off.

Doing the impossible

Based on his long experience as a career criminal, Sutton had developed his own intricate philosophy of escape. He believed that the older a prison was the harder it was to escape from because there had been more convicts who had attempted to break out and each time one of them had tried the authorities had responded by shoring up whatever weaknesses the convict had tried to exploit. One of his goals was to turn an old prison's greatest strength into its greatest weakness.

Sutton was also a master prison politician, knowing which convicts to trust and which potential "rats" to avoid. He was a master at getting cunning friends to help him assemble an intricate plan to bust out.

At ancient Sing Sing in 1932 he had somehow put

> **" No one has escaped on me yet ... All the guards have been notified to be on the alert. "**
>
> **Eastern State Penitentiary warden**

Eastern State Penitentiary: When it was built in 1829 it was the largest and most expensive prison ever constructed. It was closed in 1971 and exists today as a "preserved ruin." Like Alcatraz, it is a significant tourist attraction with Sutton's tunnel and Al Capone's cell the highlights.

such tenets together to pull off one of his most impressive feats. Somehow, he had sawed through his cell's steel bars. Then he had figured out how to get from the upper tier to the lower tier of a huge cellblock filled with 900 inmates and dozens of guards, after which he managed to penetrate a 15-foot (4.6 m) corridor that led to the mess hall. From there he entered into the mess hall cellar and snuck out into the heavily policed prison yard. This alone had required, at the very least, conquering the locks of seven very secure doors at four key intersections, three blind wooden doors, three barred gates, and finally the huge metal door in the cellar that opened into the yard. From there, as if by magic, he had deployed a specially constructed makeshift ladder to scale the 30-foot (9 m) high wall to freedom, and lowered himself without injury. Once on the street, he later said, "I felt so good that I stood up, like the King of the Hill, and looked

down on the searchlights and the general panoramic view of the sleeping prison." Then he shook his fist at it and said, "I beat you, you bastards!"

Precision work

From the time Sutton first set foot in Eastern, he did everything he could to study its strengths and weaknesses and became pals with others who could help him escape. "Planning to escape from prison takes infinite patience," he once confided. "Precision work paced over a long period of time. A plan which can be described in a paragraph may have taken two years to put together."

In Eastern's case, the obstacles were so great, it took more than a decade to plan and execute — a harrowing process of twists and turns, triumphs and setbacks. A key breakthrough occurred when one of his prison mates discovered the secret location of the main sewer beneath the prison — a fact that had eluded convicts for more than a century.

Somehow, Sutton and his co-conspirators were able to covertly acquire or make dozens of tools and other pieces of equipment they could use in digging a hidden tunnel to the sewer line. They also had to get access to the cellar location where they would conduct their dig. And they needed to carry out extensive excavation — all without getting caught and while strictly adhering to a tight schedule that allowed no room for error.

Their digging was dangerous and physically exhausting. At times Sutton almost suffocated or drowned underground. He always had to emerge at just the right moment — when friends were waiting to wipe him down and clean up the mess.

On one occasion, an alert guard noted a speck of red lead on his shoe and the authorities suspected that it might mean he had been in the cellar. Sutton talked his way out of trouble, but he and his pals had to suspend their work until the coast was clear. By then seven years had already passed since Sutton had started with his plan.

But he kept going, relentlessly. Night after night, he

> **❝ Planning to escape from prison takes infinite patience ... a plan which can be described in a paragraph may have taken two years to put together. ❞**
>
> Willie Sutton

Warder vision: Prison architect John Haviland designed a "hub and spoke" structure for ease of monitoring the cell wings. It was one of the first prisons to feature only solitary confinement cells and was designed to make it difficult for prisoners to communicate with each other.

Foiled: Eastern State Penitentiary wardens pose after the 1945 escape plan was curtailed.

break, Sutton was transferred to Holmesburg Prison, where on February 10, 1947, he was caught in the prison searchlights during another carefully plotted escape attempt. But by assuring the guards, "It's OK," the steel-nerved convict miraculously was allowed to walk away into the night unmolested.

In and out of prisons for the rest of his life, Willie Sutton later published two autobiographical books about his exploits, eventually dying in sunny retirement in 1980 at the age of 79.

climbed up to the slanted window on the roof of his cell in order to get a good view of the prison yard, memorizing every detail. After creating a secret cache in the stone floor in which to hide his tools and materials, he labored to build a life-sized dummy complete with a plaster head and painted a mask that was eerily lifelike. But prison guards discovered it in a cell shakedown and he was moved into solitary confinement.

Break out

When Sutton returned to general conferment in June 1944, he resumed digging an extraordinary tunnel with his accomplices. Masterfully designed and constructed, it was even equipped with an electrical lighting system and wooden bracing.

The work proceeded slowly in part because they had to be so careful removing and hiding the moist dirt; oftentimes a man would carry handfuls in his clutched fists and later drop the telltale evidence on the prison ball field before covering it over with dust.

Finally, after ten backbreaking months, on April 3, 1945, Sutton and 11 others coordinated their complicated escape. Sutton was the fourth man through the tunnel. But just as he stuck his head out of the hole, two beat cops happened to be reporting to the police box located at that precise spot.

End of the line

Sutton was caught. But his escape went down in prison annals as one of the greatest in history. After the Eastern

Going nowhere: Sutton's 1945 tunnel attempt was a brilliant failure which only added to his cachet as the No.1 escape artist.

Tunnel unearthed

Sutton had a convict chum, Clarence Klinedinst (aka "Kliney"), who worked in the plastering shop and was allowed to move around the prison for his trusty work. He was the one who provided Slick Willie with plaster to make his first dummy head. Even though he had little time left on his sentence, he also wanted to join in the effort. Kliney and his cellmate William Russell opted to get involved in the escape attempt. Kliney used his masonry knowledge and privileges to remove the granite blocks and dispose of the tunnelers' unwanted debris. He also was instrumental in constructing their underground marvel. When the time finally came for the crew to make their break, Kliney was the first con out — three men ahead of Sutton. He got away for awhile, but like the others, he too was later recaptured.

In 2006 a team of archaeologists from John Milner Associates excavated areas of the famed and then-abandoned Eastern State Penitentiary, looking for the legendary 122-foot (37 m) long Willie Sutton tunnel. Guided by historical accounts (including Sutton's autobiography and detailed records left by the prison staff who had inspected the tunnel after the escape) and using ground-penetrating radar and other technology, they discovered its exact location and dimensions beneath the penitentiary's southwest courtyard. After utilizing an auger to dig down 10 feet (3 m) to the underground cavity, they lowered a miniature camera into the opening to document its intact interior, searching for the wiring, sockets, and light bulbs the convicts had used to light their dark passageway to freedom; the probers showed videos of the scene to visitors on closed-circuit TV. Kliney's subterranean corridor turned out to be a wonder to behold.

The Rock

Three determined bank robbers followed through with an elaborate scheme to become the first convicts to escape from "Uncle Sam's Devil's Island" and live to tell the tale. Their brazen breakout left befuddled FBI agents scratching their heads — but did they ever make it?

Frank Lee Morris had spent much of his 35-year-old life since infancy shuffling in and out of foster homes, juvenile institutions, jails and prisons. His rap sheet included convictions for bank robbery, armed robbery, auto theft and narcotics possession. But federal prison officials had sent him to Alcatraz due to his record of persistent escape attempts. With an IQ of 133, and an occupational background as a mechanical draftsman and

The Rock: Alcatraz Island hosted Confederate prisoners from the Civil War, military prisoners from the Spanish-American War of 1898 and then civilian prisoners following the 1906 earthquake. It became a federal prison in 1933.

painter, he ranked as one of the most intelligent convicts in the federal prison system, and therefore, one of the highest risks.

From the time that Morris arrived at The Rock on January 20, 1960 as inmate #AZ-1441, he was determined to someday break out of the place many inmates considered the world's toughest prison.

He was not alone. John Anglin, aged 32, and his brother Clarence, aged 31, had been convicted of bank robbery with their brother Alfred, and the three brothers had served time together in Atlanta Penitentiary where they had met Morris. Like him, Clarence and John had been sent to Alcatraz for previous escape attempts.

Every convict at Alcatraz was assigned to a small individual cell. The Anglins occupied adjacent cells near Morris. Also adjacent to Morris was a career criminal with longer experience in Alcatraz, Allen West, who had also known John Anglin from the Florida State Penitentiary. After coming into contact again the four began plotting their escape.

For incorrigibles

Escape was a tall order. Alcatraz was situated on a tiny island that was located a little more than a mile (1.6 km) from Fisherman's Wharf, just inside the entrance to gusty San Francisco Bay. Its 12 acres (0.05 km²) of sparse, rocky, windswept sandstone jutted sharply from the water to a height of 136 feet (42 m), making it visible for miles around. The scenic locale was tantalizing because the island was surrounded by perpetually cold (never more than 52°F, or 11°C) and treacherous ocean currents that were extremely difficult to swim and, therefore, almost impossible to escape from.

That was why Attorney General Homer Cummings announced on the radio that Alcatraz was reserved for the most hardened and incorrigible convicts — inmates such as Al Capone, Alvin "Creepy Karpis" Karpavicz, and George "Machine Gun" Kelly — "so that their influence may not be extended to other prisoners who are disposed to rehabilitate themselves."

Alcatraz convicts often wore several layers of clothing to protect themselves from the cold, damp wind that whipped the island. When it eased, the air became alive with the sounds of passing boats or planes, distant foghorns, and an ever-present whoosh of waves and screeching of gulls; and when it stopped, an especially keen ear might hear someone's distant laugh from the St. Francis Yacht Club a mile-and-a-quarter (2 km) across the bay.

Observation tower: The position of Alcatraz in the cold, fast-flowing waters and tidal rips of San Francisco Bay made it very difficult to escape from. It also made it expensive to run.

Tight security

The prison's security also included the tightest level of supervision of any prison in America; there was one guard for every three convicts. Its numerous guard towers commanded a view of every part of the island; and the armed guards were not afraid to shoot. Besides the walls, the institution was encased with a 12-foot (3.7 m) tall cyclone fence, topped with barbed wire. Its steel bars were advertised as tool-proof. Convicts had to submit to 12 official counts per day and sometimes as much as 50 tallies. It was no wonder that nobody had ever successfully escaped from the place.

Escape plan

The four plotters aimed to become the first escapees. Their cause received a boost when West confided that when cleaning a prison corridor he had come across a hidden collection of several old saw blades. He also knew how to acquire other useful tools.

The plan that evolved was extremely complex, involving the design and fabrication of lifelike dummies, water rafts, life preservers, and many other ingenious makeshift items. They also utilized a variety of crudely made tools for digging and manufacturing.

After escaping from the prison, they planned to brave

> **"Here may be housed the criminals of the vicious and irredeemable type, so that their evil influence may not be extended to other prisoners who are disposed to rehabilitate themselves."**
>
> U.S. Attorney General Homer Cummings

the treacherous waters by rafting to Angel Island, located due north in San Francisco Bay. Then they hoped to cross Raccoon Strait to make their escape through Marin County, where they would steal a car and necessary clothing.

Following through

One of their tools included a homemade drill made from the motor of a broken vacuum cleaner, which they used to loosen the air vents at the back of their cells by painstakingly drilling closely spaced holes around the cover so the entire section of the wall could be removed. By May of 1962, they had also started work on the vent on top of the cellblock.

They had secretly set up a hidden workshop. Using a crude periscope they had made, one took turns keeping watch while another used a variety of contraband materials to build and hide crucial escape objects. Using dozens of stolen raincoats, they fashioned life preservers

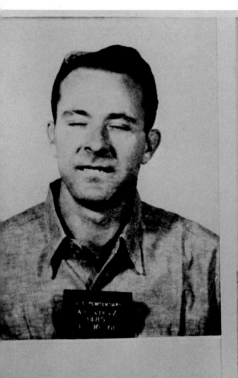

The elusive trio: The prison mugshots of the escapees. From left to right: Clarence Anglin, John William Anglin and Frank Lee Morris. After June 11, 1962, they were never seen again.

and a 6 x 14-foot (2 x 4 m) rubber raft, the seams of which they carefully stitched together and "vulcanized" using the prison's steam pipes. They created wooden paddles and converted an accordion-like musical instrument (concertina) into a tool they could use to rapidly inflate the raft. After months of constant work, the crew had completed making all of the equipment they needed for their escape, and they were still hurrying to devise their escape route out of the prison.

The ceiling was 30 feet (9 m) high, but using a network of pipes they climbed up and eventually pried open the ventilator at the top of the shaft. They kept it in place temporarily by fashioning a fake bolt out of soap so that the lid could be lifted when they were ready to escape.

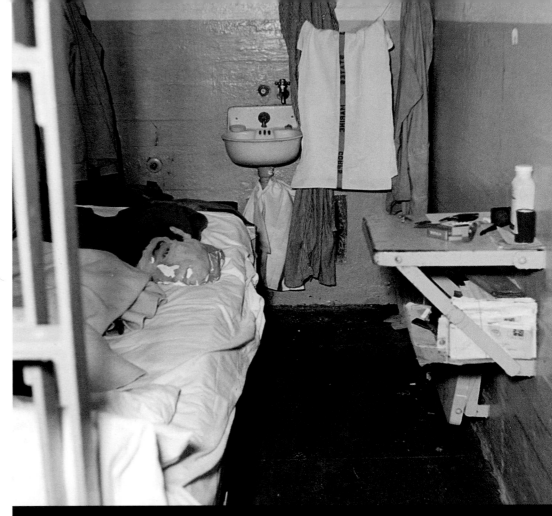

The jailbirds have flown: Photographed the day after the escape, a prison cell in Block B showing one of the dummy heads used to fool warders.

Lifelike dummy heads were created from homemade plaster, glue and paint they had fashioned from materials such as toilet paper, soap, Kool-Aid and hair they had taken from the prison barbershop.

The big night

On the night of June 11, 1962, Morris indicated that the top ventilator was loose enough, and that he felt they were ready to attempt the escape. But West had fallen behind in digging out the ventilator grill at the rear of his cell. Clarence Anglin tried to assist West in removing his ventilator grill, but it remained stuck. As a result, Morris and the Anglins decided they would have to leave him behind.

The three escapees got into the corridor, gathered their gear, and made their final 30-foot (9 m) climb up the plumbing to the cell house roof. Then they traversed 100 feet (30 m) across the rooftop. Each man carefully maneuvered down the 50 feet (15 m) of bakery smoke stack piping to the rear of the cell house on the ground level near the entrance to the shower area. When the coast was clear, each one climbed over the fence and snuck to the northeast shore of the island where they gathered to quickly launch their raft into the choppy bay.

Never found

By morning, when their escape was discovered, the three men were still gone. A massive search failed to find them. Two days later a packet of letters sealed in rubber and related to the men was recovered from the water at Marin. Later, some paddle-like pieces of wood and bits of rubber inner tube were also found in the water. A homemade life-vest was discovered washed up on Cronkhite Beach, but extensive searches did not turn up any other items in the area. The three were never seen or heard from again.

To this day, nobody knows whether they drowned or made it to freedom. The episode later became the basis

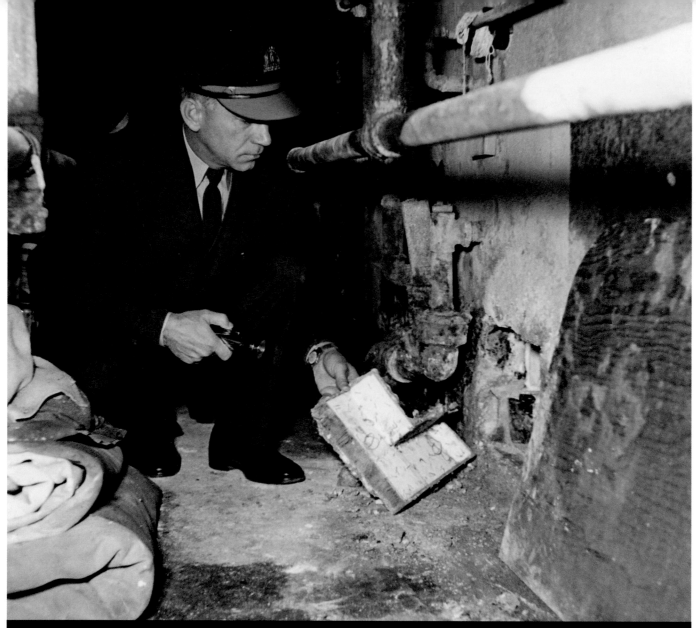

Exit route: A warden shines on a flashlight into the hole the prisoners drilled while clutching the skirting used to conceal it. Ironically, it was not escapes that drove Alcatraz to closure. At $10 a day per inmate detained, it was poor value compared to $3-a-day mainland prisons.

for countless books and television programs and a hit movie, *Escape from Alcatraz*, starring Clint Eastwood.

The escape proved to be a final straw leading to the prison's demise. Its public image was too ugly, and the operating costs too high. Attorney General Robert F. Kennedy ordered it closed. On March 13, 1963, the last convicts were finally removed from Alcatraz and the prison was officially shut down on May 15, 1963.

> When the coast was clear, each one climbed over the fence ... where they gathered to quickly launch their raft into the choppy bay.

On December 31, 1979, the FBI officially closed the escape case and turned over responsibility to the U.S. Marshals Service, which continues to investigate in the unlikely event the trio is still alive. Today the FBI's redacted file about the escape, numbering 1,757 pages, is posted on the agency's website. And more than a million tourists per year flock to Alcatraz to see the sites and relics of one of history's greatest prison escapes.

Other Alcatraz escape attempts (1936–1962)

- April 27, 1936 — Joe Bowers shot and killed climbing chain link fence.
- December 16, 1937 — Theodore Cole and Ralph Roe disappear without trace into San Francisco Bay during a bad storm.
- May 23, 1938 — James Limerick, Jimmy Lucas, and Rufus Franklin attack correction officers; Limerick shot to death, Franklin and Lucas get life sentences.
- January 13, 1939 — Arthur "Doc" Barker, Dale Stamphill, William Martin, Henry Young, and Rufus McCain discovered on shoreline west side; Martin, Young, and McCain surrender; Barker and Stamphill are shot; Barker dies.
- May 21, 1941 — Joe Cretzer, Sam Shockley, Arnold Kyle, and Lloyd Barkdoll seize hostages, then surrender.
- September 15, 1941 — John Bayless give up shortly in cold water.
- April 14, 1943 — James Boarman, Harold Brest, Floyd Hamilton, and Fred Hunter take hostages; Boarman and Brest are apprehended in water; Boarman is shot in water and body is never recovered; Hamilton later apprehended on island.
- August 7, 1943 — Huron "Ted" Walters caught on shoreline.
- July 31, 1945 — John Giles apprehended on launch at Angel Island.
- May 2–4, 1946 — Six convicts attempt takeover and escape: Bernard Coy, Joe Cretzer, Marvin Hubbard, Sam Shockley, Miran Thompson, Clarence Carnes. Coy, Cretzer, and Hubbard are killed; Shockley and Thompson are legally executed; Carnes gets life sentence.
- July 23, 1956 — Floyd Wilson discovered on shoreline.
- September 29, 1958 — Clyde Johnson caught in water; accomplice Aaron Burgett later found floating dead.
- December 16, 1962 — Darl Parker apprehended on rock off shoreline; accomplice John Paul Scott recovered from rocks near Fort Point (beneath the Golden Gate Bridge).

Acid's "high priest" flees prison

DR. TIMOTHY LEARY	September 15, 1970

With a little help from his friends and the Weather Underground, Dr. Timothy Leary, the Pied Piper of the psychedelic 1960s, went on another far-out trip. But this time, he had to bust out of a federal prison and flee from the orbit of politicians who believed him to be dangerously subversive.

Preaching the message: Former Harvard professor Dr. Timothy Leary addressing the National Student Association in College Park, Maryland, in August 1967. Leary said that LSD was here to stay and it was only a matter of time before it became legalized.

High priest of hippiedom: Leary had a gift for provocation. He aligned his LSD movement with Black Power and in 1969 announced that he was going to run for governor of California. His wife Rosemary (above) campaigned vigorously for his release from jail.

Today some facts about his escape aren't exactly clear, which shouldn't be surprising, given that the episode involved Dr. Timothy Leary, the great popularizer of psilocybin, LSD acid trips and the drug culture, who once warned the authorities to watch out because, "I have America surrounded." But maybe that is what qualifies his antics as one of history's great escapes.

Leary, a brilliant Harvard clinical psychologist who conducted research into mind-altering drugs before they were made illegal, became a highly controversial figure in the 1960s when he urged the new generation to "tune in, turn on and drop out," and persuaded millions of youths to take drugs and explore alternative lifestyles.

A fixture of the era, Leary went on drug trips with Allen Ginsberg and Jack Kerouac, got busted by G. Gordon Liddy, and sang "Give Peace a Chance" with John Lennon and Yoko Ono. Richard Nixon called him the "most dangerous man in the world," but to many freedom lovers he was the high priest of hippiedom and founding father of the counter-culture.

Constantly hassled and arrested for his drug-related activities, Leary kept getting into more and more serious legal trouble as America's social and political ferment turned ugly. In 1970, while awaiting a 10-year sentence on a Texas drug charge, he got sentenced to another 10 years in California on a marijuana charge, and found himself in prison. The two sentences were to be served consecutively, which meant that he was facing hard time.

> **❝ I was a 49-year-old man facing life in prison for encouraging people to face up to new options with courage and intelligence. ❞**
>
> **Timothy Leary**

"Consider my situation"

Believing that Leary did not pose a serious risk of violence or escape, California prison authorities sent him to the Men's Colony, the most minimum-security correctional facility, located in San Luis Obispo.

But Leary couldn't hack it.

"Consider my situation," he later wrote. "I was a 49-year-old man facing life in prison for encouraging people to face up to new options with courage and intelligence. The American Government was being run by Richard Nixon, Spiro Agnew, John Ehrlichman, Robert Haldeman, G. Gordon Liddy, John Mitchell, J. Edgar Hoover and other cynical flouters of the democratic process. Would you have let men like these keep you in prison for life for your ideas?"

As his wife, Rosemary Woodruff, raised money for his defense fund, a drug-based group called the Brotherhood of Eternal Love, swung into action. Known as the psychedelic mafia, they had often dropped acid with Leary on their sprawling Idylwild Ranch near Palm Springs, scanning the skies for UFOs and alien creatures that would expand their consciousness beyond the limits of mere mortals.

The group approached Weather Underground (aka Weathermen and Weatherman Underground), the ultra-leftist American outlaw organization that had conducted bombings and other acts to protest the Vietnam War, offering money in exchange for their assistance.

Leaders of the Weather Underground, including Bill Ayers and Bernardine Dohrn, who themselves were fugitives being sought by the FBI, agreed to help. They arranged for passports and other false identification and also made plans for Leary and his wife to escape from "Amerika" and go underground.

INTERSTATE FLIGHT - MOB ACTION; RIOT; CONSPIRACY
WANTED BY FBI
BERNARDINE RAE DOHRN

I. O. 4364
4-24-70

FBI No. 56,360 H
20 0 9 R O1O 12
L 17 R O1O

OTHER NAMES KNOWN BY: Marion DelGado, Bernardine Dohrn, Bernardine Rae Ohrnstein, H. T. Smith

Photographs taken 1969

Bernardine Dohrn

DESCRIPTION
AGE: 28, born January 12, 1942, Chicago, Illinois
HEIGHT: 5'5"
WEIGHT: 125 pounds
BUILD: medium
HAIR: dark brown
OCCUPATION: secretary
SOCIAL SECURITY NUMBER USED: 395-38-5006
EYES: brown
COMPLEXION: light olive
RACE: white
NATIONALITY: American

CAUTION
DOHRN REPORTEDLY MAY RESIST ARREST, HAS BEEN ASSOCIATED WITH PERSONS WHO ADVOCATE USE OF EXPLOSIVES AND MAY HAVE ACQUIRED FIREARMS. CONSIDER DANGEROUS.

A Federal warrant was issued on March 17, 1970, at Chicago, Illinois, charging Dohrn with unlawful interstate flight to avoid prosecution for mob action (Title 18, U. S. Code, Section 1073). A Federal warrant was issued on April 2, 1970, at Chicago, Illinois, charging Dohrn with violation of Federal Antiriot Laws and conspiracy (Title 18, U. S. Code, Sections 2101 and 371).

IF YOU HAVE INFORMATION CONCERNING THIS PERSON, PLEASE CONTACT YOUR LOCAL FBI OFFICE. TELEPHONE NUMBERS AND ADDRESSES OF ALL FBI OFFICES LISTED ON BACK.

Identification Order 4364
April 24, 1970

Director
Federal Bureau of Investigation
Washington, D. C. 20535

Most wanted: Leary's escape was engineered by the political group the Weather Underground. One of their leaders, Bernardine Dohrn, was subsequently put onto the 10 Most Wanted list of fugitives. The FBI described her as a reputed leader of the "Violence-Oriented Weatherman Faction of Students for a Democratic Society." Today she is an Associate Professor of Law.

Running barefoot

On September 15, 1970, Leary made his unlikely bid for freedom. He slipped across the prison yard, hoisted himself onto a rooftop and ran across it in his bare feet, then shimmied along a utility cable over the barbed wire and dropped to the ground outside the prison fence. At the highway a band of accomplices were waiting. Together they sped off, triggering a manhunt.

A few hours later the smiling escapee hobnobbed with Dohrn and other members of the Weathermen at their safehouse outside San Francisco.

Leary released a tripped-out "P.O.W. Statement" that read: "Brothers and Sisters, this is a war for survival. Ask Huey [Newton] and Angela [Davis]. They dig it . . . To shoot a genocidal robot policeman in the defense of life is a sacred act." Media across the world also reported the following communiqué:

September 15, 1970. This is the fourth communication from the Weatherman Underground. The Weatherman Underground has had the honor and pleasure of helping Dr. Timothy Leary escape from the POW camp at San Luis Obispo, California. Dr. Leary was being held against his will and against the will of millions of kids in this country. He was a political prisoner, captured for the work he did in helping all of us begin the task of creating a new culture on the barren wasteland that has been imposed on this country by Democrats, Republicans, Capitalists and creeps.

LSD and grass, like the herbs and cactus and mushrooms of the American Indians and countless civilizations that have existed on this planet, will help us make a future world where it will be possible to live in peace ... (signed) Bernardine Dohrn

Seized in Afghanistan

With forged passports, the couple found refuge with the Black Panthers' "government in exile" in Algiers. By February 1971, however, a rift had developed between Leary and Cleaver, who had ordered them "detained." So Leary and his wife left Algeria for Switzerland, where he spent 18 months before eventually heading to Afghanistan.

In early 1973, American agents kidnapped Timothy Leary at gunpoint in Afghanistan. They brought him to California where he was found guilty of prison escape. He spent three more years in 29 jails in California's prison system. At Folsom he once shared a cell with killer Charles Manson.

This time Leary decided to cooperate with his captors. He told the FBI, "I want to get out of prison as quickly as I can. And I believe that telling the total truth is the best way to get out of prison."

"Just say know"

After turning informer for the FBI, Leary was released on parole in 1976. The Learys divorced the same year, and Rosemary remained underground for 23 years before secretly returning to the U.S. where she died in 2002.

After his release from prison, a chastened Timothy Leary returned to the lecture circuit and urged students to "just say know." He died from prostate cancer in 1996 and his ashes were launched into space from Grand Canary Island off the Moroccan coast.

Freedom: Leary leaves the Federal Correction Center in San Diego in 1976 with new partner Joanna. He was freed on a personal bond of $5,000.

The legend of "D.B. Cooper"

Portland, Oregon	November 24, 1971

He was a nondescript man committing an extraordinary crime. The quiet passenger in Seat 18C said he had a bomb and wanted ransom money and four parachutes. When the crew landed the plane after their ordeal, they found the rear door open and the hijacker gone.

It was the day before Thanksgiving, one of the busiest travel periods of the year, and people were in a rush to get home. Northwest Orient Flight 305 had just left Portland, Oregon bound for Seattle with 37 passengers and four crew members aboard, and everything seemed to be proceeding as planned.

When the gentleman occupying seat 18C motioned to the young flight attendant, Florence Schaffner, and passed her a folded piece of paper, she assumed he was coming on to her. So she simply put the note into her pocket without reading it and continued about her business. But then he leaned closer and said, "Miss, you'd better look at that note. I have a bomb." She opened it and read the message: "I have a bomb in my briefcase. I will use it if necessary. I want you to sit next to me. You are being hijacked."

Since the 1960s air piracy had become all-too-frequent as far as the airline industry was concerned. Yet the carriers and the government had dragged their feet in instituting stricter security measures — because they didn't want to discourage flying as a result of increased costs and delays. In the United States most hijackings were political in nature, involving Castro's Cuba. But this one seemed different.

"Just follow my instructions," the hijacker said, "Exactly! And everything will be fine and nobody will be any wiser. Just report this to your captain."

Get $200,000

As Schaffner quickly tried to size up the situation, she noted that the passenger (identified at the ticket counter only as "Dan Cooper") appeared to be in his mid-40s, and

Mystery man: The police artist's impression of "D.B. Cooper" circulated at the time of the hijacking. The image has become almost iconic over time.

Takeoff point: The rear steps configuration of the Boeing 727 made it the perfect commercial airline plane to go skydiving from, with little chance of the chute being caught on a wing or rear engine.

between 5 feet 10 inches and 6 feet (177–183 cm) tall, weighing about 170 to 180 pounds (77–82 kg). He was wearing a black raincoat, loafers, a dark suit, a neatly pressed white collared shirt, a black necktie with a mother-of-pearl tie pin and black sunglasses. He appeared to be American, didn't speak with any noticeable accent and seemed rather nice. He smoked filter cigarettes.

The hijacker was demanding $200,000 in unmarked $20-bills and two sets of parachutes to be delivered to him as soon as they reached Seattle, or he would blow up the plane.

Within minutes, the pilot's distressed message passed through air traffic control, the Seattle police, and the FBI before reaching the airline president, Donald Nyrop, who instructed the pilot to cooperate. Meanwhile, the hijacker

> **❝ I have a bomb in my suitcase. I will use it if necessary. I want you to sit next to me. You are being hijacked. ❞**
>
> Cooper's note

opened his briefcase to the stewardess to reveal what appeared to be sticks of dynamite rigged to a battery. He also instructed the pilot not to land until his money and parachutes were ready.

On the ground, FBI agents hurriedly gathered the required packets of twenties, selecting bills printed mostly in 1969 that mostly had serial numbers starting with the letter L, which had all been issued by the Federal Reserve Bank of San Francisco. Then they ran the stacks through a Recordak that copied each item so they would later be able to trace every bill.

Civilian parachutes

The hijacker was also picky about what type of parachutes he would accept. He demanded four civilian

Familiar routine: Northwest Airlines flight attendant Flo Schaffner thought Cooper wanted a date when he passed her the short note.

chutes with manual ripcords, thus sending the FBI agents in a frenzy of speculation. Did he have an accomplice on board? Would he force some or all of the crew to jump?

While he waited, the passenger ordered a Bourbon and water cocktail and even offered to pay the stewardess for it.

At 17:24 hours the ground team radioed the captain with a simple message: "Everything is ready for your arrival." The plane landed at 17:39, barely 30 minutes behind schedule, and the hijacker ordered the pilot to taxi to a remote spot on the tarmac and dim his cabin lights. Then an unaccompanied airline employee was instructed to deliver the money and chutes without any funny business.

As soon as this occurred, the hijacker made good on his promise to release all of the other passengers and flight attendant Schaffner via the aft stairs. Four crew

including the captain were forced to remain on board. After refueling, the hijacker ordered the pilot to take off again and then he gave specific instructions for the craft to head for Mexico City at a slow speed of only 170 knots and an altitude under 10,000 feet (3,050 m) with its landing gear down and 15 degrees of flap. After the first officer protested that the jet could not fly to that location at that speed and altitude, he and the hijacker settled on flying to Reno, where they would then refuel.

Unpressurize the cabin

Cooper ordered the pilot to leave the cabin unpressurized, which indicated that he might be seeking to reduce the risk from incoming air if the cabin door was opened during flight. Shortly after the plane was in flight, he also directed the rest of the crew to remain in the cockpit. One crew member peeked from behind the first-class curtain to see that the hijacker appeared to be adjusting something around his waist. But that was all they could glean.

Moments later the crew in the cockpit noticed a light flash indicating that Cooper had attempted to operate the door. The pilot quickly asked over the intercom if there was anything they could do for him, but the hijacker replied curtly, "No!"

Soon the crew started to feel their ears pop, indicating a change of air pressure in the cabin. The plane was being pelted with heavy rain in the darkness. At the end of a harrowing, two-and-a-half-hour flight, they landed in Reno with the aft stairs dragging.

The hijacker was gone.

Where did he go?

FBI agents swarmed over the plane, searching for clues. The briefcase and money bag were gone, along with two of the four parachutes. Other than a few possible fingerprints, and some cigarette butts, one of the few things he had left behind was his tie clip.

Aircraft experts examined the damaged airstair that had been deployed during flight — something that had never happened before in history.

The Air Force F-106 jet fighters accompanying the airliner had not observed anything in the cloudy, rainy night. Agents quickly calculated that the hijacker had jumped from the plane somewhere over the vicinity of Ariel, Washington, about 25 miles (40 km) north of Portland. At that time the air temperature at 10,000 feet (3,050 m) would have been about 19°F (-7°C).

Although the plane had been traveling at a speed slightly faster than the 170 knots (about 195 miles, or 315 km, per hour) the hijacker had ordered, some skydiving experts concluded that the jump may have been survivable. They suggested that the 727-100 aircraft probably had been picked for its design: with three engines, one high on the fuselage immediately in front of the vertical tail fin and two others on either side of the fuselage just above the horizontal tail fins, neither the engine intakes nor exhaust would have interfered when he lowered the aft steps and stepped out into the night sky. The cockpit door had no peephole, and the jet was not equipped with any remote cameras or other monitors to enable the crew to spy on the man in the cabin.

Police and military personnel mounted a massive manhunt that lasted for several weeks. But nothing was found.

Mistakenly dubbed by the media as the "D.B. Cooper" case, after a suspect by that name who was later cleared, and designated by the FBI as "NORJAK," the incident remains one of the greatest unsolved escapes in modern history.

Scattered clues

Over time, only a few scattered clues have surfaced. In late 1978 a placard containing instructions on how to lower the aft stairs of a 727, which was later confirmed to be from the rear stairway of the plane from which Cooper jumped, was discovered just a few flying minutes north of Cooper's projected drop zone.

Two years after that, an eight-year-old boy, Brian Ingram, stumbled across a wad of $5,880 in decaying $20-bills along the banks of the Columbia River near Vancouver, Washington. The money proved to be part of the original ransom and the youth was allowed to keep half of it. But experts could only speculate over how and when it had landed there.

Hundreds of other purported clues have failed to materialize. Otherwise, no trace of the man known as Dan Cooper has ever turned up. He may be dead. He may have survived. But stories about his amazing and mysterious escape will be told for a long time to come.

Nine years later: Eight-year-old Brian Ingram of Vancouver, Washington, points to the spot where he found three bundles of decomposed $20-bills in February 1980. The serial numbers matched the notes given to D.B. Cooper.

Midnight express

BILLY HAYES | **October 1975**

Faced with 30 years in hellish Turkish prisons for trying to smuggle hashish out of the country, a young American tourist made a daring move to escape. What happened next made Billy Hayes a worldwide celebrity and put Turkey's record on human rights in question.

Midnight Express: Actor Brad Davis played Billy Hayes in Alan Parker's successful 1978 movie. The film was criticized for embellishing the degree of violence and corruption in the Turkish prison system, a charge that screenwriter Oliver Stone has subsequently admitted.

Refuge: Having escaped from Imrali, Hayes made his way to the city of Bursa to lie low. He decided to make himself less conspicuous in the city by dying his blond hair a darker color.

On October 6, 1970 Billy Hayes was just another young, freewheeling American tourist drifting around Europe in search of fun and excitement. Raised in Patchogue, Long Island, he'd grown up in suburban comfort, aided by parents who helped support his solid middle-class lifestyle. Now 23 years old, he had dropped out of Marquette University the previous year and was hoping to stay one step ahead of the military draft that was forcing so many young men from his generation into having to go fight the unpopular war in Vietnam.

Despite his short hair, Hayes was becoming a free spirit. In the course of his adventures abroad, he had ventured into Turkey, which was an especially popular hippie mecca due to its exotic culture and super-cool hashish. He had liked it a lot. One of his favorite hangouts was the Pudding Shoppe in Istanbul, where he had enjoyed sipping Turkish tea with interesting foreigners and heard many fascinating stories.

Since he was preparing to fly back to the States, Hayes naively reckoned that he could make some easy money by bringing back some cheap hash to later resell. In fact, he had scored about 4.4 pounds (2 kg) of the stuff for

$200 with the expectation of unloading it to some of his friends in New York for $5,000. It didn't seem like such a big deal at the time.

But now that he was at Istanbul's Yesilkoy International Airport, preparing to try to board a Pan Am flight that would take him to Frankfurt, London and New York, he worried about getting caught.

Busted

Hayes had donned a trench coat and hat and covered his eyes with dark aviator sunglasses in an effort to try to appear more respectable. Concealed under his arms he had taped the two wrapped bricks of hash, in order to make it through customs. Now he was nervous and afraid. Sweating everywhere.

One thing he didn't realize was that recent PLO hijackings of commercial airliners had put many airports on alert for suspected terrorists — and Istanbul was one of the places most affected. The police were on the lookout for nervous young men his age. Hayes stood out.

So, as he tried to slip through the passenger line, an alert security officer noted something suspicious about him and administered a quick body frisk that detected a telltale object taped to his torso. At first the policeman had feared it was a bomb and he pulled out his gun to subdue his suspect. When it turned out to merely be hashish, the relieved officer seemed almost happy. But for Hayes, the discovery meant he was in serious legal trouble: Turkey was known to punish drug offenders very severely.

Thirty years

The young American was tossed into filthy Sagalcilar prison with hundreds of prisoners, where he was beaten and tortured and witnessed many horrible things. He also joined the prisoner subculture, learning how to bribe guards for privileges and how to survive in a corrupt world.

Tried and convicted of drug possession, Hayes was sentenced to four years in prison, which was bad enough. But after the prosecution appealed the sentence, his penalty was increased to 30 years as a deterrent to other drug smugglers.

After serving time in Bakirkoy Prison, another hellhole, he came to the conclusion that he had to escape or he would lose his life in prison. Fortunately, he was transferred to a "half-open" prison — one that offered better living conditions and maybe a better chance of escape as well.

Imrali Prison was located on an island in the Sea of Marmara, an inland sea cutting across the northwestern tip of Turkey between the Black Sea and the Aegean. It enabled him to spend more time outside, doing work or

> " The message of *Midnight Express* isn't 'Don't go to Turkey,' it's 'Don't be an idiot like I was, and try to smuggle drugs.' "
>
> Billy Hayes

Press conference: New York, October 1975, a gaunt-looking Hayes displays the passport issued to him by the American embassy in Athens to get him home. The photo on the passport shows him with dyed hair.

swimming in the bay. At first it seemed like a paradise compared to his previous holding places, but Hayes could not get over the fact that he was still in prison, still condemned to spend his most productive years behind bars.

The plan

On September 28, 1975 Hayes wrote a letter to his father, hinting that he had come to some sort of important but risky decision. Don't worry, he said.

By then he had studied his options and developed a plan to escape from the island. He had observed that when storms set in, many of the fishing boats came in from the sea to dock in the island's harbor. He figured that he might be able to reach one of the boats and use it to get away.

He waited until the weather was right and the waves were churning, knowing that many boats would soon be anchored nearby. That afternoon (October 2) he retrieved the most important items he would need for such a journey — a map, a small knife, and some money — and put on his darkest clothes.

At dusk he absconded from his guards and hid in a concrete storage bin overlooking the coast. Then, when it was dark, he snuck out and evaded the searchlights and machineguns. Slipping down to the beach, he entered the water and swam the breaststroke as quietly as he could until he had reached an available fishing boat and climbed aboard.

Then he started rowing over the waves. It was hard work rowing in the rough sea, but he finally landed ashore and made his way to the city of Bursa, where he hid out and tried to disguise his appearance by dying his blonde hair. Eventually, he bought a ticket to Istanbul and from there went to Edirne.

At last on October 5, exhausted and ragged from the trip, he snuck over the border into Greece and was arrested by Greek police. Taken before the Greek authorities, he got help from his family and the American Embassy to convince the Greeks to deport him back to the United States rather than returning him to Turkey. Billy Hayes was free.

Upon returning to New York on October 24, 1975, Hayes held a press conference with his lawyer to tell the world press about his ordeal. Three years later he teamed up with writer William Hoffer to write a book about his experiences that he entitled *Midnight Express*, based on Turkish prison slang for an inmate's escape attempt.

Oliver Stone's "overdramatization"

The best-selling book by Hayes and William Hoffer was adapted for the screen by an up-and-coming movie writer, Oliver Stone. Brad Davis (above left) played Billy Hayes. Alan Parker directed the film in 1978. It was a huge box-office hit that was nominated for six Academy Awards and won the Oscars for Best Music, Original Score (Giorgio Moroder) and Best Writing, Screenplay Based on Material from Another Medium (Stone).

The Hollywood version presented Turks as incredibly corrupt, brutal and sadistic. Stone's screenplay also embellished the true story to make it more sensational, adding scenes in which Hayes gets sexually attacked in prison, bites off the tongue of a prison informant and accidentally kills a sadistic warden while fending off a rape attempt; the movie also fictionalized Hayes' escape to show him walking out the front door in a stolen uniform, which was untrue.

In interviews with the news media, Hayes himself later acknowledged the inaccuracies and said he regretted that the film adaptation unfairly "depicts all Turks as monsters." Even Oliver Stone later publicly apologized for "overdramatizing" his script.

Since the late 1990s, however, human rights organizations have stepped up their criticism of Turkey for operating some of the world's most notorious prisons. *Midnight Express* remains one of the most popular prison escape movies ever made.

By helicopter — again!

It was business as usual for two of Greece's most notorious criminals as they prepared to escape from a high-security prison by helicopter. The big problem for the authorities was that it was Groundhog Day — they had already got away with it once before.

Serial armed robber and kidnapper Vassilis Paleokostas and his sidekick, the professional hitman Alket Rizaj, were two of Greece's most notorious criminals. They were days away from trial for their dramatic 2006 helicopter escape from the Korydallos high-security prison in a densely populated western suburb of Athens. On that occasion a helicopter had landed in the prison's central yard at exercise time and whisked them away. Guards reportedly had failed to react because they thought it was a visit by prison inspectors. Police had finally caught them after two years on the run.

Besides their pending charges, Paleokostas, 42, was already serving prison sentences of more than 25 years for 16 bank robberies, arms possession, and his 1995 kidnapping of industrialist George Mylonas, who had been released after paying a huge ransom. Police still had not recovered all of the kidnap money. Rizaj, an Albanian immigrant, was serving a life term for murder and he was facing charges of two more contract killings while on the run from their earlier prison escape.

Prosecutors claimed the pair's previous breakout had been planned by Paleokostas's older brother, Nikos, who was currently being held in another prison, having spent 16 years on the run following his own 1990 prison escape. Government officials assured the public that since the 2006 brazen fly out, Korydallos prison had put tighter prison security procedures in place to protect society from dangerous criminals.

Lightning strikes twice: Police officers investigate an area near Athens where a helicopter carrying Greece's most wanted criminal Vassilis Paleokostas and Albanian convict Alket Rizaj, landed after the two inmates escaped Korydallos high-security prison.

The country's embattled administration had a lot riding on the outcome of what was sure to be a high-profile trial. All three men were powerful members of organized crime and Greek law enforcement was riddled with corruption; its prison system was known the world over for its rampant escapes, hunger strikes, riots and bribe-taking. Many socialists speculated as to what new scandals might pop up next in court. But little could they imagine that the surprising answer would come from the heavens, not from the trial.

From the sky

At 3:30 p.m. on Sunday, February 22, 2009, a brightly colored chartered helicopter suddenly flew in low over the high-security prison and landed on a flat-topped roof of one of the cellblocks. Somebody quickly dropped down a rope ladder and two figures scrambled up onto the roof, then jumped into the chopper's cabin.

Gunshots rang out as someone in the helicopter engaged in a firefight with prison guards. A moment later, the aircraft lifted very slowly and peeled away into the overcast sky amid sounds of scattered small-arms fire, wailing sirens, and wild cheering from inmates, who had been watching with delight as the startling rescue unfolded.

A nearby video camera caught the events on tape, from the time of the helicopter's approach to its casual flight away, complete with some of the eyewitnesses' catcalls and whistles.

Paleokostas and Rizaj had done it again — at the same prison, in the same outlandish way.

Resulting probe

Police later found the helicopter abandoned in the northern suburb of Kapandriti. It had a bullet hole in its fuel tank. The pilot was discovered bound and gagged with a hood over his head, later telling investigators that he had been hijacked by a man and a woman brandishing an assault rifle and a hand grenade. But the fugitives and the shooter were gone.

Reporters soon had a field day recounting the events, including the fact that the helicopter company offered "escapes . . . to idyllic destinations," although the pilot insisted that wasn't any kind of escape he had bargained for. Observers noted that the aircraft was abandoned near a main highway leading towards Greece's central mountain range, an area where Paleokostas had successfully hidden out over the years.

Other helicopter escapes

In 1996, four leftist guerrillas escaped from a high-security prison in Chile by jumping into a large basket dangling from a helicopter and flying away amid gunfire. Three years later Lucy Dudko hijacked a rented sightseeing helicopter and forced the pilot to land at Australia's largest maximum-security prison to pick up her lover. In 2002, two inmates were rescued from the prison yard of the São Paulo penitentiary, and five convicted murderers were taken out of a high-security prison in Puerto Rico. In 2004, three French convicts were rescued from a jail in the French Alps, and two years later a convicted killer flew out of Grasse prison in Toulon, France. On October 31, 2007, the Belgium gangster Nordin Benallal got away from prison despite his helicopter crashing in the attempt. In April 2009, French cult leader Juliano Verbard escaped in a hijacked helicopter (pictured above) from the Domenjod jail on the French island of La Reunion in the Indian Ocean. Verbard, a sect leader who was serving 15 years for sex offenses, was hauled on board the helicopter by three accomplices. The group made off in a van after abandoning the aircraft.

5
Man-made disasters

The flaming wreck of the *Hindenburg*

For those trapped inside a flaming and plummeting airship, escape had to be almost instantaneous. As *Hindenburg*'s descent was caught in motion pictures and shocked commentary, everyone wondered how anybody could possibly survive the crashing inferno.

Feat of engineering: The workers who put together Luftschiff LZ-129 proudly pose for a photo. *Hindenburg* was on the first of 10 planned round-trips between Europe and the United States in 1937 when it crashed at Lakehurst.

The evening air was warm and humid as the awestruck crowd eyed the approaching giant. *Hindenburg* was the largest airship ever built, stretching 813 feet (248 m) — more than two-and-a-half football fields long — with an odd bomb-like shape and otherworldly movement that resembled that of some strange creature or vehicle coming down from outer space, its silver-colored skin glowing in the dusk and tail emblazoned with huge swastikas.

High over NYC: The *Hindenburg* skirts New York's skyscrapers. The airship had originally been designed to be lifted by non-flammable helium gas, but the U.S. would not export it to the Germans and they had to opt for the more dangerous hydrogen.

Built the previous year in Nazi Germany, the huge, hydrogen-filled blimp had just crossed the Atlantic at a cruising speed of 78 miles per hour (126 kph), making it faster than any ocean liner and able to fly farther than any large airplane of that time. Its passengers lounged in luxurious cabins that each had its own shower or bath, and the craft boasted an elegant clubroom with an aluminum grand piano, as well as a carefully insulated smoking room where travelers could enjoy their obligatory cigarettes and cocktails. *Hindenburg's* kitchen prepared the finest foods and her waiters provided the best service. There were even telephones and other modern conveniences.

As ground crews scrambled to prepare for the airship's "high docking," attention focused to the ground lines that would be used to secure the floating blimp to the top of the tall radio-tower-shaped mast. The craft was now so close that some of them could see passengers waving and smiling through the windows.

Flash

Then, at 7:25 p.m. one of the most dramatic scenes of modern times began to unfold. As one passenger noted, there was a remarkable stillness, the diesel motors were silent, and "it seemed as though the whole world was holding its breath." Then he noticed that people on the ground had suddenly stiffened. And he heard "a light, dull detonation from above, no louder than the sound of a beer bottle being opened." Turning his gaze toward the bow, he noticed "a delicate rose glow, as though the sun

were about to rise," and it was then that he realized the airship was aflame.

Several witnesses on the port side saw yellow-red flames, at first just forward of the top fin, around the vent of cell 4. Other witnesses on the port side noted the fire actually began just ahead of the horizontal port fin, only then followed by flames in front of the upper fin. Another person viewing the starboard side saw flames beginning lower and farther aft, near cell 1. But it happened so fast. Fire raced across the silver skin, blasting out a fuel tank and cracking the passenger decks. The bow lurched upwards and the tail fell into a dive.

Quick escape

Inside the cabin, the passengers included notables from many walks of life. The lucky ones had been situated near the windows and the unlucky ones were unable to get away in time.

Clifford L. Osbun, a 37-year-old Chicago business executive, had been talking with fellow passengers in the dining salon, looking through the observation window, watching the ship being moored, when the disaster occurred. The blast blew him through the window and threw him to the ground, where he suffered injuries that later required his hospitalization.

Herbert O'Laughlin, another business executive from Chicago, was packing his belongings in his cabin in the forward part of the airship when he felt a slight tremor shaking the ship. That was the explosion that had rent the tail and was tearing the dirigible apart. Hearing people

Spark: As the airship came into land at Lakehurst, the unthinkable happened. "It's burst into flames!" radio announcer Herbert Morrison proclaimed in a classic broadcast. "It burst into flames and it's falling! It's crashing! Watch it! Watch it! Get out of the way!"

run past his door, he stepped out and was walking toward the promenade deck when the second jolt occurred. Nobody was screaming or panicked yet, but by the time O'Laughlin reached the promenade deck, the airship's nose was about 20 feet (6 m) above the ground and he knew he had to escape. Climbing onto the windowsill, he was just about to jump when he was catapulted to the ground from a height of about 15 feet (4.5 m). Finding himself uninjured, O'Laughlin stood up to see the ship's captain stumbling with his hair and coat afire, so he hurried over and beat out the flames, burning himself in the process.

Joseph Späh, a 32-year-old German-born acrobat and contortionist, had been happily leaning out one of the *Hindenburg*'s forward-most portside observation windows, taking home movies of the landing crew. He had just aimed his camera at Lakehurst's massive Zeppelin hangar when he saw the hangar surface reflecting an orange glow and suddenly he realized the Hindenburg was on fire.

As the ship descended with its tail down at an angle of about 45 degrees, Späh held tight to a rail as others nearby slid 15 or 20 feet (4.5–6 m) down the floor to the back wall of the observation deck. An instant later, as it dropped to about 20 feet (6 m) above the ground, he let

go and fell to the surface, injuring his ankle. Before he could pull himself together, a U.S. sailor ran over and hauled him out of the enveloping inferno.

Life and death

As the *Hindenburg*'s tail crashed into the ground, a burst of flame shot out of the nose, killing nine of the 12 crew members in the bow. Still the airship kept falling with the bow facing upwards, part of the port side directly behind

Inferno: A few seconds later, as the gigantic zeppelin collapsed to earth in flames, Morrison became overwrought with emotion, "Oh," he cried, "the humanity!"

the passenger deck collapsed inward and the gas cell there exploded, erasing the scarlet lettering "*Hindenburg*" while the airship lowered its bow. Then the gondola wheel touched the ground, causing the airship to bounce up again before finally crashing bow first for the last time.

The time from the first flash to the final crash took only about 34 seconds, much of it involving terrified human figures who were struggling to escape the raging fire. Of 97 persons on board, 35 people died in addition to one fatality on the ground. But 62 persons from the *Hindenburg* miraculously escaped through the flaming wreckage, many of them sustaining only minor injuries.

Herbert Morrison's shaken eyewitness radio report from the landing field and all of the spectacular newsreel coverage and newspaper accounts captured world attention for a long time to come. Although the actual cause of the fire remains officially unknown, many believe that an electric charge in the atmosphere likely ignited some of the highly flammable aluminum powder filled paint varnish that coated the airship's sleek skin.

Hindenburg's career

Germans called their dirigibles "zeppelins" after Count Ferdinand von Zeppelin, who had pioneered their use. Although such aircraft had proved unfeasible for combat during World War I, by the early 1930s the Zeppelin Company had successfully adapted them for long-range passenger travel.

The immense *Graf Zeppelin*, launched in 1928, seemed to be only the precursor for even greater things to come. Named after Germany's president, Paul von Hindenburg, LZ 129 *Hindenburg* was almost as large as the ill-fated *Titanic*, and much bigger than any other blimp ever constructed. It was less expensive to build and maintain than huge ocean liners and it set the world record time for a trans-Atlantic crossing.

In 1936 it had made 10 trans-Atlantic flights from Germany to New York and six trips to Rio de Janeiro, carrying a total of 2,656 passengers. In 1937 it flew from Germany to Rio, then returned to Germany. On May 3rd, 1937, 97 passengers paid $400 to fly from Frankfurt to New York.

But immediately after the *Hindenburg* disaster, Hitler ordered all passenger zeppelins grounded until further notice. Investigations into the cause of the crash failed to restore public confidence in dirigible travel. The imagined "wave of the future" for travel ended within a few seconds at Lakehurst, New Jersey. The *Hindenburg* memorial at Lakehurst (left) was dedicated on May 6, 1987.

Escaping a sunken submarine

When one of the U.S. Navy's new submarines blew a valve during its sea trials off the New Hampshire coast, the result was catastrophic. The vessel was stuck on the seabed with its oxygen running out and the technology to rescue its crew had yet to be put into practice.

USS *Squalus* (SS192) was one of the new fleet of submarines designed to replace the old World War I-vintage vessels. Built at Portsmouth Naval Shipyard in March 1939, *Squalus* had performed well during her initial sea trials. Eighteen test dives went smoothly, but on the morning of May 23 she was near the Isles of Shoals, 10 miles (16 km) from the New Hampshire coast, when her skipper, Lieutenant Oliver Naquin, ordered the first test of the day — a "crash dive."

Everything seemed to go smoothly, but then there was

Crew photo: The crew and officers of the ill-fated sub, USS *Squalus*, before their departure from Portsmouth, New Hampshire.

a frantic call over the intercom line, "Flooding in the engine room!" A 31-inch (79 cm) diameter ventilation valve that should have been shut had remained open, and as the sub submerged, tons of seawater gushed into the rear engine compartments, killing nearly half the crew and sinking the vessel.

Naquin immediately tried to halt its descent, but the crew's desperate actions were thwarted by electrical failures and explosions that cut off all lights and left the disabled vessel plummeting onto the icy seafloor, 243 feet (74 m) below the surface.

Everyone else took refuge in the forward torpedo compartment, but the 33 sailors remained trapped inside the pitch-black hull. Wet, cold, and low on oxygen, they were keenly aware that nobody had ever survived such a predicament. Naquin ordered his men to lie down, relax, and not use up too much oxygen.

Momsen Lung

Although they were without radio contact, Naquin released a messenger buoy and smoke bombs in hopes of summoning aid. Five hours later, their sister ship, *Sculpin*,

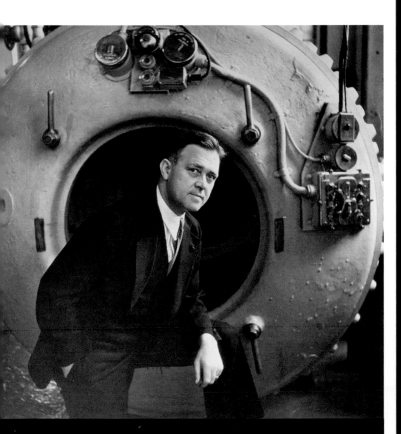

Rescue vehicle: Commander Charles "Swede" Momsen with his diving bell, known affectionately as "the Momsen Lung."

"... History in the making."

The first time the diving bell broke the surface and bobbed around near the rescue ship, *Falcon*, a CBS radio announcer broadcast the events live to millions of listeners via short-wave transmitter WAAU. From his position on a vessel close to the lead Coast Guard rescue ship, Jack Knell reported seeing rescue workers straining to unscrew the pressurized bolts on the hatch cover. Finally they were able to force it open and they reached down into the bell, where a man's head appeared: "The first survivor rescued from the sunken submarine *Squalus* is out and safely aboard the rescue ship," he said. "Another man is out now, and they're reaching inside to aid another... We are seeing history in the making." Knell's suspense-filled report captured the dramatic underwater escape. It was also a tremendous relief to the families of the trapped crewmen (above).

Rescued: Some of the rescued crew of USS *Squalus* SS 192 on the coastguard cutter *Harriet Lane*, shortly after they were brought up to the surface, still numb from the cold and stress.

arrived, followed later by other rescue vessels. Twenty-six hours after the sinking, a diver was sent down and landed on *Squalus*'s deck near the forward escape hatch. Inside the crew heard his footsteps above and they tapped on the hull to let him know they were still alive.

Rescue efforts were greatly helped by the presence of Commander Charles "Swede" Momsen, who was the Navy's leading expert on submarine rescue. But he quickly determined that their options were extremely limited.

Waiting for the submarine to be raised would take too long — the crew would never survive. The only other choice was to attempt individual rescues from the stricken ship using the newfangled Submarine Escape Appliance ("Momsen Lung"), which was a kind of large diving bell designed to attach to a disabled sub's hatch and ferry survivors to the surface.

> ❝ **Another man is out now, and they're reaching inside to aid another … We are seeing history in the making.** ❞
>
> **Jack Knell's radio commentary**

But the Lung had not been tested beyond 207 feet (63 m) and rescuers worried that the men were already very cold and undoubtedly weak from the foul air and tension. It also was designed to accommodate only seven passengers plus two chamber operators at one time, which meant that multiple trips would have to be made. Momsen estimated such an operation would take at least ten hours if the weather held up.

Deteriorating conditions

The situation worsened as seawater mixed with battery acid in the forward battery compartment and slowly filled the compartment with deadly chlorine gas. While the crew was able to protect themselves by sealing off the problem compartment, some of them would later have to go through it to escape. Rougher seas were also on the way.

At 11:30 a.m. the chamber made its first descent. An hour later its operators were handing food and drinks to the crew in the forward torpedo room and fresh air was being pumped into the submarine. By 1 p.m. the chamber was ready to return to the surface with its first group of survivors. The first party was successfully brought to the surface.

But elation over the rescue of the first group was tempered by fears that the others could not survive eight more hours in the bad air at such temperatures. Therefore, after the chamber had been lowered twice, it was decided to bring up nine survivors instead of seven. It was a risk they had to take.

By the time of the final trip, conditions aboard *Squalus* had deteriorated alarmingly. The temperature was only 4 degrees above freezing and the air was full of deadly chlorine gas. Naquin was the last man to climb into the chamber.

Dramatic conclusion

During the last ascent a line became tangled, causing an abrupt stop and the chamber dropped back down to 210 feet (64 m), where it required a diver to intervene. More divers were required to get the chamber untangled and it finally reached the surface, allowing the last of 33 survivors to make it aboard the rescue ship nearly 40 hours after their ordeal began.

The first rescue of its kind, the *Squalus* incident became known as the greatest submarine rescue in history. The successful operation turned what would have otherwise been a complete disaster into a maritime tragedy costing 26 submariners' lives.

Salvage: Two months later and the *Squalus* is hauled to the surface by a naval salvage team only for it to sink back down to the depths again. The submarine would eventually be recovered in September and be recommissioned as USS *Sailfish*.

Apollo 13

After a catastrophic rupture of a vital oxygen tank put their space craft and their lives in danger, the crew of the Apollo 13 and Mission Control raced to find a solution to their dwindling air supply. However, they were 200,000 miles (320,000 km) from home and heading the wrong way.

Flush from the success of the first manned landing on the Moon and other triumphs, Apollo 13 was planned as the third manned lunar-landing expedition, part of the National Aeronautics and Space Administration's fabled Project Apollo.

In an age of astronauts who were hailed as heroes and stars by an adoring media and public, Apollo 13's crew were depicted as some of the best and brightest exemplars of American enterprise and technological innovation, and every aspect of the flight received extensive media coverage. After some last-minute reshuffling, the three-man combo was set and ready to go. Commander James A. Lovell was making his fourth trip into outer space, and Command Module pilot Jack Swigert, and Lunar Module pilot Fred Haise were venturing there for the first time.

Standing behind them at the bustling Lyndon B. Johnson Space Center in Houston was the hub of NASA's space program — Mission Control — billed as the greatest collection of aeronautical know-how and space-age engineering ever assembled under one roof.

Narrowly defined, the Apollo 13 mission was supposed to explore the Moon's Fra Mauro formation, or Fra Mauro highlands, named after the 50-mile (80 km) diameter Fra Mauro crater located within it. But in its broadest sense, the mission was intended to reassert and demonstrate once again America's status as the

NASA mixer: As part of the press build-up to the launch, NASA released pictures of a social mixer at Mission Commander Jim Lovell's house in February. From left, Lovell, Thomas Mattingly (who was replaced shortly before the launch), Marilyn Lovell, Mary Haise, Fred Haise and Susy Young, wife of backup astronaut John W. Young.

Ready to go: The initial Apollo 13 crew in their space suits. From left to right: Fred Haise, James Lovell and Thomas Mattingly.

world's dominant super power. The nation's prestige was at stake. In short, the United States had a lot riding on it.

Problems

Apollo 13 lifted off from its launchpad with awesome thrust on April 11, 1970 at 13:13 CST, lighting up the sky with glorious rocket flame. But its center (inboard) engine of the second-stage boost cut out 132 seconds early, due to dangerous pogo oscillations that could have blown the spacecraft apart. The failure would turn out to be the first of many problems on the ill-fated flight. Some were too technical for the public to understand, but others would turn out to be too glaring and fundamental to be overlooked.

Two days, 7 hours and 54 minutes into the flight,

when the spacecraft had traveled approximately 200,000 miles (320,000 km) from the Earth en route to the Moon, Mission Control in Houston asked the crew to perform a routine stir of the craft's oxygen and hydrogen tanks. The tanks' supercold fluids — the ship's only source of oxygen and electricity — tended to stratify,

> ❝ We're venting something out into space. It's a gas of some sort. ❞
>
> Commander James A. Lovell

Lift off: Apollo 13 (spacecraft 109/Lunar Module 7/Saturn 508) lifts off from Pad A, Launch Complex 39, Kennedy Space Center, at 2:13 p.m. on April 11, 1970.

Losing oxygen and power

Initially the crew thought a meteoroid may have struck the spacecraft, but finding no sign of meteor impact, they had to search elsewhere for the cause. Lovell looked out a window and saw a gaseous substance escaping at a high rate of speed. "It looks to me that we are venting something," he radioed. "We're venting something out into space. It's a gas of some sort." Immediately seeing that it was their oxygen that was running out, he realized they were in grave danger.

"Houston, we've had a problem," Lovell reported.

Mission Control was frantically trying to cope with an incredible barrage of information, struggling to make sense of the data stream. Its collective brainpower didn't yet know what to do about it. They had to solve the problem, and fast.

Whatever the cause of the explosion, the most serious issue became its effect, for the explosion had wrecked the number two tank and damaged the other oxygen tank or its plumbing, resulting in a complete loss of oxygen and electrical power, leaving the command module on limited battery power.

Lifeboat

Apollo 13 consisted of three main components: the Command Module (CM) in which the crew traveled to

making it hard to accurately measure them. NASA's simple solution was a fan in each tank. A so-called "cryo stir" was a regular feature of all Apollo flights.

Neither Mission Control nor the crew knew it yet, but damaged insulation on the teflon wires to the stirrer motor in oxygen tank 2 caused them to short-circuit and ignite the insulation. The resulting fire rapidly increased pressure beyond its nominal 1,000 PSI (7 Mpa) limit and either the tank or the tank dome failed. Sixteen seconds later, one of the two oxygen tanks in the Service Module — tank number two — exploded, giving off a loud thump.

Mission control: After Jim Lovell uttered the famous lines, "Houston, we've had a problem," the control room gather to monitor the data coming back from the ship.

and from the Moon; the Service Module (SM) that powered the Command Module and contained the engine that would put the ship back into orbit around the Moon and bring it back to the Earth; and the Lunar Module (LM), the frail-looking craft in which two of the crew would land on the Moon and later take off inside to rejoin the Command Module.

With the Service Module (SM) irrevocably damaged, the Command Module — codenamed Odysscy — was fast on its way to becoming inoperable as well. All that would be left to possibly save them was the LM (codenamed Aquarius).

Ninety minutes after the explosion, Houston said, "We're starting to think about the LM lifeboat."

Mission Control concluded that they had to save remaining oxygen by closing valves. But that was irreversible, for once the valves were closed, they couldn't be reopened. Nevertheless, it was a gamble they had to take.

The crew was told to shut down the CM completely and to use the LM as a "lifeboat" for their return to Earth. This had been suggested during an earlier training simulation but had not been considered a likely scenario. Without the LM, the accident would certainly have been fatal. The damage to the Odyssey made a lunar landing impossible. Instead, the best they could hope was that the Moon's gravity would be used to return them to Earth.

Little power left

But turning the Lunar Module into a lifeboat was no easy task. Luckily, Haise was the astronaut in the space program who was most familiar with the LM, and he made his way through the narrow tunnel connecting Odyssey and Aquarius, and assessed the situation.

Short-term fix: Interior view of the Apollo 13 Lunar Module, showing some of the temporary hose connections and apparatus when the three astronauts moved from the Command Module to use the Lunar Module as a "lifeboat." Astronaut Swigert, command module pilot, is on the right. On the left, a fellow astronaut holds the feed water bag from the Portable Life Support System.

White knuckles at the White House: President Richard Nixon and Secretary of State Henry Kissinger (center) watch the splashdown with staff in the White House.

innumerable obstacles. It was getting darker; the cabin temperatures were cold and plummeting, the men had not slept for almost two days.

Splashdown

Nevertheless, the crew and Mission Control worked together to guide the spaceship back from space. Another hurdle was crossed when the heat shield appeared to withstand the re-entry.

Finally, on April 17 at 1:07 p.m., the world watched as Apollo 13's damaged space capsule parachuted down from the heavens and splashed into the South Pacific near American Samoa. Within minutes the capsule opened to reveal the three waving astronauts.

Apollo 13 had failed in its mission, but historians took to calling it the "most successful failure in history." NASA had pulled off the greatest escape from outer space.

Apollo 13 had only 15 minutes or so of power left. To power up the LM normally took two hours. Haise and Lovell worked feverishly to do it as fast as possible. This required them to go through an extremely complicated series of motions by hand, without the benefit of a computer. Neither they nor Mission control knew if the LM's motor could be fired to place Apollo 13 on a free-return trajectory needed to get them back to Earth. There was a lot they didn't know.

Moreover, the LM was designed to support two persons for 48 hours. Now it would have to support three men for perhaps 100 hours. Luckily, they were able to power up the LM.

But that was only the first step. The crew labored under worsening conditions. They were becoming dehydrated and slowly suffocating. Yet oxygen was the least critical consumable because electric power and water were also needed to power the LM. Therefore, they had to conserve their power and water as much as possible for re-entry.

Despite great hardship caused by severely limited power, cabin heat, and potable water, the team overcame

Recovery: With the astronauts already safely back on ship, the Command Module is hauled aboard the USS *Iwo Jima* after splashdown on April 17.

The crew

Center: Commander James A. "Jim" Lovell, Jr. (1928) — graduate of U.S. Naval Academy, former U.S. Navy captain, selected in 1962 for the second group of astronauts. **Right: Command Module Pilot John L. "Jack" Swigert** (1931–1982) — ex-U.S. Air Force fighter pilot, earned master of science degree in aerospace science from Rensselaer Polytechnic Institute; the only bachelor astronaut in the space program. **Left: Lunar Module Pilot Fred W. Haise, Jr.** (1933) — graduated from University of Oklahoma with bachelor's degree in aeronautical engineering; US Marine Corps fighter pilot; served as U.S. Air Force test pilot.

Astronaut Thomas Mattingly (1936) trained for the Apollo 13 mission as Command Module pilot. But it was discovered he had been exposed to the rubella virus (German measles) — a disease to which he was not immune — so three days before their launch he was pulled from the crew and replaced by Jack Swigert. As it would turn out, he never contracted the measles and went on to fly as CMP of Apollo 16.

Forgetting to close the bow doors

Hundreds of trapped passengers fought to escape as their crowded ferry capsized in the English Channel. People and objects were hurled through the air and into the freezing water in pitch-black darkness.

Roll On, Roll Off: The *Herald of Free Enterprise* was a "Roll On, Roll Off" (RORO) ferry designed for a quick turnaround in port. It shuttled across the English Channel between Dover and Calais, but on the day of the disaster it was routed to Zeebrugge.

Rescue: Capsized in the dark, the stricken ferry is attended by rescue boats. One of the biggest problems facing rescuers was that there was no proper log of the passengers traveling onboard.

The *Herald of Free Enterprise* ferry of the Townsend Thoresen line left the Zeebrugge dock shortly before 7 p.m. bound for Dover with hundreds of cars and 539 persons aboard, many of them English newspaper readers who had taken advantage of the papers' offer on cut-price day trips to the Continent.

The loading time at Zeebrugge seemed to take forever because there was only room for access to a single ramp onto the car deck. Water also had to be pumped into the ballast tanks to lower the level of the ferry. But now they were underway and passengers would be treated to a pretty, star-lit cruise across the English Channel.

Nineteen-year-old Simon Osborne was returning from a day trip to Belgium with seven of his high school friends. They were in warm spirits, having enjoyed a good day in Ostend. After boarding the ferry a few minutes earlier they had gone their separate ways and arranged to meet later in the bar. By the time the ship had only

traveled about 100 yards (91 m) from shore, still in shallow water, Osborne was in the lounge at the duty-free perfume counter, waiting to be served, when it suddenly became clear that something had gone wrong.

The passengers didn't know it yet but the crew had forgotten to shut the bow doors and the vessel had left port with the doors open and the extra ballast still in her tanks. Now seawater was flooding onto the car deck, making the ship wildly unstable.

Tipped over

At first the ship experienced a violent jolt, which didn't alarm too many passengers. However, within a few seconds there was a much more violent jolt and the heavily laden vessel suddenly flipped over. Passengers heard a terrible, immense, metallic grinding noise, as cars were hurtled through the air, bottles and debris went flying, and the unwarned passengers and crew were

Shallow grave: The full horror came to light the following day. Only a lucky roll onto a sandbar at the last moment had prevented the ship from going down in much deeper water. Had that happened, the loss of life would have been far greater than 193.

thrown screaming into the ocean or smashed against steel walls. Inside the crowded lounge, bodies somersaulted from floor to ceiling as water burst through the portholes and deck doors. Then the ship's lights went out and those passengers who were still aboard and conscious felt the rushing icy water.

Within 90 seconds of leaving shore they were fighting for their lives. Many were trapped inside the capsized ship as she filled with water. Some were breaking windows to get out, and clambering onto the ship's side to avoid being drowned.

Trapped inside

Osborne was trapped inside the lounge, terrified that the ship was going to sink to the bottom with him still inside. But luckily they were still in shallow water and it came to rest on a sandbank, leaving some air pockets and avenues of escape.

He tried to remain as calm as possible when floating in the frigid water. But he knew he had to get out or he would die. "I could see in the not-too-far distance — maybe 20 or 30 meters away — where windows had been broken and ropes had been lowered down," Osborne later said. "So I pulled myself through life jackets, through the debris of the disaster, and unfortunately through dead bodies, to get to beneath a window. By the time I'd done that there were rescue teams in the ship and very quickly a harness was put around me and I was winched onto the side of the ferry. I was very lucky to get out alive."

Some of his fellow passengers were not so lucky. A husband formed a human bridge for his wife and daughter to climb to safety, but when the wife called to him to follow there was no response. He was gone.

Another man rushed about the ship carrying a baby by holding its clothing clenched in his teeth. A little girl, perplexed by the unfairness of their distress, turned to an adult and said, "I've been ever such a good girl. I've never told any lies."

Rescue

The mishap occurred before the crew could send an SOS. But rescue helicopters, including two RAF Sea Kings, were at the scene within minutes. Dutch and Belgian boats in the area were also diverted to help in the rescue operation. Divers climbed inside the vessel looking for survivors, but some of them had their wet suits slashed by broken glass.

Over the next several hours more than 400 people were brought out of the ship alive and rushed to shore. Many were taken to hospitals in Bruges and Blankenburg suffering from cuts and bruises, hypothermia and shock.

But the trauma for the survivors and their loved ones was far from over.

For some it would take days to learn for sure if their relative or friend was among the dead, in part because the ferry did not maintain a complete passenger list before departing and some travelers had showed up at the last minute without having made reservations. There was no central information clearinghouse with definitive information about the survivors or the dead.

Maureen and Frank Bennett, from Sussex, had been on a day trip with their daughter and her boyfriend to celebrate their wedding anniversary. Maureen Bennett did not know about her daughter's fate until a hospital staffer brought her the news, sending the mother into tears. "She's alive," she cried, "she's alive. Thank God."

Sharon Gibbons agonized for many hours about the welfare of her husband, Ryan, a 37-year-old truck driver, who still hadn't been found. Finally, she was informed that he had been brought out of the ship alive after spending nine hours in an air pocket in the ferry's car deck.

But a forlorn young man wept over the apparent loss of his girlfriend, Christine Long, 32, who had been seated with him in the ship's restaurant when the vessel tilted and "the window just gave way." He said the entire restaurant looked like a goldfish tank. "She's lost," he added, "I don't know for sure, but I suspect the worst given the struggle she had."

Osborne later learned that two of his high school friends had perished in the accident.

> **I pulled myself through life jackets, through the debris of the disaster, and unfortunately through dead bodies, to get to beneath a window.**
>
> Simon Osborne

Outcome

The final death toll was 193, making it one of the worst passenger ship disasters in years. In 1994 MS *Estonia* sank with the loss of 850 lives. The worst peacetime maritime tragedy occurred in 1987 in the Philippines when the ferry *Dona Paz* sank after colliding with the tanker *Vector* in the Sibuyan Sea, killing 4,375 passengers of the liner and 11 crew members from the tanker. The most famous sea tragedy was the sinking in 1912 of the steamship RM *Titanic* on her maiden voyage from Southampton to New York, which killed at least 1,496 persons. Many of the *Herald* survivors continued to suffer from post-traumatic stress disorder that lasted for years after the tragedy.

Scrap metal: The disaster spelled the end for the Townsend Thoreson ferry brand and the company fleet was renamed P&O Ferries. All existing Townsend Thoreson ferries had the TT logos removed from their funnels and the ships were repainted blue.

Race from the South Tower

Two strangers, Brian Clark and Stanley Praimnath, trapped high in the flaming South Tower of the World Trade Center, scrambled to escape together. Surviving the plane's impact was lucky enough, but then they had to race down and out before the structure collapsed.

September 11, 2001 started as a perfect Fall day in New York. The twin towers of the World Trade Center — the North Tower and the South Tower, center of world commerce — stood 110 stories, or more than 1,000 feet (305 m), high above Manhattan in the bright, clear sky.

Brian Clark arrived on the South Tower's 84th floor at 7:15 a.m., ready for business. As usual, he entered his Euro Broker office, grabbed a cup of coffee and a sweet roll, and walked the floor, greeting his co-workers. Then he sat down at his computer to read his e-mails.

Three floors down, and little more than an hour later, Stanley Praimnath, an assistant vice president of Fuji Bank, sauntered into his office on the 81st floor with a raisin bagel and coffee. It was just another workday for thousands of white-collar workers at one of New York's most fashionable business addresses.

The two had never met nor could they ever have

> ❝I just happened to raise my head ... I saw this giant aircraft ... coming in slow motion towards me. ❞
>
> Stanley Praimnath

Moments from impact: The second plane, United Airlines Flight 175 approaches the South Tower of the WTC, while the North blazes.

imagined what bond they would soon be sharing.

North Tower is hit

At 8:47 a.m. Clark heard an enormous blast and he spun around to look out his window. But instead of seeing the Hudson River and the World Financial Center there was nothing but a huge fireball raging against the glass. A large plane laden with jet fuel — American Airlines Flight 11 — had slammed into the neighboring North Tower at a tremendous speed, cutting a huge gash angling through seven floors.

Clark, who was designated as a fire marshal for his floor, urgently sought guidance for what to do. Some tenants decided to trudge the 1,512 steps from the 84th floor to the ground lobby.

But Clark heard the announcement over the public-address system that told everyone the building was secure and everyone should return to his or her office. The fire authorities in charge of the South Tower apparently believed that their tower was safe because it hadn't been hit and they didn't want persons from their building to needlessly complicate the emergency evacuation of the North Tower, or get injured in the process.

Shock and awe: Traffic comes to a standstill as onlookers in lower New York see the twin towers ablaze, never dreaming that within minutes both will collapse.

Sent back up

Meanwhile, Stanley Praimnath, an assistant vice president of the Fuji Bank, had been on the 81st floor of the South Tower when the plane hit the neighboring building. He and 17 others dutifully left their floors.

Praimnath had walked out with a woman who was working there as a temp assistant; they immediately caught an elevator that took them down to the 78th floor — the "sky lobby" way station — where they boarded the express for the lobby.

had mistakenly concluded. "All is well here. You can go back to your office. This building is secure."

Most of the senior executives of the Japanese bank dutifully obeyed, but a few demurred. Praimnath hopped back on the elevator with his boss, Kenichiro Tanaka, and several other top managers.

Plane hits South Tower

Back at his office, Praimnath was talking on the phone with a colleague who was watching the disaster unfold on TV and telling the caller he felt safe, everything was fine. As he was speaking he happened to look out the window over the New York Harbor and the Statue of Liberty when his eye caught a strange sight. It was 9:02:59 a.m.

As Praimnath later put it: "I just happened to raise my head watching the Statue of Liberty and as I watched I saw this giant aircraft [...] coming in slow motion towards me — eye level, eye contact. And I just froze."

Finding the plane so close that he could clearly see its red and blue markings and realizing it was aimed directly at him, the shocked banker screamed and dove under his desk.

South Tower collapse: After burning for 59 minutes, the steel structure of the South Tower, already weakened by the plane impact, collapses and the building falls.

Praimnath reached the South Tower lobby about 10 minutes after the plane had struck the other building. But a security guard stopped them from going further.

"Where are you guys going?" the security guard asked.

"We saw fireballs coming down," said Praimnath

"No, no," said the guard, repeating what his superiors

An instant later, the Boeing 757 (United Airlines Flight 175) slammed into the building, with part of it plunging right through his room, bringing down the ceiling, breaking computers and overturning every desk — except the one Praimnath had ducked under. Part of the wing was wedged into his office door barely 20 feet

(6 m) from where the bank executive huddled in terror.

Trembling and crying, Praimnath called out, "Lord, don't leave me here to die!"

Impact of the crash

Three floors up, Brian Clark had been consoling a co-worker, Susan Pollio, who was distraught after watching people jump to their deaths from the North Tower inferno.

Clark's decision to walk her to the ladies room all the way over on the west side of the tower probably had saved his life.

He was standing along the west wall of the office on the 84th floor of the South Tower of the World Trade Center when the plane hit and the building was rocked, causing everything around him to fall apart.

The building swayed to the west, toward the Hudson, farther than anyone had ever felt it lean before, and then it proceeded to rock and shake as if trying to right itself. People screamed.

Search for survivors: A policeman with a sniffer dog looks for survivors in the aftermath. Even with both towers down the rescue work was hazardous. The North Tower collapsed at 10:28 a.m., but it wasn't until 5:20 p.m. that the smaller 7 World Trade Center came down.

Shaken but alive: Rescue workers attend to the many walking wounded. A total of 343 firefighters and paramedics and 84 Port Authority workers lost their lives in the attack.

Clark grabbed his flashlight, gathered with six others and headed down stairway A — as it turned out, it was the only one of three stairways in the upper floors of the South Tower not blocked by debris.

At the 81st floor, a woman stopped Clark and his group, telling them not to go down further due to the smoke. Instead, she urged them to go up and get above the smoke before descending at another spot.

"We've got to help this guy"

Praimnath, meanwhile, was just coming to his senses after the blast. Smelling fuel and screaming, he had begun to crawl on top of the rubble and ended up behind a mangled wall. He punched a small hole in it, but was otherwise unable to go anywhere. He was trapped. Just then Clark heard banging and a strange voice coming from inside.

> **" Come on Ron, we've got to help this guy. "**
>
> Brian Clark to his colleague Ron DiFrancesco

"Help! Help! I'm buried," somebody was crying. "Is anybody there?"

Clark grabbed another man in his group, Ron DiFrancesco, and said, "Come on, Ron, we've got to help this guy."

But the smoke and dust made it hard to see and breathe. DiFrancesco became overcome and turned back up the stairs, but Clark continued to probe for the trapped man in distress. Shining his flashlight through the hole, he spied an animated face.

Clark told the stranger to run up the wall in an effort to jump over, but the man's first attempt fell short. Then the man tried again and when he did the dutiful fire marshal reached up and grabbed him by the armpit, then pulled his body over the top of the obstruction, causing the two men to fall into a heap on the floor.

Hugging each other, they exchanged names and retreated to the stairs as fast as they could move.

Making it out

Although they were the same stairs the woman had warned him against, Clark and Praimnath headed down the slippery staircase, scrambling as fast as they could.

By the 68th floor, the air became clearer, the stairs drier, and the lights were on to show the way. En route they passed Jose Marrero, one of Clark's co-workers at Euro Brokers who'd led several people down and was going up for more. Clark would never see him again.

On the 44th floor, they came upon a security guard who was insisting on remaining with a wounded man until help came, and Clark hesitated, but Praimnath kept urging him to hurry, saying he feared that the tower might fall.

Finally, they reached the bottom. They rushed outside and hurried away. Four minutes later, there was a great roar.

"It was like steel bending and creaking," Praimnath later said. "It made this — I can't explain the last sound but it was an eerie sound."

"We heard the boom, boom, boom — like a series of gunshots," said Clark. "It disappeared into its own dust so quickly. We didn't run initially; we just stared at it in awe." Somehow they had escaped.

Evacuation: Stunned and choking, workers carefully make their way down a crowded stairwell. Many suffered respiratory problems from the sheer volumes of dust inhaled on the day.

Last man out of the North Tower

Richard "Pitch" Picciotto | **September 11, 2001**

Richard Picciotto, a fire chief responding to the World Trade Center disaster, found himself trapped with his fellow firefighters between the sixth and seventh story of the collapsing North Tower. A stairwell somehow cushioned them, but they knew it couldn't remain standing for long.

Chief Richard "Pitch" Picciotto marveled at the beautiful morning as he cruised down the New York State Thruway to his job on Manhattan's Upper West Side. A former New York City police officer, the 28-year veteran of the FDNY had served as a fire marshal, arson investigator, lieutenant and captain, prior to becoming chief of Battalion 11 in 1992. Picciotto had won numerous departmental awards and citations for his bravery and meritorious service, but above all he loved his work as part of the close-knit fraternity of fire fighters.

At the firehouse he and his brothers always bowed their heads whenever the department bell system sounded its signal of five bells, four times in a row. The "four fives" as they called it meant that one of their members had been lost. "We'll all meet at the big one," many of them would say.

At 8:46 a.m., Picciotto was at his firehouse at 100 West 100th Street when a Boeing 767 laden with jet fuel flew into the North Tower of the World Trade Center in lower Manhattan, creating an impact hole that stretched between the 92nd and the 98th floors. Emergency radios throughout the city crackled with the first

Sifting through the ruins: Two days after the shocking event, Richard "Pitch" Picciotto (left) and his colleagues are back on site with the slim hope that they can still pull someone out alive.

Responding: 9/11, a firecrew races to the scene after the South Tower collapses. The buildings had been designed to withstand an impact from a Boeing 707, and both absorbed the impacts from Boeing 767s. The effects of an intense jet-fuel fire had not been factored in.

sketchy reports of a major fire. As police and firefighters raced to the scene, television screens began to carry live shots of smoke pouring from the top of the 110-story-high structure.

Picciotto stared at the live coverage in disbelief. All he could say was, "Holy shit!"

Second plane hits

By the time he grabbed his gear and headed out the door, 18 fire companies had begun to respond to the blaze, setting up a command post in the tower's glass-lined lobby. World attention was becoming focused on the dramatic events unfolding in New York.

At 9:03 a.m. another large plane, United Airlines Flight 175, crashed into the southwest face of the South Tower of the WTC, causing a gash that extended from the 78th to the 83rd floors, leaving no doubt that a terrorist attack was underway. Its fire at first seemed less deadly, however, and the elevators remained operational. But nobody knew what lay ahead. America was under attack.

No elevators

Picciotto was one of the early responders. He knew the Twin Towers well, especially the North Tower. In 1993 he

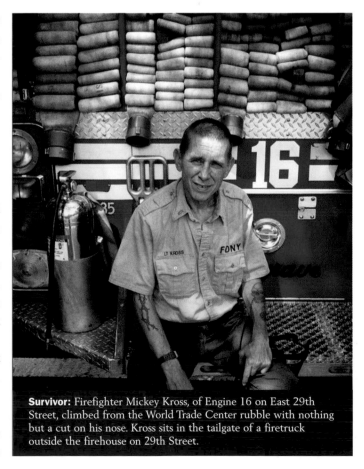

Survivor: Firefighter Mickey Kross, of Engine 16 on East 29th Street, climbed from the World Trade Center rubble with nothing but a cut on his nose. Kross sits in the tailgate of a firetruck outside the firehouse on 29th Street.

had been in charge of the evacuation there after a thousand-pound bomb planted in the underground parking garage had gutted the bottom seven stories, six of them underground. That evacuation had gone remarkably well, saving thousands of lives, and not even such a massive explosion had proved able to knock down one of the world's tallest structures.

But this time, as soon as he arrived, Picciotto could see that this new blow was much worse.

All of the elevators had been knocked out and the raging fire from 10,000 gallons of burning jet fuel prevented any person above the 91st floor from being able to escape. The chaotic scene already was posing incredible dangers. As Lieutenant Danny Suhr of Engine Co. 216 stood on the ground outside, he was killed by the body of a woman who had hurtled to escape the fiery inferno. Shortly afterward, a fire chaplain, Mycal Judge, knelt to administer the last rites to his fallen comrade; Judge too was fatally struck by falling debris.

Picciotto rushed into the tower to help. There were hundreds of shaken people, many of them injured or disabled, to evacuate. Unencumbered by the 100 pounds of equipment that each of his men had to carry with them, he quickly made his way as high as the 35th floor of the North Tower when suddenly he heard and felt an enormous roar and heard over his crackling radio the

Buried for 13 hours: Two New York Port Authority police officers who survived, William Jimeno (left) and John McLoughlin, later were portrayed in Oliver Stone's movie, *World Trade Center*. Jimeno and three other officers were trapped under the concourse between the twin towers by the collapse of the South Tower. Only Jimeno and McLoughlin survived, with another officer, Dominick Pezzulo, surviving the initial collapse, only to be killed by the collapse of the North Tower.

staggering news. The voice simply said, "The tower came down," alerting everyone that the South Tower had collapsed. Within ten seconds it was gone.

All firefighters in the North Tower were ordered to evacuate as soon as possible. For Picciotto, the words, "We'll all meet at the big one" came to mind, along with flashes of fear and danger.

Stairway B

Moving down with the others, at the 12th floor he encountered about 50 disabled persons who were congregating with their wheelchairs and crutches, unable to get past obstructions, and he helped them get to the only open stairwell, Stairwell B, which led to the lobby.

But before he could reach the bottom, at about 10:27 a.m. he heard a deafening roar and felt the building shake and instantly realized that it was about to fall. A few seconds later he was still bounding down the stairs, on the landing between the sixth and seventh floors, when chunks of concrete began tumbling down and some of it struck him, knocking off his helmet and he found himself being swept down in a thunderous cascade.

"Mayday!"

Somehow, he ended up in a black void or cave that cushioned his fall and protected him from the hundreds of thousands of tons of collapsing steel and concrete, away from the raging fire with its temperatures of more than a 1,000°F (538°C). He didn't know if he was alive or dead and dreaded the next stage of his ordeal.

Within minutes, he called out and began hearing scattered voices, some of them belonging to men he knew. In the darkness they discovered that several of

Happy ending: Genelle Guzman, who was just below the surface and suffering fom a crushed leg and other injuries, was rescued more than 27 hours after the towers fell. She enjoyed her dream wedding in July 2002. She was the last person pulled from the wreckage.

> The voice simply said, 'The tower came down,' alerting everyone that the South Tower had collapsed.

them, and a 59-year-old grandmother, had somehow been spared instant death and now they were hanging in a house of cards that could collapse at any moment or which could end up as their tomb. Traumatized, bruised and exhausted, and blinded and choked by dust and smoke, they struggled to communicate in order to find their way together and manage an escape.

Using radios that had failed them in the past, they called out Maydays that eventually were detected by a firefighter who was searching outside the rubble, and with a few crude tools Picciotto discovered a light about four stories above, and he climbed toward it and realized it was the sky. At last he crawled up and looked out to see "unfathomable, mind-boggling destruction."

Picciotta reached down and helped pull up one after another of his fellow survivors. He and a few others were rescued. But 343 other firefighters never made it out and they were lost at Ground Zero in one of the most shocking moments in American history.

Crawling from the rubble

Tom Canavan	September 11, 2001

After realizing that his pants were on fire, a dazed victim, Tom Canavan, tried to crawl out of a netherworld before the World Trade Center's North Tower fell. Dragging another survivor behind him, they searched for an opening out of the hot, smoldering rubble.

At 42 years old, the happy-go-lucky banker Tom Canavan weighed about 205 pounds on his 5 foot ten inch (178 cm) frame, scarcely anticipating that his excess bulk might mean the difference between life and death.

After the first plane hit the North Tower, Canavan lingered longer than he should have in his bank office on the 47th floor, in order to place securities in the vault for safekeeping before he evacuated his post. He was moving down the stairs when the second plane struck at 9:03 a.m. By the time he finally made it down the congested stairwell and passed through the revolving glass doors into the eerily darkened shopping mall directly below the Twin Towers, the floor was already littered with glass and sprinklers were pouring water. Alarm bells were ringing. Rescue workers were motioning dozens of frightened workers along the primary evacuation route.

He had just put his arm around an office colleague, Antoinette Duger, joking: "Do you want me to go back up and get your umbrella?"

But she wasn't buying it. "How can you be so calm?" she asked.

"Don't worry. We'll get out of here," he replied.

Canavan had just lifted his arm from her shoulder to help an elderly couple navigate the revolving door when suddenly there was a giant rumble caused by the South Tower's collapse. Within seconds, everything came down upon them and he was knocked to the ground, encased by slabs of concrete that somehow had left a small pocket for him to reside.

The fires below

Unable to hear any voices, he thought he was dead. But

Scene of devastation: The tubular walkway over Vesey Street close to where Tom Canavan emerged, mercifully just before the North Tower came down.

The Sphere: The sculpture by Fritz Koenig that had stood on the World Trade Center plaza has now been relocated to Battery Park, complete with 9/11 dents, scrapes and holes.

The Sphere, the famous globe-shaped bronze sculpture that had always stood as the main landmark outside the World Trade Center's entrance, but which now looked like a prop in some apocalyptic movie.

He tried to squeeze through the hole but his body was too thick. Pulling back, he helped the slender young man get through and saw him exit. Reaching out, he expected his companion to help pull him through, but the fellow simply began staggering away.

Canavan called out to him to stop but the man kept walking away, heading east toward Church Street, turning only to wave back. Canavan threw a rock at him in anger, but it was no use. He disappeared.

Afterwards Canavan found a larger opening and made it out onto the rubble. It was so hot it burned his soles. Within minutes he had walked north to Vesey Street when he heard the second great rumble and felt the North Tower collapsing.

then he tasted the dust and smelled smoke, which led him to realize that his pants were on fire. By tossing handfuls of dirt on the cuff, he managed to squelch the flames but burned his fingers in the process.

Bent face down in his coffin-like cocoon, he discovered there was only a narrow space about four inches (10 cm) wide above his head. The only light seemed to come from burning paper.

As he shifted his body to try to crawl forward through the opening, a man's voice cried out, "Don't leave me!"

Canavan asked who was it.

To which the man replied, "Maybe they'll find us here."

But Canavan knew he had to try to escape. "We'll suffocate if we stay," he said, telling the stranger, "I'm going," as he started his movements.

The man grabbed his ankle and Canavan continued to crawl, pulling the man with him through the dark void. Together they made their way over and under beams and slabs, joined like two caterpillars.

Finding *The Sphere*

After 20 minutes of claustrophobic wiggling and slithering in the suffocating maze of smoking debris, Canavan got his first breath of cool air and found a small hole that was about the size of a saucer. Forcing his head through it, he gasped for oxygen and looked out to see

Preserved: The "Survivors' Staircase," which had connected the WTC's outdoor plaza with the street, was one of the few surviving structures from the ruins to be preserved.

By most estimates, 13,000–15,000 persons successfully evacuated the two World Trade Center (WTC) towers on September 11.

A large number of the survivors began to leave as soon as possible after one or both of the planes struck. The majority of those, aided by police and firefighters, were successful in getting away before the buildings collapsed. Evacuation plans and drills, as well as the experience of the 1993 evacuation from the North Tower and many subsequent improvements to the exit signs and stairwell lighting, all contributed to the high survival rate.

However, the occupants of the towers faced many obstacles that hampered their ability to escape the flaming towers. In some instances, the poor physical condition of the victims or their reliance on high-heel shoes or other inadequate footwear, or their decision to delay for a minute in order to make a telephone call or gather up their personal items, meant the difference between life and death. Fire and structural damage prevented many workers from escaping according to plan, and broken elevators and crowded corridors also blocked their movement. It was a long way down.

Nobody could have imagined that both towers would fall within 102 minutes of the first air strike, giving everyone precious little time to respond.

Although hundreds of evacuees narrowly escaped death, only a tiny number — just 19 persons — survived once the towers fell.

Tom Canavan, a bank worker who had exited from the 47th floor of the North Tower to the lobby and been buried by debris from the South Tower's collapse, crawled 70 feet (21 m) through the rubble, aiding another man to safety just before the North Tower collapsed.

Fourteen people survived in the North Tower's Stairwell B and crawled to safety. They included Firefighters Billy Butler, Tommy Falco, Jay Jonas, Michael Meldrum, Sal D'Agastino, and Matt Komorowski of Ladder 6; Firefighter Mickey Kross of Engine Company 16, Firefighters Jim McGlynn, Rob Bacon, Jeff Coniglio, and Jim Efthimiaddes of Engine 39; Port Authority Police Officer Dave Lim; Battalion Chief Rich Picciotto of the 11th Battalion; and civilian Josephine Harris.

Two WTC employees also survived in Stairway B after the North Tower collapsed. Pasquale Buzzelli, a structural engineer for the Port Authority, and Genelle Guzman, a secretary, had remained in their work areas on the 64th floor until the South Tower's collapse shook their office and smoke started pouring in, at which time they and several others began to descend down Staircase B. The pair had reached the lower floors when the tower began to come down. Buzzelli awoke three hours later on a hill of rubble and she was extracted to safety. Guzman, who was just below the surface and suffering from a crushed leg and other injuries, was rescued more than 27 hours after the tower fell.

Two Port Authority Policemen, John McLoughlin and William Jimeno, were rescued after being buried in rubble around a freight elevator for about 13 and 21 hours.

A one-story-high portion of Staircase B, consisting of about 35 steps, has been preserved for display in the planned World Trade Center Memorial Museum.

"Miracle on the Hudson"

Flight 1549	January 15, 2009

Passengers and crew were asked to brace for impact. If the plane stayed in one piece, they would have to escape drowning after their crowded jetliner landed in the freezing cold Hudson River. Millions of viewers held their breath as the surreal "miracle on the Hudson" unfolded on live television.

It started as another normal flight. US Airways Flight 1549 had just left New York's LaGuardia Airport for Charlotte/Douglas with 150 passengers and five crew members aboard, and the plane was still climbing.

Most of the passengers were about to settle in for a nap or preparing to do some work on their laptops. But at least a couple of families had been required to split up in their seating arrangements, and they were trying to

Textbook landing: Nobody had landed a commercial airliner on water before without loss of life, let alone serious injury, but Chesley Sullenberger managed this unique feat.

adjust. Martin Sosa had been placed with his four-year-old daughter, Sophia, while his wife Tess was seated four rows back with their nine-month-old son, Damian. The harried mother was feeling uncomfortable about the separation, but a gentleman in the seat beside helped to make her feel more at ease by taking an interest in the baby. In another instance, a middle-aged father and his grown son also had to forgo sitting together for the flight.

At the controls was the first officer, 49-year-old Jeffrey B. Skiles, a 23-year veteran of the airline, who had just logged 35 hours of flying time in this particular kind of aircraft, the Airbus A320. Sitting beside him was the plane's captain, Chesley B. Sullenberger III, 57, a former fighter pilot who had been flying for the airline since 1980 and who was more accustomed to flying that model of airplane.

The birds

The craft had been airborne for only two minutes and reached an altitude of about 3,200 feet (975 m), going at a

Up close: The photo that was an Internet phenomenon. Janis Krums snapped this close-up shot from a commuter ferry that responded to the US Airways plane crash.

speed that was now up to about 250 miles (402 km) an hour, when Captain Sullenberger — who had been busy monitoring the cockpit instruments, managing the radios and checking the charts — looked up to see the windscreen suddenly filled with birds. His first instinct was to duck, but the loud sounds coming from the wing made him realize that something terrible had happened.

The aircraft had collided with a flock of hardy Canadian geese — something that had become an increasingly common occurrence near many airports located along the water, but one that, in this instance,

gravely worried Sullenberger as he smelled something burning and saw from his instrument panel that some of the creatures had apparently struck both engines. It was then that he knew that both engines were out.

Dave Sanderson, 47, of Charlotte, a married father of four who was heading home after a business trip, was seated in seat 15A on the left side of the plane when he heard an explosion and saw flames coming from the left wing. This isn't good, he thought.

After hearing the loud thump, the plane's two veteran flight attendants were shocked to note that the cabin had

User error: After getting the plane down in perfect shape, a panicked passenger rushes to the rear door and opens it before a crew member can stop them. Water rushes in weighing down the tail.

The nearest runway in sight was Teterboro Airport across the Hudson, but Sullenberger — who was also an experienced glider pilot — sensed that they wouldn't make it, so that was ruled out. LaGuardia Airport was considered, but Sullenberger said they were already going "too low, too slow," and besides, they were in the middle of one of the most heavily populated areas in the world — and he didn't want to crash into one of the city's endless buildings: the casualties from that would be catastrophic. All he could say to the controller was "Unable, we may end up in the Hudson."

fallen eerily silent: there was no sound at all coming from the engines.

Sullenberger immediately took the controls and began trying to assess the situation.

Back in the passenger cabin, Tess Sosa had also heard the thud and she turned to the man beside her for reassurance. He calmly looked up from his reading material, gazed out the window, and said in a matter-of-fact tone, "Oh, something hit the engine."

"Are we going to be OK?" she asked.

"Yes," he said.

"Are you sure?"

"Yes." Then he explained they were heading back to the airport. "We're going to be fine," he told her.

Actions in the cockpit

Captain Sullenberger was fighting to gain control. Both engines were stopped. Although the flight was at a low altitude, the fact that the aircraft had sharply lost its thrust and speed required him to lower the nose even further to keep the plane from going into a death dive. As he was straining for control, he had Skiles tear through a three-page checklist of procedures for restarting both the engines. Neither man was fully aware that the checklist was intended for planes flying at altitudes of 35,000 feet (10,668 m) or more.

> **Too low, too slow ... we may end up in the Hudson.**
>
> Captain Sullenberger

River below

That meant their only hope would be to land in the Hudson River. But to do that Sullenberger first had to steer the plane over the 604-foot (195 m) high George Washington Bridge, then glide down onto the water in just the right way — an extremely difficult maneuver for such a large plane, and something that in many previous air crashes had often resulted in a catastrophic breakup and massive casualties.

As a student of air science, Sullenberger knew that his river landing had to be perfect in several ways. He needed to touch down with the wings exactly level. The nose had to be slightly up, but not too far down in the tail. He had to touch down at a rate that was just above the aircraft's minimum flying speed, but not below it, or the plane would come apart in the process. And finally, he needed to make all these things happen simultaneously.

Sullenberger's task was made harder due to a little-known design feature involving the flaps, which on the Airbus A320 included a "ram air turbine" that essentially amounted to a small propeller that was supposed to automatically drop down into the wind to produce the electricity necessary for the crew to lower the flaps.

As the crew was struggling to master this unknowable feature, Sullenberger saw a boat on the river and was reminded of a point from his fighter training that if a plane has to ditch, it should be done near a vessel. Luckily for Flight 1549 the Hudson River was home to many boats, none of which were in the plane's landing path at that precise time.

As the plane glided down over the river, the passengers remained mostly quiet, except for the sound of some persons praying. Many were thinking about dying; some were trying to make last-minute cell phone calls to bid farewell to loved ones.

Denise Lockie, a passenger in Row 2 of first-class, consulted a pilot from another airline who was sitting nearby. She asked him if they were going down and he just nodded his head. The man in the next seat kept saying, "We're gonna make it. We're gonna make it."

"Brace for hard impact"

Sullenberger gave his final instruction over the intercom: "Brace for hard impact," and the flight attendants told everyone to get ready.

"What did he say?" a disabled woman of 85 asked her daughter, at which time her daughter held her in her arms and said, "I love you mom. We're going down."

Nearby, the kind stranger sitting next to Tess Sosa offered to take the baby out of her hands so she could steady herself, but she held on. Behind her she could hear her daughter crying for her and she turned around and yelled back to her, "We're gonna be OK, Sophia. We're gonna be OK."

Just then the plane made its sharp, abrupt impact on

Drama in Manhattan: Nearby ferries rush to aid the stricken aircraft, as their crews had been trained to do in case of such an emergency.

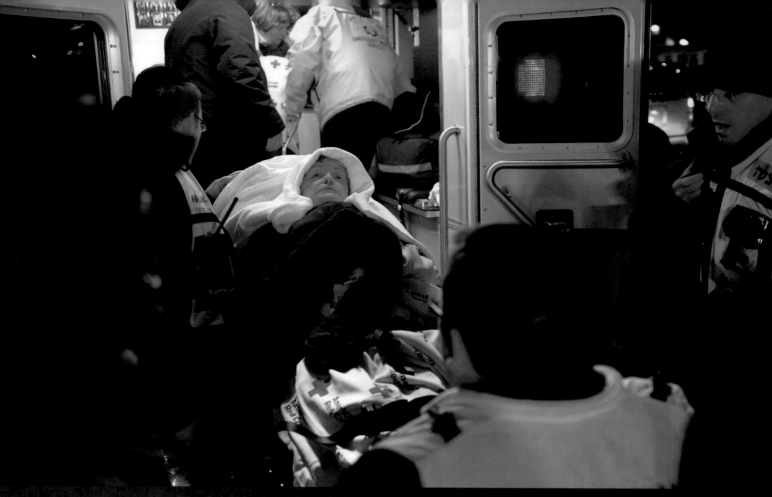

Precautionary checks: A passenger from the US Airways Airbus A320 is loaded into an ambulance on the West Side Highway at 40th Street. In all, 24 people were treated in hospitals for minor injuries and hypothermia. Flight attendant Doreen Welsh suffered a lacerated leg.

the water. The jolt was strongest in the tail, where items in the galley went crashing in every direction, severely gashing the leg of the flight attendant who was stationed there. But every place was like a roller coaster as the craft shot onto and through the water, banging passengers' heads into seats, snapping necks and knocking off eyeglasses, amid a cacophony of cries and shrieks.

When the splashdown finally seemed to be over and the plane was gliding on the water or sinking, many passengers immediately jumped to their feet and began trying to get into the aisle.

Miraculously, the airbus was still afloat, but everyone knew they had to evacuate as soon as possible, even if they didn't know what might await them outside.

Surprised that his landing had been so smooth and the plane hadn't broken up, Sullenberger breathed a sigh of relief and turned to his co-pilot, saying, "Well, that wasn't as bad as I thought."

By the time he could issue the order to evacuate, the flight attendants already were assisting passengers to open the exits.

Evacuate

The disabled matriarch in row 17 told her daughter, "Just leave me — you go," but her daughter refused, as she tried desperately to get someone to help her lift her mother out of the seat.

Cold water was already gushing into the plane from cracks in the fuselage, particularly in the rear of the passenger cabin where a passenger had opened the rear door even though that part of the plane was submerged. The water level deepened as many passengers scurried toward the rear exit, shifting even more weight to the back of the plane and threatening to sink it. And the boat-like plane was starting to turn and sweep with the current, heading toward the ocean.

Two flight attendants were in the front, one in the rear. The one in the front opened a door that was also armed to activate a slide, however the one on the port side did not immediately deploy.

Although hindered by her severely cut leg, the flight attendant in the rear had attempted to reseal the rear door; she was not successful, so she was urging passengers to move forward by climbing over seats to escape the rising water within the cabin. Soon she was in ice-cold water up to her chest, and a passenger in seat 23A was floundering up to his neck in the numbing torrent.

Besides slipping into their life jackets, some passengers were trying to rip off their clothes to be better able to swim; others were climbing over seats and clambering toward the exit doors. But considering the situation they were in, the evacuation was proceeding without panic.

In danger of drowning

Outside the cabin the frigid air temperature was only about 18°F and the water was 36°F — too cold for anyone to swim to shore or remain immersed for more than a couple of minutes. But some passengers slipped on the fuel-slickened wings, or smelling the strong scent of leaking diesel fuel and fearing that the wrecked plane might next explode, some of them dove into the water in a frantic effort to avoid being incinerated. Within a few seconds, each realized they would never survive in the killing cold and they thrashed to get out of its lethal grip.

The Sosa family joined together on the wing, standing in water that was already climbing up the adults' legs. From the shoreline, hundreds of stunned residents were looking out of their waterfront apartments to see dozens of figures standing on the wing in the middle of the river.

Rescue

Even before the splashdown, 911 calls had begun flooding in to report the plane on the Hudson. Emergency frequencies crackled with urgent dispatches. Within three or four minutes, tourist ferryboats and other vessels were racing toward the crash site, most of them with crews that had been specially trained and drilled to respond to just such an emergency. A small armada of police boats, fireboats, tugboats and Coast Guard craft

Hazard to shipping: The wreck of the Airbus A320 as it is towed to shore by tugs, the forward escape chute still inflated. Captain Sullenberger checked that the aircraft was empty before being the last to leave.

converged on the scene, and some of them snubbed up to keep the jetliner afloat. Helicopters dropped wet-suited police divers into the icy water to rescue those who seemed to be in the most distress. Emergency rescue personnel tossed life rafts and life preservers at the stranded victims. One by one, they hoisted the victims out of the water and off the wing into waiting boats, where they were wrapped in blankets and borrowed coats and hurried ashore on both sides of the river.

Before it was over, Captain Sullenberger walked up and down the watery cabin, double-checking that nobody had been left behind.

Hours later leaders of many of the lead rescue agencies gathered with top officials at a hastily called new

" I believe now we've had a miracle on the Hudson. "

Gov. David A. Paterson

conference. Gov. David A. Paterson stepped to the microphone and said, "I believe now we've had a miracle on the Hudson. This pilot, somehow, without any engines, was somehow able to land this plane, and perhaps without any injuries to the passengers. This is a potential tragedy that may have become one of the most magnificent days in the history of New York City agencies."

Remarkably, all 155 persons aboard Flight 1549 had escaped death, marking one of the most dramatic airplane crash rescues in history. The success was the result of extraordinary piloting, textbook responses by the rest of the crew and passengers, and a perfectly executed rescue effort by well-trained emergency response personnel.

Wintery scene: The plane was recovered from the Hudson three days later. The ice floes gathering around the salvage crane are testament to the fortune of the passengers. While many pilots could have got the plane down in the river, the chances that they could have done so and kept the plane in one piece are slim.

Profile of a hero — Chesley Sullenberger

In more than 50 years of commercial jet aviation, nobody had ever landed an airliner on water without fatalities. But Chesley B. Sullenberger III wasn't just any pilot. He was the ideal flyer to have at the controls of Flight 1549 over New York that day: the right person in the right place at just the right moment.

Sullenberger (pictured above with New York Mayor Michael Bloomberg) had devoted the last 40 years of his life to flying. After graduating from the U.S. Air Force Academy, he had spent more than six years as a fighter pilot, and he later earned advanced science degrees at Purdue University and the University of Northern Colorado. In his 29-year career as a commercial pilot for U.S. Airlines he had gained a reputation as a "pilot's pilot," going on to become an instructor and Air Line Pilots Association (ALPA) safety chairman. His ALPA safety work led to the development of a Federal Aviation Administration (FAA) Advisory Circular. The painstaking pilot had committed himself to trying to help his employer learn from prior mistakes and he was instrumental in developing and implementing his airline's Crew Resource Management (CRM) course that was taught to hundreds of his colleagues. He had also founded and presently served as president and CEO of Safety Reliability Methods Inc., a company that provides emergency management, safety strategies and performance monitoring to the aviation industry.

Sullenberger's cool, calm and collected style not only had been honed by decades of challenging flight experience and research on safety issues — it had also become his way of life. As his wife, Lorrie, later put it: "He loves the art of the airplane."

6
World War II

The Inn of the Eight Happinesses

GLADYS AYLWARD	**March–April 1940**

A tiny missionary, Gladys Aylward, led 94 frightened and destitute orphans on a miraculous escape across mountainous terrain in war-torn China. To evade butchery by the invading Japanese army, they somehow overcame hunger, disease and exposure to the elements.

Rising sun: Japan's invasion of China gained pace in 1938. In January they celebrated the fall of Nanking from the city's crumbling walls. As the war spread into the countryside, so Aylward's orphanage came under threat.

When Gladys Aylward set her sights on something, she was not one to always take the easy course. The 38-year-old English spinster had arrived in China in 1930, hoping to become a missionary. After years of working as a parlor maid, she had devoted herself to Christian service and used all of her life's savings to book passage to Yangcheng, China, to work with an elderly missionary, Mrs. Jeannie Lawson.

However, because China and the Soviet Union were at that time engaged in an undeclared war, in order to get there by train she had to go to Vladivostok, Russia and sail from there to Japan and from Japan to Tientsin; then she had to go by train, then bus, then mule, to the inland city of Yangcheng, in the mountainous province of Shanxi, a little south of Peking (Beijing).

When she left home, all she took with her was her passport, her Bible, her tickets and two pounds nine pence for the trip. Upon arriving at her destination, she found herself in an alien world where the Chinese peasants were conditioned to regard her as a "foreign devil" — not very inclined to be receptive to her gospel teachings. In order to carry out their mission, the two women restored an old building into an inn, which they called The Inn of the Eight Happinesses.

But when old Mrs. Lawson died, Aylward was left to run the mission alone. Somehow, she succeeded.

The Virtuous One

Shortly after Mrs. Lawson's death, Aylward met the Mandarin (local leader) of Yangcheng, who arrived with great fanfare, in a fancy sedan chair and accompanied by an impressive escort. He told her the government had decreed an end to the ancient practice of footbinding of young girls.

For centuries, it had been customary for the upper and middle classes that a woman's feet should be wrapped tightly in bandages from infancy, to prevent them from growing. Thus adult women came to have extremely tiny feet, which was seen as a sign of grace; however it also meant that they had great difficulty walking. The government needed a foot-inspector to patrol the district, enforcing the decree. However, the work would

Film of the book: Aylward's mission was made famous by the film *Inn of the Sixth Happiness* starring Ingrid Bergman, after the missionary's life story was published in the book *The Small Woman*.

Escape: Bergman as Aylward organizes the evacuation of the children from the orphanage. By early 1940, Aylward was looking after almost 200 children, as well as tipping off local Chinese Nationalist leaders about Japanese troop movements. The Japanese branded her a spy.

require a woman who did not have bound feet. Aylward was hired for this role and she accepted the position believing it would provide good opportunities to spread the Gospel.

A year later the Mandarin was so pleased by the job she had done, he summoned her again. This time the challenge was much greater. The convicts had rioted in the prison and the soldiers were afraid to intervene. Aylward agreed to serve as a negotiator and she worked out a peaceful agreement. As a result, she became known as *Ai-weh-deh*, which means "The Virtuous One."

By 1936 she had adopted five children, becoming a Chinese citizen, a favorite of the Mandarin, and an accepted member of the community. She lived frugally and dressed like the local people.

Saving the orphans

Japan's invasion of China spread into the countryside. In the spring of 1938, Japanese planes bombed Yangcheng, killing many civilians and causing the survivors to flee into the mountains. Then the Japanese Imperial Army occupied the city and left, then returned and left again.

During the hostilities, Aylward helped treat the wounded and assist the refugees. She also used her status as a Briton to carry messages past the Japanese lines, later learning that the Japanese had labeled her as a spy and offered a reward for her head and that of the Mandarin.

By early 1940 the indomitable Aylward was looking after almost 200 orphans. After arranging to send more than half of them to the government orphanage in the Nationalist-controlled city of Sian (Xi'an), 100 miles

(161 km) away, she continued to supervise the others until she could arrange their transfer as well.

But another Japanese advance threatened to make them all captives and most likely result in their deaths. Therefore, Aylward moved quickly in an effort to lead them to safety.

Yellow River

The 94 children included a few who were 11 to 15 years old, but most were only four to eight and a few were toddlers. They had no money or supplies other than two days' worth of food, yet she estimated that the 100-mile (161 km) journey to Sian would doubtless take at least 12 days — if they made it.

The trip required them to walk the entire distance over difficult terrain, including high mountains and somehow cross the formidable Yellow River, known as "China's Sorrow" because it had claimed so many lives. Simply shepharding so many young ones for such a distance would pose an enormous challenge.

They spent the first night on the road sleeping at a rat-infested Buddhist monastery; otherwise, they had to camp out in the open air. They drank from polluted streams. Some of the older children were sent to scavenge

> **❝ The journey was made more difficult because we couldn't walk on the main trails ... we had to get across the Yellow River. ❞**
>
> Gladys Aylward, interviewed by Alan Burgess

for food. Everyone became hungry, thirsty and exhausted.

Upon reaching the Yellow River on the twelfth day, they discovered there was no way to get across. All boats had been seized to keep them out of Japanese hands.

After being stuck for three days Aylward and her flock knelt and prayed for help from the Lord. A Chinese officer who was with his patrol heard their song and rode over to ask them what they were doing. After hearing their story, he helped get them a small boat, which they used to ferry everyone across one small group after another.

Illness

As soon as they reached safety, Aylward collapsed. She was discovered to be suffering from typhus, pneumonia and malnutrition, and spent several months in hospital fighting for her life.

She never fully regained her health. However, after returning to England in the late 1940s, a British author, Alan Burgess, learned about her exploits saving the children. In 1957 he published a book about her, *The Small Woman*, which was later made into a Hollywood movie, *The Inn of the Sixth Happiness*, starring Ingrid Bergman. Aylward died in 1970.

Back in Britain: When she returned to Britain in 1949, the *Inn of the Sixth Happiness* movie made her famous, but she found the film distressing. A modest woman, she was upset by the inaccuracies of a movie version of her life, and in particular, the obligatory love interest that was shoe-horned into the film.

The one that got away

Oberleutnant Franz von Werra, an inveterate escapee, aimed to break away from a prisoner-of-war train in Canada and make it all the way back to Germany. In order to succeed, however, the arrogant officer had to clear innumerable obstacles, one step at a time.

In September 1940, as the Battle of Britain raged in the skies overhead, farm workers in Kent, England heard a burst of gunfire from a nearby Lewis battery and saw a disabled German BF109 fighter make a crash landing in the field about a quarter of a mile away. Moments later the German pilot climbed unhurt from the wreckage and he was captured at gunpoint — another Axis prisoner-of-war of defiant Great Britain.

For captured members of the German armed forces, this meant the war was over for them. But for Luftwaffe *Oberleutnant* Franz von Werra, it was just beginning.

Taken away for interrogation and processing that lasted for three weeks, the cool and arrogant German pilot was sent to Camp No.1, at Grizedale Hall in the Lake District, Cumbria. Although von Werra was convinced that Germany would win the war in a few weeks, he wanted to be part of the conquest and was determined to escape. Shortly after arriving in the camp he submitted an escape proposal to the *Ältestenrat*

(the governing council) that the Germans had established to oversee not only camp discipline and conditions but also escapes. The committee approved his request.

First escape

The plan called for von Werra to run away from a daily morning walk that prisoners were allowed to take outside

Flight delay: Hardy Kruger played von Werra in the film *The One That Got Away*. This scene recreates the moment when von Werra pretended to be a Dutch airman keen to take a test flight. He was stopped at gunpoint by a Royal Air Force (RAF) squadron leader.

Crash landing: Von Werra got his plane down in one piece near Marden, Kent, and was promptly captured by the unarmed cook from a nearby army unit. He was sent to the London District Prisoner of War detention center for interrogation.

the camp's grounds. At 2 p.m. on October 7, 1940 von Werra and 23 of his fellow officers were led out for their exercise, escorted by 10 armed guards, an officer and two sergeants, one of whom was mounted on a horse. As some of his fellow officers helped to divert attention, von Werra slipped into a passing cart and got away into the rugged countryside.

> **It's the duty of an officer to try and escape.**
>
> Franz von Werra, from the film
> *The One That Got Away*

A manhunt ensued and three days later two members of the Home Guard discovered him hiding in a *hoggarth* (stone farm shed) and they arrested him. But as he was being brought back to camp, he overpowered his guards and escaped again. Two days later he was spotted submerged in mud and he was recaptured. This time he was transferred to Camp No. 13, the Hayes Camp, in Swanwick, Derbyshire.

Another escape

There von Werra joined with several of his fellow prisoners in a group they called "*Swanwick Tiefbau A. G.*" (Swanwick Excavation Company) that was intent upon digging an escape tunnel. When completed in December 1940, the escape tunnel was only 43 feet (13 m) long, but it served in getting von Werra and four of his fellow POWs beyond the perimeter, from where they would split up. Von Werra traveled alone, trying to pose as a Dutch pilot serving with the RAF in order to gain access to a plane that he would then use to fly back to Germany.

After a series of close calls, he ended up sneaking into a Rolls Royce aircraft factory where he succeeded in gaining some instruction about a warplane's cockpit controls and he was about to turn on the engine and take it for a ride when he was apprehended at gunpoint. This time the escape-prone inmate was transferred 3,000 miles (4,828 km) across the Atlantic to a prisoner-of-war camp in Canada.

In January 1941 the British began the process of transporting their German POWs to Canada. Von Werra and the others were driven to Greenock on the River Clyde and put aboard the troop ship, the *Duchess of York*. On January 10 the ship left port carrying 1,250 German prisoners and 1,000 Royal Air Force recruits, who were going to Canada to receive their training.

While assigned to Cabin 35, von Werra began to plot his next and most ambitious escape. After the convoy landed in Halifax, Nova Scotia, the POWs were loaded aboard two trains. He was put on one that he discovered was bound for the new Gravenhurst Internment Camp on the north shore of Lake Huron, Ontario.

Upon consultation with others, he realized that his next journey would bring him very close to the border with the United States, which was then a neutral country. Therefore, he decided to try to escape over the border and then gain assistance from the German Consulate.

Escaping from the train

Von Werra was closely guarded but he decided that when they came close to the border he would try to jump headlong out of a train window. The cold weather meant that the windows were kept closed and they were also frozen shut with ice. So he and some accomplices worked on ways to thaw the ice, using their body heat in an attempt to raise the cabin temperature.

After the train left Montreal station, the prisoners succeeded in melting away the ice of one window without attracting suspicion. Before the locomotive had picked up

Over the wall: His first escape was over a dry stone wall while exercising at Grizedale in Cumbria. He was picked up five days later immersed in a muddy depression in the moorland fells.

speed, von Werra signaled his helpers that he was ready. One of them stood up and opened a blanket at the corners as if he was folding it, which served to conceal the fact that von Werra was opening the window and preparing to jump. Then he dived out of the open window and rolled down the embankment. He was unhurt.

Von Werra had landed in the small town of Smith Falls, Ontario, 30 miles (48 km) from the St. Lawrence River that formed the border with the United States. His absence would not be noted until the following afternoon. Six other prisoners also jumped out the window but all except von Werra were recaptured.

Crossing the river

Shortly after entering the town, he obtained a local map from a garage and determined that the nearest point of the river was at Prestcott, Ontario, and he walked there. Upon his arrival, he was happy to discover that the wide and swift-running river had frozen over. In the darkness he could see lights on the other side that he supposed were coming from the town of Ogdensburg, New York, so he walked two miles downstream and began crossing the ice.

When he reached the middle of the river, however, he found that cutters had opened a channel in the ice and therefore he couldn't get across. So he returned to the shore and found an upturned rowboat at a deserted summer camp. Struggling in the cold, he dragged the heavy and unwieldy boat across the snow-crusted ice all the way to the channel. Then he pushed it in and got inside. Soon he was stepping onto the shore on the American side of the river. Now he was on neutral soil.

Finding himself at the New York State Hospital, he walked over to the first policeman he could find, showed him his uniform and papers, and convinced him that he was an escaped German prisoner of war. The suspect was allowed to contact the German Consul and to obtain the services of a lawyer in order to block his extradition back to Canada.

Hailed as a celebrity

Von Werra's story became front-page news and the escaped fighter pilot milked his celebrity for all it was worth. While his lawyer tied up the immigration proceedings, Baron Franz von Werra announced that he liked the United States "because there is no barbed wire here," and saying that he wished to go on a sightseeing

Canadian border: Having picked up no serious injuries after throwing himself from a train window, von Werra set off for the Canadian border and the safety of neutral U.S.

tour of New York City. Representatives of the German government put him up at the Astor Hotel on Times Square and scheduled press conferences for him to score propaganda victories. In one of them he said he would find his way back to Germany "as well as I found my way out of prison camps three times."

Before American authorities could arrange with Canada and British authorities for his return to Canada, it was learned that he had already returned to Berlin, via the Mexican border, Rio de Janeiro, Barcelona and Rome. Von Werra returned home to a hero's welcome. Adolf Hitler awarded him the Iron Cross.

But on October 25, 1941, while flying a routine patrol from Holland, his engine failed over the sea and his plane disappeared without a trace.

The story of von Werra's escape was later made into a book and a film, *The One That Got Away*, starring Hardy Kruger in the title role. He is generally regarded as the only Axis POW to successfully escape and return back to Germany.

Escaping Hitler's "escape-proof" castle

AIREY NEAVE | **January 1942**

Airman Airey Neave made his audacious attempt to become the first British prisoner-of-war to make a "home run" from Colditz Castle. His detail-oriented German captors were just as determined to block any avenue of escape.

Airey Middleton Sheffield Neave was a young Eton-educated nobleman who had joined the British Army as an officer in the Royal Artillery only to be wounded and captured by the Germans at Calais in May 1940.

After he had made several thwarted escape attempts, in May 1941 the Gestapo classified him as a trouble-maker and sent him to Oflag IV-C at Colditz, a special camp for officer prisoners-of-war (POWs) who were either escape risks or high-profile VIPs. (Oflag was the abbreviation for *Offizierslager*, "officers' camp.")

Situated high on a cliff overlooking the town of Colditz near Leipzig in Saxony, the medieval castle had been built in 1014, withstanding countless sieges, wars, and regime changes over the centuries. Since taking it over in 1939, the Nazis had added several modern improvements in an effort to make it their most famous, "escape-proof" prison.

Colditz's granite battlements rose to a height of 75 feet (23 m) of solid rock. Below them the Germans had strung an eight-foot-high double barbed-wire fence. Armed sentries patrolled the perimeter round the clock and below the wire the ground gave way to a sheer drop of 150 feet (46 m) down to the valley floor. Crack shots in 18 sentry towers equipped with searchlights and machineguns scanned the exterior.

Making it even more formidable for any would-be

Colditz Castle: Given the determined nature of many allied prisoners to escape, German authorities decided to house their most troublesome and most valued prisoners together in one secure unit.

escaper was the fact that Colditz had the highest level of supervision of any prison in World War II — three guards for every POW.

For you and your fellow prisoners, the Germans told Neave, the war is over. There is no escape.

The escape factory

Behind the fortress walls, however, a collection of Polish, British, French and Dutch officers conspired to prove them wrong. Refusing to comply, as a matter of honor they were determined to break out of Hitler's prison and rejoin the war against Nazi Germany.

By putting so many escape-prone prisoners in the same institution, the Wermacht had unwittingly created an escape academy. Inside its walls were the Allies' largest

Inner courtyard: The nationalities interned in the castle varied throughout the war. At first it housed mainly Polish prisoners, then it was dominated by French officers. From 1943 onwards it housed only British, Canadian and American prisoners of war.

> ❝I learned at Colditz that the escaper must have absolute confidence in his success. ❞
>
> Airey Neave

concentration of schemers, tunnelers, forgers, smugglers, lock-pickers and escape artists who could trade skills. For the rest of the war, Colditz would become the scene of a never-ending cat-and-mouse game between the famously efficient German captors and some of their most daring and enterprising adversaries. At Colditz, the art of escape developed into a science.

The British Secret Service was so determined to succeed at that science that they instituted a special, super-secret unit, code-named MI9, to remain in touch with and hopefully assist prisoners in enemy hands. As the war progressed, its operatives devised escape plans and produced a range of ingenious escape gadgets that could be concealed in everyday objects and sent to the POWs via the Red Cross private parcel system that

allowed prisoners to receive "comforts" such as cigarettes and candy.

Over the next four years, the German security officers would record more than 300 escape attempts at the castle, of which 130 prisoners managed to break out and 18 actually made it back to rejoin their country's military forces.

If at first you don't succeed

Three months after his arrival in Colditz, Neave attempted his first escape. On August 28, 1941 he donned a disguise (a discarded Polish army tunic and a cap he had covered over with paint so that it resembled a German non-commissioned-officer's uniform) and he boldly proceeded to walk out of the prison. However, his ruse was revealed when the searchlights betrayed its oddly colored appearance.

Escape outfit: Airey Neave in one of his German uniforms. The clothes were painted and the insignia made of cardboard.

Dutch officers: Sixty-eight Dutch officers arrived in July 1941 and by August 13 two had already escaped. Six Dutch officers would eventually make it back to England.

the pair emerged from an unoccupied room and headed through a corridor that led over the prisoners' yard and into an attic above a German guardroom. When the guards were away, they descended into the empty guardroom and walked outside, then strolled across the courtyard and exited the main gate. Then they turned east and under cover of darkness clambered over an unguarded wall along the road. Afterwards they boarded a train, then made their way to Liepzig, Ulm, and Singen before crossing over to Switzerland on January 9.

Neave became famous as the first British officer to score a "home run" (completed escape) from the castle. "I learned at Colditz that the escaper must have absolute confidence in his success," he later said. "He must never be influenced by the gloom of his companions or he is lost."

Afterward, he published best-selling accounts about his adventures and Colditz became the subject of many popular books, movies, TV shows and games. After becoming a Member of British Parliament for Abingdon, he was assassinated in 1979, the victim of an Irish terrorist car bomb.

Although he might have been shot, he got off with a light punishment and opted to try again.

On the night of January 5, 1942, Neave teamed up with a Dutch officer, Anthony Luteyn, to slip away from a theatrical production using a specially cut trap door beneath the stage. Wearing more convincing uniforms,

Plan of the castle: Prisoners had access to a detailed plan of the castle courtesy of an original in the British Museum which was copied and smuggled in via a Red Cross parcel.

British airmen: Following numerous attempts to get out of the various Stalag Lufts, many British airmen found their way to Colditz, including fighter ace Douglas Bader (center, front row).

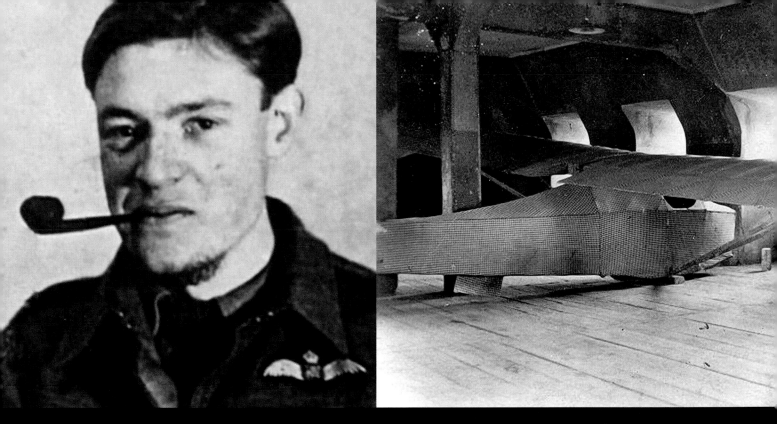

The Colditz glider

In December 1943, a Colditz prisoner named Bill Goldfinch (above) was looking out his cell window over the town in the valley below when he noticed something. A Royal Air Force man with some experience in aviation and a mind intent on escape, Goldfinch studied the sight before him. Although the wind was blowing in his face, the snowflakes were drifting up in the wind currents. Watching intently, he could see the way the wind worked so smoothly around the castle.

This gave him an idea. What if somebody jumped off the castle roof in a glider and flew away!

Colditz's roof stood 300 feet (91 m) above the ground. If a runway could be improvised along the 40-foot (12 m) ridge, then by using ropes, pulleys and a counter weight, a prisoner might be able to catapult over the ramparts and glide silently over the sleeping inhabitants, across the river, and onto what appeared to be a perfect landing place along the distant shore.

Goldfinch discussed his audacious idea with some of his RAF mates. Consulting the prison library, they found a textbook with information on building a glider (shown above). Then they drafted one version after another of a craft that was designed to carry two persons.

Other prisoners aided them in stealing the necessary materials. Homemade tools cut and shaped the wood, which was stuck together with glue bribed from the German guards. The prisoners used lookouts and signals to evade detection as they worked to construct their makeshift skeletal frame. Time and time again they had to hide every piece to avoid discovery.

Cotton gingham bed sheets were used to cover the frame. Then they had to make it aerodynamic by making it stiff, the way a child dopes his model plane. From their meager rations, the prisoners concocted a unique recipe to make the starch. By grinding and boiling some millet, they made the necessary substance.

The war ended before they had the opportunity to fly away.

Across the Pacific

PHILIPPINES TO AUSTRALIA	1942

A plucky dive-bomber pilot and an infantry officer ran from their barbarous Japanese captors and sailed off in a leaky tub to escape 3,200 miles (5,150 km) across the enemy-held Pacific. The Yanks' only navigational tools were a simple compass and a torn page from an old magazine.

Lieutenant Damon "Rocky" Gause of the Army Air Corps stood five feet, five-and-a-half inches (166 cm) and weighed a muscular 165 pounds (75 kg), with a face that bore some resemblance to screen star Edward G. Robinson.

A product of Jefferson, Georgia, he had grown up in the great outdoors and playing sports; he later left home to join in the Coast Guard and spent time roughnecking on an oil rig in South America — a background that would serve him well in the wartime military. Now he was a flyer in the Army Air Corps.

Stationed in Manila, the 26-year-old dive-bomber pilot became a prisoner of the Japanese when the Philippines fell shortly after Pearl Harbor. In April 1942 he was doomed to be among the 70,000 half-starved American and Filipino soldiers forced to walk what would later go down in history as the infamous Bataan Death March, a grueling 64-mile (103 km) forced march to prison in which at least 10,000 captives were shot or bayoneted, or perished from disease and dehydration.

But in the first of Gause's many amazing feats, he managed to overpower a Japanese guard and kill him with his own bayonet, then flee into the jungle. Then he swam through three miles (4.8 km) of shark-infested waters to the rock island fortress of Corregidor, where he joined with the 2nd Battalion, 4th Marines to wage a last-ditch fight against the Japanese.

An estimated 2,300 military and civilians had escaped from Bataan to Corregidor. Together they endured horrid privations and brutal shelling. But soon they could hold out no longer.

When Corregidor fell on May 6, Gause again eluded

Death road: The infamous Death March of Bataan. American and Filipino troops captured at Bataan and Corregidor were forced to carry their wounded comrades across the Bataan peninsular to prisoner-of-war camps. They suffered summary shootings, beatings and beheadings from the Japanese en route.

capture by swimming and sailing a stolen boat to a neighboring island. A Japanese army patrol passed his body washed up on the beach and assumed he was dead. For three months he moved from one island to the next, always staying one step ahead of enemy patrols. Aided along the way by courageous Filipinos, he tried to meet up with someone who could help him get over to the Allied side.

Australia or bust

On the jungle island of Mindoro, he met a fellow escapee from Bataan, Captain William Lloyd Osborne, who was just as determined as he to avoid recapture by the barbarous Japanese.

Fantastic voyage: Equipped with an old map torn out of *National Geographic* magazine, Damon "Rocky" Gause and William Osborne pose in front of the storm-battered *Ruth-Lee*.

Together they commandeered a 20-foot (6 m), native-built, diesel-powered skiff and consulted with the Filipinos about sailing routes and possible dangers they might encounter by attempting to make the epic nautical journey south to Australia.

Christening their little boat *Ruth-Lee* after their wives, they stocked it with as many supplies as they could gather and in mid-August 1942 they sailed off for what they hoped would be an uneventful, four-month cruise. Neither man had ever sailed a boat before. Their only navigational tools were a compass and a tattered map of the Far East from an old *National Geographic* magazine.

The boat proved to be leaky and poorly equipped, with an inadequate sail and an unpredictable motor. Waves crashed over the prow and threatened to sink the vessel, but they nursed their craft as best they could, using whatever meager materials they had available.

Hazards along the way

Hopscotching from one island to the next, they encountered a leper colony, tropical storms, illness, man-eating sharks, and a jagged coral reef that damaged their hull, but their battered craft held together. Sometimes they had to subsist on coconuts and shark flesh.

To fool Japanese warships and planes, they camouflaged the boat with coconut leaves or created a makeshift Japanese flag, but in one instance as they approached the Australian battle zone a Japanese fighter

pilot flew down and strafed their helpless vessel with machine-gun slugs, narrowly missing them and setting fire to some of the coconut oil. They were lucky to stay afloat.

Finally, 159 days after setting sail, they reached the northwest coast of Australia — a journey of 3,200 nautical miles. Australian troops greeted them with glee and took them to the hospital to be treated.

Meeting MacArthur

As soon as they were ready, a plane brought them to the headquarters of the American commander, General Douglas MacArthur, where they found him in his palatial hotel. The scruffy pair slithered along the marble floor in their bare feet and saluted sharply.

"Sir, Lt. Gause reports for duty from Corregidor!"

MacArthur returned the salute and exclaimed, "Well, I'll be damned!"

On October 21, 1942, MacArthur decorated them with the Distinguished Service Cross, making Gause and Osborne two of America's early heroes of the Pacific war.

Gause resumed his Army Air Corps service and was promoted to major. Shortly before D-Day, he died testing a P47 dive-bomber over the Isle of Wight.

For more than 50 years, the journal he had written about his escape experiences was stored in a soldier's footlocker. Edited by the son he never knew, his memoir was published in 1999 as *The War Journal of Damon "Rocky" Gause: The Firsthand Account of One of the Greatest Escapes of World War II*.

Norway's greatest war hero

| JAN BAALSRUD | March 24–June 1, 1943 |

A Norwegian resistance fighter's epic flight from the Nazis took him through some of the most brutal landscape in northern Europe.

Jan Baalsrud was a 26-year-old instrument maker in Kolbotn, Norway when the 1940 German invasion forced him to flee to neutral Sweden. But after his conviction for espionage, he was expelled and eventually ended up in Great Britain, where he joined the Norwegian resistance organization Kompani Linge.

In March 1943, Baalsrud and three other British-trained Norwegian commandos embarked on a dangerous mission to destroy a German air control tower in Northern Norway and recruit operatives for the resistance movement.

Sailing from Scotland on a 75-foot (23 m) fishing boat that was laden with 8 tons (8,000 kilos) of explosives, the agents reached the desolate and icy coast on March 29, preparing to destroy the air control tower.

However, this mission was compromised when Baalsrud and his fellow resistance men sought out a shopkeeper, who was a trusted resistance contact, only to alert the wrong person. The terrified resident ran to a telephone to warn a local official, who betrayed them to the Germans.

The morning after their blunder, a German gunship steamed into the bay where they were anchored. Realizing they were trapped, the Norwegians hastily set a time-delayed charge and fled for shore in a small boat just as the fishing boat exploded. Before they could reach land, their boat was sunk, leaving them swimming for their lives through the frigid Arctic water.

The only survivor
Three of the four men were shot as they scrambled up the slippery shoreline, but Baalsrud made it into a snowy gully, pursued by several German soldiers. Soaked and freezing, he had lost one shoe and was only lightly armed. After evading immediate capture, he used his pistol to shoot and kill the lead German officer and wounded a second enemy. Two other Germans fled, but bullets were thudding in the snow all around him as he continued his getaway.

The man on the plateau: Jan Baalsrud, pictured after the war. Despite almost losing both his feet to frostbite he returned to Norway to work behind the lines later in the war.

By the time he had climbed to the summit, about 200 feet (60 m) high, he realized that part of his numb foot had been shot off and the rest was badly frostbitten. Nevertheless, he continued to flee over the barren landscape. Finally, he reached the shore of the small island and spotted a rock about 1,500 feet (457 m) offshore.

Incredibly, despite the extreme cold, he dove in the sea and swam to it, then collected himself and set out for another small island less than an eighth of a mile (200 m) away.

Against all odds: Norway's Lyngen Alps in winter. Baalsrud got lost attempting to cross them. Desperately weak, frostbitten and hallucinating, he stumbled into the man who would save him.

The frozen swimmer barely survived the ordeal and fell onto the shore, where two small girls discovered him. Luckily for him, their mother, Fru Pedersen, supported the resistance, and she with another friendly neighbor, Fru Idrupsen, took in the fugitive and tended his wounds — knowing that the Gestapo would kill them all if they found out. The next morning, the two women rowed Baalsrud to a safer spot, where residents kept him under wraps.

Over the mountains

Passed from one safehouse to another, he spent the next six days evading the Nazis as he headed south toward the mainland, from which he hoped to slip into Sweden. But in order to reach Lyngenfjord, he would have to cross the formidable 3,000-foot (900 m) high Lyngen Alps alone and hobbling on his injured foot.

Shortly after he embarked, the weather worsened and he became lost in the snow. Frostbitten, snow-blinded and hallucinating, he wandered through the wilderness for days until stumbling into a home of another brave Norwegian, Marius Grönvold, a farmer and former part-time journalist. Grönvold saved his life, first by nursing him back to health, and second by smuggling him across the fjord to a safer location at Revdal.

Hidden there in a tiny wooden hut that the grateful Baalsrud called his "Hotel Savoy," he passed in and out of delirium. Now his injuries were life threatening. Using a pocket knife and some brandy, he was forced to amputate nine of his toes to stop the gangrene from spreading.

At one point, he was left on a high plateau on a stretcher in the snow, barely alive, as German troops swarmed through the area. Eighteen days later, Grönvold and another supporter were finally able to return. Seeing his "ghastly waxen face," they thought he was dead. But he said, "I'm not dead, damn you."

After transporting him by stretcher to the Finland border, they put him in the care of a party of Lapps, who hauled him by reindeer-pulled sled across Finland. On June 1, the badly injured Norwegian was carried into neutral Sweden where he was safe at last. From Saarikoski in northern Sweden a Red Cross seaplane rushed him to Boden for emergency medical treatment.

Recovery

After spending seven months in a Swedish hospital, he flew back to England and went to Scotland to train other resistance fighters. In 1944 the British awarded him with the MBE (member of the Most Excellent Order of the British Empire) and his own country bestowed the St. Olav's medal with Oak Branch. Considered Norway's greatest hero of World War II, he died in 1988.

Baalsrud's escape story was told in David Howarth's book, *We Die Alone* (1955), and in *Defiant Courage — Norway's Longest WW2 Escape* (2001) by Astrid Karlsen Scott and Tore Haug, as well as in the popular Norwegian movie *Nine Lives* (1957).

The great escape

Imprisoned Allied airmen connived to engineer the greatest mass escape of the war by tunneling out of one of the Third Reich's most security-conscious prisoner-of-war camps. But how did they conceal their actions — and all of that dirt — from the vigilant Germans?

Germany's Luftwaffe created the Stalag Luft III (*Stammlager Luft*, or Permanent Camp for Airmen #3) as a prisoner-of-war (POW) camp to house captured airmen. It was located deep behind German lines in Upper Silesia near Sagan, Poland, about 100 miles (161 km) southeast of Berlin.

The first prisoners (or "kriegies," as they called themselves) were British Royal Air Force and Fleet Air

Over the wire: The watch tower, fence and perimeter guards at Stalag Luft III, located near Sagan in Poland. By March 1944 the number of prisoners had risen to 11,000, the majority being American airmen.

Nordic airmen: (Left to right) Jan Staubo, Peter Bergsland, Halldor Espelid and Jens Müller photographed in 1943. The three men on the right were part of the 76 who made it out of the tunnel. Bergsland and Müller, posing as Norwegian electricians, headed for the port of Stettin and were able to talk their way onto a boat to Sweden. Espelid was one of the 50 officers captured and murdered by the Nazis.

Army officers who arrived in April 1942. Flyers from the U.S. Army Air Corps began arriving in significant numbers in October 1943. By March 1944 the area was expanded to 60 acres and the numbers swelled to 2,500 RAF officers, 7,500 Americans, and 900 officers from other Allied air forces, for a total of 11,000 inmates.

According to the Geneva Convention governing the treatment of military prisoners of war, and due to the Germans' desire not to have their own captured airmen mistreated, conditions in the camp were relatively good compared to the horrific concentration camps. The international rules also generally limited penalties for escape to 10 days in solitary confinement, which often did not deter POWs on both sides from attempting to escape.

The wooden horse

The Stalag Luft III site had been specifically selected to prevent escapes. Its location would require any would-be escapee to flee hundreds of miles from German-held territory. Moreover, the camp was situated in very sandy subsoil that was extremely ill-suited for tunneling; its telltale bright yellow color was easily detected if left on clothes or dumped on the grey ground surface.

The Nazis had also added many additional security features to prevent escape. The prisoners' barracks were raised several inches above the ground to reveal possible tunneling and the Germans had even installed seismograph microphones around the perimeter of the camp to detect any suspicious sounds.

The first successful breakout occurred as a result of an ingenious scheme based on the classic Greek story of the Trojan Horse. Prisoners had used some of their Red Cross package plywood to construct a gymnastic vaulting horse which they brought into the yard each day for group exercise. Unbeknownst to the Germans, the kriegies had concealed men, tools and containers of dirt inside the horse. Each day the horse was carried to exactly the same spot near the perimeter fence and the prisoners commenced their noisy drills. Meanwhile, below the contraption, other prisoners dug furiously before covering the hole and replacing the surface dirt.

WWII classics: Paul Brickhill, a pilot in the Royal Australian Air Force, was shot down over Tunisia in 1943. He was interned in Stalag Luft III and helped organize the mass breakout. After the war he wrote three classic war tales, *Great Escapes, The Dambusters* and Douglas Bader's life story, *Reach for the Sky.*

For three months, three RAF officers worked in shifts, using bowls and metal rods to construct a 100-foot (30.5 m) long tunnel. On October 29, 1942 the trio made their break and two were able to reach the port of Stettin where they stowed away on a Danish ship and eventually made it back to England. The third escaped by train to Danzig and from there stowed aboard a Swedish ship that ultimately enabled him to return home as well. After the escape, the Germans became even more vigilant.

Master plan

In January 1943, a British officer, Roger Bushell (who was also a champion skiier), devised a more ambitious escape plan. His scheme called for the simultaneous construction of three separate hidden tunnels, codenamed "Tom," "Dick," and "Harry." If one were exposed, there would still be two in reserve. The tunnels would need to be dug over 300 feet (91 m) long, to pass under the perimeter wire and into the forest 20 feet (6 m) beyond it. This would allow 200 people to escape on a single night.

Each entrance was carefully selected and concealed to ensure it would not be detected by the guards. "Tom" originated in a darkened corner of a hall in one of the buildings. "Dick's" entrance was concealed in a washroom drain sump. "Harry" was hidden under a stove.

To avoid detection by the microphones, the tunnels were located 38 feet (11.6 m) deep and measured only two square feet in size; the passage would extend hundreds of feet in length — a massive undertaking. There would have to be workshops, staging areas, a pump house and other features. Its sandy walls would have to be reinforced with wood and other stolen materials.

> For three months, three RAF officers worked in shifts using bowls and metal rods to construct a 100-foot tunnel.

The Great Escape: John Sturges directed the 1963 film of Paul Brickhill's book. Steve McQueen played Virgil Hilts, a fictitious character partially based on British serviceman and seven-time escapee Eric Foster.

After the murders: A church service held in the camp to honor the memory of the executed 50. The incoming German commandant of the camp was so appalled by the actions of the Gestapo that he allowed prisoners to build a memorial to their comrades.

The construction required the close collaboration of more than 600 inmates. Men were assigned as planners, builders, scavengers, lookouts, diggers, hiders, messengers, forgers and mappers. The prisoners removed boards from their beds and every scrap they could find, especially the tin cans of powdered milk they had received from the Red Cross. They also devised an elaborate code system to communicate among themselves.

Building the tunnels

All digging was confined to only about a 10-minute period each day, so the workers had to work like racecar crews to complete their tasks in time while others above ground also carried out their duties.

As the tunnels grew longer, it became extremely difficult to breathe underground, so one inmate invented an air pump that could be created from scrap items such as discarded hockey sticks and milk tins. Blankets were hung to muffle the sounds. Down in the tunnels the prisoners even rigged up an electric lighting system and they constructed a miniature rail system to help them quickly remove the sand.

One of the biggest obstacles proved to be hiding all of the excavation material they had dug. Some prisoners devised special clothing that would enable them to scatter some quantities of their telltale dirt. But the volume eventually became so large that they resorted to using "Dick" as a dumping place and storage shed.

A major setback occurred when the Germans discovered the entrance to "Tom." But the loss later worked in the prisoners' favor for it made the Germans mistakenly think they had foiled the only major escape attempt.

Using "Harry"

"Harry" was finally ready for use in March 1944. The escape was set for the moonless night of Friday, March 24. One by one, each of the nervous escapers showed up at the designated hut. The order of entry was strictly determined according to each man's likely ability to elude capture.

At 10:30 p.m., at the top of the vertical shaft outside the perimeter, digger Johnny Bull broke through the last inches of soil and breathed in the fresh air. But the tunnel had turned out to be a little too short. Because it hadn't reached the woods, the escapers were in danger of being spotted by the patrolling sentries.

The prisoners devised a signal device to warn the next escapee if the sentry was near. Two tugs on the rope meant the coast was clear. The escape resumed.

Each man took roughly 10 minutes to crawl through the tunnel and out the exit shaft. But at midnight another

---

By 2 a.m., 38 prisoners had made it through the tunnel and the pace was frenetic.

---

glitch occurred. An air raid caused the Germans to shut off all electric power, including the power used in the tunnel. For an hour the pipeline was closed. By 2 a.m., 38 prisoners had made it through the tunnel and the pace was frenetic. But at 5 a.m., there was a mix-up with the rope signal and the 77th man emerging from the tunnel was spotted. Shots rang out, immediately stopping the breakout.

Back in the camp, prisoners scurried to hide all of the evidence, burning documents and concealing tools.

The Germans commenced a massive manhunt that snagged 73 of the 76 escapees. Three others remained on the loose.

After the escape

At Stalag Luft III the camp *Kommandant*, Fritz von Lindeiner, was removed for court-martial and the Gestapo carried a ruthless investigation. Their inventory disclosed the following amazing list of missing items: 4,000 bed boards, 90 beds, 52 tables, 34 chairs, 10 single tables, 76 benches, 1,219 knives, 478 spoons, 582 forks, 69 lamps, 246 water cans, 30 shovels, 1,000 feet (305 m) of electric wire, 600 feet (183 m) of rope, 3,424 towels, 1,700 blankets, and more than 1,400 milk tins.

Hitler demanded that all 76 escapees be executed, but his advisors got the number reduced to 50 and General Artur Nebe was required to select the condemned. The doomed airmen were taken away and shot. The remaining 23 were sent back to prison, four of them to Sachsenhausen concentration camp, two to Oflag IV-C

Colditz, and the remaining 17 back to Stalag Luft III. Meanwhile, the three fugitives (two Norwegians and a Dutchmen) were able to evade capture: Jens Müller and Per Bergsland made it to neutral Sweden first, by boat, while Bram Van der Stok traveled through France before finding safety at a British consulate in Spain.

The new camp *Kommandant*, Oberst Braune, was so appalled by the executions that he allowed the prisoners to build a memorial, which stands to this day. Several of the Gestapo officers who carried out the torture and executions were later tried and executed or imprisoned as war criminals. The story of both escapes were later immortalized in several books and movies, including *The Wooden Horse* and *The Great Escape*.

Sagan today: Though the ground has been claimed by trees, there is now a monument to the allied servicemen who took part in the escape, with memorial stones for those who were executed.

On the run from Auschwitz

Working against all odds, two desperate Slovak inmates, Alfréd Wetzler and Rudolf Vrba, devised a cunning scheme to escape from the deadliest place on earth — the Auschwitz-Birkenau death camp — in order to warn the world of the ongoing atrocities going on there.

Auschwitz-Birkenau: The grimly familiar outline to the notorious concentration camp, Auschwitz II. Building work began in October 1941 to ease congestion at Auschwitz I, which was converted to an administration block on completion of the main camp.

Auschwitz — a huge complex of hellish concentration camps located near the rail line in southern Poland — comprised three main camps and 39 auxiliary camps that the Nazis maintained in World War II. Hundreds of thousands of prisoners were worked to death in them, but the most deadly, Auschwitz II (Auschwitz-Birkenau), functioned as the secret extermination center for more than one million men, women and children.

Though the *Schutzstaffel* (SS) employed machinelike efficiency, brute force, and special technology, including ravenous gas chambers and crematoria to carry out mass murder, nothing was more crucial to the success of their "Final Solution" than secrecy

Fenced in: Vrba worked in the part of the camp where Jews' possessions were sorted and redistributed. It was cynically nicknamed "Canada" because many Polish families were used to receiving parcels from relatives who had emigrated there.

and deception. Without it Hitler's SS probably never would have been able to gain so much compliance and cooperation from their unwitting victims.

Had the prisoners known they were being sent to gas chambers disguised as showers, there would have been more resistance, rebellion and worldwide condemnation. But very few inmates lived long enough to discover the real inner workings of Auschwitz and of those who did, very few survived to talk about it. Scarcely 7,000 of an estimated 1.1 to 1.7 million Jews who arrived there left it alive.

Vrba and Wetzler

By early 1944 Alfréd Wetzler and Rudolf Vrba were among only a handful of Jews in Auschwitz II who had survived more than a year in the camp. Two Slovak Jews, both had been sent there for slave labor. Now Wetzler was 24 and Vrba was barely 19.

> Scarcely 7,000 of an estimated 1.1 to 1.7 million Jews who arrived at Auschwitz left there alive.

Wetzler had been transferred there from a camp at Sered in southern Slovakia on April 13, 1942, and for the last two years had witnessed some of the worst atrocities known to man. Assigned to the Birkenau mortuary, his job was to record the number of prisoners who died other than by gassing; he also had to keep track of the amount of gold extracted from their teeth. His mind was full of unspeakable horrors.

Vrba had arrived at Auschwitz I at the end of June 1942, following two weeks at the Majdanek concentration camp near Lublin, Poland.

After befriending a Viennese prisoner who was trusted by the SS, he got assigned to a storage area nicknamed the "Canada," where the goods stolen from the doomed deportees were kept before being sent to Germany and the dead bodies from the arriving freight trains were disposed of. Later his duties involved digging up the bodies of more than

Going nowhere: Vrba was set to work sorting the possessions of the Jews who had been gassed. He soon realized from the contents of their baggage that they had no idea of their ultimate fate.

On January 15, 1943, Vrba was transferred to Birkenau, the death camp, where he continued to work as part of the "Canada" work team. Upon his arrival he was "selected" to go to the right rather than the left, which meant he had been chosen to work instead of being sent to the gas chambers.

Vrba possessed a photographic memory and he attempted to use his gift to commit to memory the numbers of Jews entering and the place of origin of each arrival. By observing when most of the Jewish deportees arrived, and sorting out the belongings of the ones who were gassed, he was able to make rough calculations of how many had been sent to Auschwitz, and how many of those were killed. Based on his observations of the confiscated luggage, he also became convinced that the arriving Jews were ignorant of their fate and expecting to live there for the long term.

According to Vrba's calculations, by April 1944, he estimated that 1,750,000 Jews had already been killed in the camps — and he was sure that the Nazis would not leave any survivors or other incriminating evidence.

On the eve of Passover

Vrba and Wetzler had known 100,000 Jews who had already been killed or died, so they could be incinerated and the traces of Nazi crimes destroyed.

Thus, in the course of his work, he too came to learn important details about the Nazis' machinery of death.

each other in their hometown, and upon encountering each other in the camp, they began to exchange information that convinced them they must try to escape — both to save their own lives and also to alert the world about the genocide that was being committed.

Other inmates from the camp resistance agreed to assist them and together they hatched a plan. Both men were assigned to work outside Birkenau's electrified barbed-wire inner perimeter but inside the external perimeter that guards kept erected during the work day, which gave them a great advantage.

On the day in question, Vrba and Wetzler bravely stuffed their pockets with the most incriminating items they could gather — a crude ground plan of the camp, construction details of the gas chambers and crematoria and a label from a discarded canister of Zyklon poison gas. Then they made their move.

At 2 p.m. on Friday, April 7, 1944 — the eve of Passover — the two men slipped away from their guards and climbed inside a hollowed-out hiding place in a wood pile that was being stored there.

Other prisoners already had placed boards around the hollowed-out area and sprinkled the vicinity with

> At 20:33 hours, the commander of Auschwitz II was informed by teleprinter that two Jews had escaped. The Nazis activated their escape response procedures.

Documenting the holocaust: Rudolf Vrba's escape was significant not just on a personal level, but also because it alerted the authorities to the barbarities of the Nazi regime.

pungent Russian tobacco soaked in gasoline to fool the guards' dogs; a trick they had learned from Russian prisoners of war (POWs), particularly Dmitry Volkov, who had escaped from Auschwitz but later been recaptured. Volkov had also advised them to travel lightly, with no money, and only at night, and to trust no one with their plans. Nazi torturers had a way to loosen even the most resolute tongue.

Hiding inside the secret compartment, the pair braced themselves and waited for the manhunt to begin. At 20:33 hours that evening, the commander of Auschwitz II was informed by teleprinter that two Jews had escaped. The Nazis activated their escape response procedures.

Stay still

Vrba and Wetzler knew from accounts of previous escape attempts by other prisoners that once their absence was noticed during the evening roll call the guards would continue to search for them for three days. Therefore they remained in hiding until the fourth night — an interminable period of almost fatal fear and deprivation.

At one point they narrowly avoided getting caught when a German guard stood on top of the wood pile right above them. Somehow they remained undetected.

On April 10, wearing Dutch suits, overcoats, and boots they had taken from "Canada" and managed to stash in the woodpile, they made their way south, walking parallel to the Sola river, heading for the Polish-Slovakian border, 80 miles (133 km) away. Their only guide was a ripped page from an old children's atlas.

After 11 days they crossed into Slovakia and a farmer put them in touch with a Jewish doctor, who in turn connected them with the Jewish Council in Zilina.

Reporting to the world

Even as they struggled to recover from their ordeal, Wetzler and Vrba labored feverishly to compile an extraordinarily detailed report on the organization and functioning of Auschwitz. Wetzler wrote the first part, Vrba the third, and the two wrote the second part together. Then they collaborated on rewriting it several times until it was completed. It was 32 pages long and packed with vital information.

Initially drafted in Slovak and hastily translated into German and Hungarian, the report would be translated into numerous languages so that the international community would know what was happening at Auschwitz. Most urgently the report aimed to warn Hungary's Jews of the Nazi regime's imminent plans to annihilate their community.

For reasons that remain hotly debated, however, the Hungarian Jews did little to prevent the systematic deportation that began in mid-May 1944. After only two months, approximately 440,000 Jews had been forcibly removed from Hungary and most had been sent to their death in Auschwitz.

The publication of the report in the Swiss press, however, finally raised so much indignation abroad that in early July 1944, under political and military pressure from the Allies, the Hungarian Regent, Admiral Miklós Horthy, was forced to forbid further deportations. But the persecution of Hungary's Jews continued.

The Vrba-Wetzler Report reached the British and U.S. governments by mid-June 1944. Details from it were broadcast by the BBC on June 15, and on June 20, *The New York Times* published the first of three stories about the existence of gas chambers in the notorious German concentration camps at Birkenau and Oswiecim (Auschwitz).

But many observers remained very skeptical, dismissing the accounts as exaggerated propaganda — Auschwitz fell to Soviet forces and subsequent proof of the atrocities confirmed that they had been right.

The Wetzler-Vrba report was later used as among the most important pieces of documentary evidence presented at the Nuremberg War Crimes Trials in 1945 and it figured in the trial of Adolf Eichmann in 1960.

Wetzler died in Slovakia in 1988. Vrba later moved to Canada where he died of cancer on March 27, 2006. Their story was later told in several books and television documentaries, yet their courageous actions and the world's tragic failure to heed their cries remains one of the most overlooked episodes of the Holocaust.

Alfréd Wetzler: Photographed in the 1970s, Wetzler was hailed as a hero. The report he wrote with Rudolf Vrba was instrumental in stopping the Jews of Budapest being deported to their deaths.

Auschwitz escape attempts

Recent studies by the Polish historian Henryk Swiebocki for the Auschwitz-Birkenau Memorial and Museum have identified at least 802 inmates (757 men and 45 women) who attempted to escape from Auschwitz from July 6, 1940 to January 18–19, 1945. According to his calculations, 396 Poles (including 10 women), 179 Soviet citizens (15 women; 50 of the men were POWs), 115 Jews (3 women), 38 Gypsies (2 women), 31 Germans (9 women), 23 Czechs (4 women), 2 Austrians, 2 Yugoslavians (1 woman), and 16 others (including 1 woman) of unknown nationality. Hundreds succeeded, but escape by Jewish inmates was much less frequent: 76 Jews are known to have gotten away.

Most prisoner escapes took place from worksites outside the camp and required assistance from both other inmates and local civilians. Many elaborate plans involved stolen SS uniforms, disguises and weapons. Multiple prisoners usually tried to escape together. A group of seven Soviet POWS successfully escaped in the Fall of 1941; the biggest involved two groups of 11 Poles — some of them dressed in SS uniforms — that escaped in September 1944. Aided by the Polish underground, many of the escapees went on to fight against the Germans.

Besides Vrba and Wetzler, three other former prisoners — a Pole, Jerzy Tabeau, and the Jews Arnost Rosin and Czeslaw Mordowicz — later wrote reports about their escapes that informed Allied forces about the atrocities being committed at Auschwitz and may have succeeded in transmitting useful information back to the camps that enabled other prisoners to escape.

Most Auschwitz escape attempts, however, ultimately ended in death. On June 24, 1944, Edward Galinski, a Pole, disguised himself as an SS man and "escorted" Mala Zimetbaum, a Jewish woman, through the closed zone around the camp. Caught ten days later and brought back to Auschwitz, they were tortured at great length before they were executed.

The long way home

Long after the end of the war, a German prisoner of war, "Clemens Forell," set out to escape from a Soviet Gulag camp on a 8,400-mile (1,352 km) trek to his homeland. Once he got away, he faced impossible odds, but he trudged on in an indefatigable attempt to reach his wife and children.

On the war's brutal Eastern Front, soldiers on both sides often fought to death, in part because they knew that few would survive as prisoners of war. For the vanquished Germans, those who were not killed on the spot were all forced to endure horrendous treatment in Soviet prison camps, the worst of which were located in Siberia. Their defeat at Stalingrad claimed casualties of 85 percent; of 90,000 troops marched into captivity, only 5,000 emerged alive. The remaining survivors would not be released and repatriated until 1956.

Oberleutnant Clemens Forell (a pseudonym, in real life his name was Cornelius Rost) was the exception to the rule. After leaving home in Bavaria for the Russian front in 1944, the married father of two was dropped behind the Ural Mountains and captured as a prisoner of war. Unbeknownst to his family or anyone else in Germany, in October of 1945 he was sentenced at Moscow to life imprisonment of hard labor.

Simply getting there was a major test of endurance. The hellish journey to northeast Siberia took almost a year, by foot, horse-drawn sleds, dogsleds, and box cars, and claimed the lives of all but 1,236 men of 3,000 who were sentenced. Nobody back home knew for sure if he was dead or alive.

In Forell's case, the destination was the Soviet Gulag lead mines at Cape Dezhnev located between the Bering Sea and the

All that remains: A now-abandoned Gulag administration building in northeastern Siberia shows the crushing winter conditions that Forell (Rost) was forced to endure.

Chukchi Sea, 51 miles (82 km) across from Cape Prince of Wales in Alaska. The cape forms the easternmost point of Eurasia, on the Chukchi Peninsula in Chukotka Autonomous Okrug of Russia, being one of the most remote arctic regions on Earth.

He concluded that he would need to take a circuitous journey of as long as 8,000 miles to reach home.

barest minimum, and assailed by extreme cold and disease. Many succumbed to lead poisoning or exposure.

The camp had no fence or watchtowers; the Russians assumed they were not necessary, believing that its totally remote location and frigid climate made escape virtually impossible. Yet Forell was determined to try.

The camp was just across the Bering Strait from Alaska, which was an American possession. However, the Soviet Union and the United States had legal agreements stating that any escaped prisoner would be returned to

Life in the Gulag

Condemned to hard labor in the dangerous underground mines, the prisoners were subjected to extraordinarily brutal conditions; beaten by the guards, fed only the

No place to hide: The former Soviet Gulag at Pevek sits in a landscape that has no need of a barbed-wire enclosure.

On the run: Forell's story was made into a German movie, *As Far as My Feet Will Carry Me*. Native Yakute herdsmen gave Forell a dog after they found him left for dead. Forell called the dog Willem. Willem was shot by a guard at the Chinese border and Forell had to flee for his life.

Soviet custody. Therefore, Forell concluded that he would need to take a circuitous journey of as long as 8,000 miles (12,875 km) to reach home.

After his arrival, he tried to run away and was caught after 11 days. Part of his punishment entailed a nearly fatal beating at the hands of his fellow inmates, who were expected to exact revenge for the punishment he had caused them. As a result of his injuries and ensuing illness, Forell was sent to sick bay until he could recover.

Assisted to escape

It was three years before he tried to escape again. Forell was aided by the camp doctor, a fellow German officer who had acquired some vital contraband that he had intended to use for his own escape. However, the physician had become incurably ill and knowing that he would never be able to use the precious items, he offered them to Forell. The supplies included a map, compass, money, food, heavy clothing, skis, boots, and even a handgun with bullets.

On October 30, 1949 Forell slipped away from the prison hospital and picked up the hidden stash of contraband. Then he set off into the night on foot. From the East Cape he hurried to methodically cover as much ground as he could — 20 and even 30 miles (32–48 km) a day — in order to reach what he thought would be the pursuing guards' outer limit. He used his compass and counted his steps to record his progress. He also took every precaution he could to evade detection, abstaining from lighting any fire and trying to avoid contact with any living person.

His only food was an occasional seal he had killed along the way. Simply surviving in the vast frozen wilderness represented a monumental achievement.

> Simply surviving in the vast frozen wilderness represented a monumental achievement.

Epic journey

For the next two years he continued on his epic journey, starting with the trek across Siberia, where he came into contact with several helpful or treacherous strangers — nomadic herdsmen, gold diggers, and scoundrels — and had several close calls. To better elude capture, he passed himself off as Pyotr Jakubovitsch. By then it was the summer of 1951 and he was still 800 miles (1,287 km) from Manchuria. Pretending to be a Latvian, he came upon an outpost of woodcutters and finagled a major coup: his new job enabled him to ride a train to Chita, complete with a travel permit. From there he continued moving west.

By early 1952 he had reached Novo-Kasalinsk, east of the Aral Sea, where he met a member of the local underground who could tell that he was a German fugitive. Although the man was an Armenian Jew, and despite what the Germans had done to the Jews, he provided Forell with forged travel papers and detailed instructions as to how to get across the Russian border into Iran. Eventually, after months, the fugitive crossed the border to Tabriz, Iran, and went straight to the police.

After hearing his incredible story of escape from the Siberian Gulag, the Iranians concluded he was probably a Soviet spy and they imprisoned him for interrogation and possible execution.

Finally, he convinced them to allow him to receive a visit from his uncle, who lived in neighboring Turkey. But when the uncle came, he didn't recognize Forell because his physical appearance had changed so much. After his ordeal, he hardly looked human. Luckily, Forell was able to identify pictures from a family photograph album the

uncle had brought with him, and they realized he had been telling the truth.

From there, Forell's uncle assisted him in traveling on to Ankara, Athens, Rome and Munich. He arrived home shortly before Christmas in 1952, three years and 8,400 miles (1,352 km) since he had started his escape.

Telling his story

In 1954 a Munich publisher introduced Forell to a well-known German author, Joseph M. Bauer, as someone who had an incredible story to tell. At first the former fugitive was too emotionally affected to discuss what he had experienced. But after several months Bauer got him to sit down for a long series of tape-recorded interviews. Fearful that he might suffer reprisals from the KGB, the escapee used the name of Clemens Forell. Their book, *So weit die Füße tragen* (*As Far as My Feet Will Carry Me: The Extraordinary True Story of One Man's Escape from a Siberian Labor Camp and His Three-Year Trek to Freedom*), became a best-seller in Germany and went on to sell 12 million copies in 15 languages. Many Germans who read it found hope that other prisoners of war might also turn up alive. In 1959 the story became the basis for a popular German television series, and in 2001 Bauer's book was adapted as a German feature movie. Cornelius Rost died in 1983 at the age of 61.

Train: Forell covered the most distance quickly when he could travel by train. The railroad had taken him east in 1945. In 1951 he was given the chance to travel west with a consignment of timber and reached the Mongolian border.

7
Modern warfare

1966 Laos POW camp
Lt. Dieter Dengler

1991 First Gulf War
Chris Ryan

1995 Shot down over Bosnia
Capt. Scott O'Grady

2004 Second Iraq War
Thomas Hamill

Surviving in the jungle

DIETER DENGLER	June–July 1966

After seven determined prisoners of war of the Pathet Lao broke away from their captors, only two, Dieter Dengler and Pisidhi Indradat, were thought to have survived. Dengler's exploits have gone down as one of the most unusual American feats of the Vietnam War.

On July 20, 1966, U.S. Navy Lt. Dieter Dengler was flying a secret mission over Laos when his Skyraider was shot down over dense jungle. Although the 28-year-old pilot tried to evade the enemy, he was captured by Pathet Lao troops and tortured.

Eventually he was marched to a small prison camp (Ban Houei Het Pathet Lao Prison) where he joined six other emaciated prisoners. Two were American, one was Chinese, and three, including Pisidhi Indradat, were Thai. By the time Dengler arrived, the others had already been imprisoned under abominable conditions for more than two years.

During the Vietnam War, Indradat had been employed as a "kicker" for Air America, the CIA's airline. His job was to kick boxes of rice from planes to aid friends on the ground. He had been held since September 1963.

When one of the Thai prisoners overheard their captors plotting to shoot them in order to make more food available to the guards, they decided to act on an escape plan they had devised.

Their hastily drawn up plan was to take over the camp and signal an American C-130 Hercules flareship that made nightly visits to the area. Dengler managed to loosen logs under the hut that allowed the prisoners to squeeze through. The idea was for him to go out when the guards were eating, seize their weapons, and pass the guns to Indradat and another Thai prisoner while his fellow Americans, Duane W. Martin and Eugene DeBruin, grabbed guns from other locations.

Battle for survival

On June 29, while the five guards were eating, the group slipped out of their hand and foot restraints and grabbed their unattended weapons, which included M1 rifles, Chinese automatic rifles, an American carbine and at

Hard labor: Asian POWs of the Pathet Lao are put to work in the fields of Laos under armed guard.

least one submachine gun. When the Pathet Lao guards spotted some of the other prisoners trying to escape, a shootout ensued in which three were killed or wounded and two ran off to get help.

The seven prisoners split into three groups. Indradat went with the other Thai prisoners; DeBruin stayed with the Chinese man, who had been too ill to continue with the escape; and Dengler and Martin headed for the Mekong River, hoping to escape into Thailand.

Dengler and Martin, however, soon found themselves lost in a deadly jungle filled with leeches, insects and snakes. Incessant rain soaked them to the bone and they were soon close to starvation. After many futile attempts to build a fire that would signal the C-130, they finally succeeded in lighting torches that were spotted by a flareship pilot.

The following day, when no plane had come to rescue them and they were weak from lack of food and the effects of malaria, Martin felt he had no choice but to approach a neighboring village for food. At first the gamble appeared to have paid off. But as Dengler watched from a distance, he was horrified to see a villager hack his friend to death with a machete.

That night, Dengler angrily set fire to the village huts when a C-130 flareship passed over, but again, there was no rescue mounted.

Finally, Dengler found a flare in a discarded parachute and he used it to signal a plane. An Air Force pilot spotted the flare and saw Dengler waving something white. At last a helicopter landed. As the Americans pulled the emaciated figure aboard, a snake slithered out of his tattered clothes. He was taken away for medical treatment and survived.

Jubilant: Dieter Dengler at his press briefing, September, 1966.

The others' fate

Meanwhile, on the second day after the escape, Indradat had separated from his two Thai companions. After 32 days in the jungle, he lapsed into unconsciousness and was recaptured and taken to a prison camp with a large number of Royal Lao POWs. After the CIA learned of his whereabouts, on January 7, 1967 they successfully rescued him with 52 other Laotian and Thai prisoners. Indradat later returned to Thailand.

For his heroism, Dengler received the Navy Cross, Distinguished Flying Cross, Air Medal, Purple Heart, and Prisoner of War Medal. In 1979 he published a book, *Escape from Laos*, about his experience, and his story was dramatized in several films, including *Rescue Dawn*. In 2001 he died of Lou Gehrig's Disease.

Other POWs who escaped

Of 771 Americans known to have been captured and interned during the Vietnam War, at least 113 died in captivity and 658 were returned to the U.S. The longest held POW — Army Ranger Capt. Floyd J. "Jim" Thompson, commander of a Special Forces detachment in Quang Tri Province — was released after nearly nine brutal years in captivity, making him the longest held POW in American history.

The Defense Prisoner of War/Missing Personnel Office (DPMO) lists only 36 successful escapes; 34 of them in South Vietnam and two in Laos. Many more prisoners broke out of their prisons but were never seen again. In 1973 Operation Homecoming completed 54 flights to bring back POWs of the North Vietnamese; only 10 emerged from Laos.

Bravo Two Zero

CHRIS RYAN

January 1991

Dropped behind enemy lines in western Iraq in brutal weather during the first Gulf War, an eight-man squad of British Special Forces soldiers waged an epic struggle to scrub their mission and make it back alive. Only one escaped. But what really happened?

Like Akira Kurosawa's classic 1950 film *Rashomon*, which presented views of the same dramatic event from different and often conflicting perspectives, the multi-faceted ordeal of several British Special Forces soldiers of the Bravo Two Zero squad during the First

Gulf War both captured world attention and left many observers wondering what had really happened.

The night that Operation Desert Storm began, on January 22/23,1991, an eight-man squad of Britain's most elite commandos was helicoptered into Northern

SCUD launcher: The allies were concerned about the strike power of mobile missile launchers which were dispersed through the country and difficult to target without men on the ground to pinpoint their location. Scud spotting was one of Bravo Two Zero's objectives.

Insertion: The Bravo Two Zero squad were dropped short of their target by Chinook helicopter. Their clothing and equipment turned out to be wholly inadequate given some of the worst winter conditions experienced in northern Iraq.

Iraq near the Amman-Baghdad Highway and deep behind enemy lines. The team was commanded by Sergeant Andy McNab (a pseudonym), and included Sgt. Vince Phillips; Corporal Chris Ryan (a pseudonym), Mike Coburn and four others: Trooper Dr. Malcolm (Mal) Graham McGowan, a dentist, formerly of the Australian First Commando Regiment; Trooper Robert (Bob) Gaspare Consiglio, a former Royal Marine; and Lance Corporal Ian Robert "Dinger" Pring and Trooper Steven John "Legs" Lane, who had both passed selection for the elite SAS after serving in the Parachute Regiment.

> **As the sound of the helicopter engines faded in the distance we heard dogs barking not far off to the East. Obviously they were around some building. They'd heard us even if nobody else had.**
>
> Chris Ryan, *The One That Got Away*

Each soldier was carrying a pack of equipment and supplies in a "bergen" that weighed between 210 and 260 pounds (95 to 120 kg). Together they were laden with M16/M203 assault rifles, FN Minimi light support machine guns, ammunition, 66mm LAW rockets, PE4 plastic explosives, Claymore and Elsie anti-personnel mines, detonators, rucksacks containing food and medical supplies, water, sandbags and observation post equipment, and other assorted gear. They also had a PRC 319 patrol radio, four tactical beacon radio devices to communicate with allied aircraft, a Magellan GPS, and a night sight.

Their mission was to report on enemy positions and call in aircraft to take out any worthwhile targets; they were also supposed to cut designated Iraqi fiber-optic lines that linked many of the Scud missile sites. Operation Desert Storm had other teams assigned to similar work.

Disaster strikes

Bravo Two Zero's first task was to move their equipment to an observation post. The mission had been put together in haste with little chance to survey the area they were expected to monitor.

> " We binned our bergens. Couldn't move quick enough with them. We heard contacts far in the distance. But they weren't shooting at us. "
>
> Andy McNab, *Bravo Two Zero*

Inserted on the ground, the soldiers found the area to be featureless with few natural places to hide out. Although the unit quickly found a gully to hole up in, their mission soon suffered some major setbacks. "Bravo Two Zero" was their radio call sign. But their radios were apparently tuned to the wrong frequencies and didn't work. Also, the vital fiber-optic switching boxes were not located where they were supposed to be. And finally, the unexpectedly cold temperatures underlined the fact that they had come with no specialist clothing for winter

Pivotal: Though the mission had been compromised by limited reconnaissance, the key mistake came when the squad got split into two groups during a night march. Actor Paul McGann played Chris Ryan in the TV movie *The One That Got Away*, and is seen trying to contact Andy McNab's group. Ryan wrote his side of events after McNab's *Bravo Two Zero* book became a huge bestseller.

operations. In short, they were ill-prepared.

To make matters worse, on the afternoon of January 24, a goat herder stumbled upon them and appeared to have spotted their post. Believing that their mission had been compromised, they therefore decided they had no alternative but to try to escape. But to do so they would need to evade the enemy and make it out of Iraq. The eight men hurriedly abandoned their excess equipment and prepared to set out into the desert.

But as they were about to leave, they heard what they thought to be a tank approaching their position, and they took up defensive positions. The tank turned out to be a bulldozer, and the driver immediately retreated. Realizing that they had now definitely been compromised, the patrol quickly withdrew from their position. They were supposed to head south for Saudi Arabia, but they ended up aiming through the desert to the Syrian border, more than 75 miles (121 km) to the northwest — a change of plan that would greatly hamper the ability of allied forces to provide support or rescue.

On the night of January 24th, the beleaguered eight-man team inadvertently became split into two groups after McNab stopped to try and make contact with the

Going it alone: Actor Paul McGann as Chris Ryan, pictured after his trio lost Vince Phillips and he became separated from the remaining squad member.

malfunctioning radios and the message to stop was not passed down the line. McNab and four others found themselves in one group and Ryan and two others in the other. Each group continued on to Syria.

McNab's team carjacked an Iraqi taxi and drove toward the border until they were stopped in a queue of vehicles for an army checkpoint. The Iraqis had armored personnel carriers and heavy machineguns. Early in the morning of January 27, during their running firefight with Iraqi irregulars that killed as many as 60 soldiers, one of the troopers — Bob Consiglio — was shot to death after he ran out of ammunition. Two troopers attempted to swim across the Euphrates to Syria but one, Steve "Legs" Lane, died of hypothermia and the other (Lance Corporal Ian Robert "Dinger" Pring) was captured. McNab was also captured. Mike Coburn, the trooper

McNab in Baghdad: After the fall of Saddam Hussein, Andy McNab was able to return to the places he was imprisoned during the Gulf War — this time, without a blindfold. He got to see the interior of the Iraqi Directorate of Military Intelligence and the Hakmiya Intelligence Center in Baghdad. Though criticized by many for revealing too many SAS secrets, bending the truth and for some of his command decisions, without the initial publication of his book, one of the greatest military escape stories might never have been told.

from the New Zealand SAS, who was wounded in the arm and ankle, ran out of ammunition and he was also taken prisoner.

The three captives were transported to Baghdad's Hakmiya Intelligence Center for some brutal interrogation. McNab later reported that the Iraqis broke his teeth and assailed his exposed nerve with power drills, but said that after several beatings, the Iraqi intelligence officers appeared to have been convinced by the squad's prearranged cover story that they were simply medics sent to rescue a downed allied pilot.

> **If I was in Syria the people might be friendly. If I was still in Iraq I was going to have to threaten to kill them, get a drink and carry on.**
>
> Chris Ryan, *The One That Got Away*

The fate of Ryan's team

Meanwhile, Ryan's three-man team had continued to travel west on foot. Unlike the others, who had regular issue army boots, Ryan wore a pair of £100, "brown Raichle Gore-Tex-lined walking boots." On January 25, after encountering extreme cold, Sergeant Vince Phillips became separated and died of hypothermia. The remaining two encountered an Iraqi civilian who convinced Ryan's remaining companion, "Stan," to go with him to a local settlement. Ryan, suspicious of the Iraqi, parted company and continued on alone.

Shortly afterward, Stan ended up getting drawn into a brief firefight and he was subsequently captured. When two vehicles later approached Ryan, he fired on them and escaped into the night. Afterwards he killed two Iraqis and hid their bodies in the river.

Alone and running out of rations, Ryan was constantly exposed to freezing cold or baking sun. He battled dehydration, hypothermia, starvation and exhaustion as he continued trying to get into Syria. He would travel at night, and lay up during the day to reduce the risk of being spotted. Short of water he was forced to drink from polluted sources to quench a raging thirst.

In order to survive, he ended up traveling 190 miles (300 km) on foot in seven days without getting caught. In the process he suffered sleep deprivation and other discomforts. The ordeal was so bad he lost 36 pounds (16 kg) of his body weight and all his toenails.

But finally he made it to Syria, where, after some initial rough treatment from the secret police, he recovered from his near-death experience and was eventually flown back to SAS HQ in Saudi Arabia.

"Chris Ryan" made history with the "longest escape and evasion by an SAS soldier or any other British soldier," for which he was awarded the Military Medal. Ryan spent his final two years in the Special Air Service training recruits.

At the end of the war, the allied prisoners, including the captured SAS men, were released by the Iraqis and returned home. McNab received the Distinguished Conduct Medal.

Differing accounts

The Bravo Two Zero story generated extensive news media coverage and several books and films based on accounts by the principals, at least three of whom launched writing careers with the story.

McNab was first to publish a book titled *Bravo Two Zero* which became an international bestseller. But the now ex-SAS man refused to sell the movie rights to the highest bidder, insisting that he had control of how the movie would look.

Realizing that there was more than one person who could tell the Bravo Two Zero story, film-makers approached Corporal Chris Ryan and got his story written before adapting it for the screen. Ryan's book was called, aptly enough, *The One That Got Away*. The TV movie that followed was critical of McNab's leadership and also criticized Vince Phillips, the man responsible for

the squad splitting up on their fateful night march. An SAS reserve veteran, Michael Asher, later interviewed some witnesses and published *The Real Bravo Two Zero*, in which he critiqued both McNab's and Ryan's accounts. Another book, *Soldier Five*, by Mike Coburn, also took issue with both of their stories and aimed to "set the record straight."

Notwithstanding the discrepancies, *Bravo Two Zero* and *The One That Got Away* emerged as two of the best-known combat-and-escape tales of the First Gulf War and a warts-and-all account of what can and does go wrong when soldiers are faced with difficult decisions in the combat zone.

Best-selling author: Unlike McNab, fellow best-selling author Chris Ryan is happy to appear on film without his image obscured.

Shot down by Serbs

After his F-16 fighter is blown apart by a Bosnian Serb missile, a U.S. Air Force pilot ejects over enemy territory. After being hunted through the forest for six days by men eager for revenge, he makes a desperate bid for freedom. What happens next becomes an international news event.

On June 2, 1995, two U.S. Air Force fighter pilots were assigned to help enforce NATO's no-fly zone over war-torn Bosnia. Scott "Zulu" O'Grady and his flight lead, Capt. Robert G. "Wilbur" Wright were flying close to each other at an altitude of about five miles (8 km) above Mrkonjic Grad, unaware that the Bosnian Serb Army had laid a trap for incoming aircraft by switching off their radar on one of their SA-6 surface-to-air missile batteries.

O'Grady, aged 29, from Spokane, Washington, had been commissioned six years earlier, after graduating with honors from Embry-Riddle with a degree in aeronautical science and studies that included physics, meteorology and calculus. Known among his jaunty fellow fighter pilots as something of a straight arrow, he took his work extremely seriously and prided himself on his highly developed sense of honor.

He was not a cowboy. But he was about to get the ride of his life.

"Missiles in the air!"

At precisely three minutes after 3 p.m., Scott O'Grady received a radar warning on his headset, alerting him that he was "spiked" or targeted by a surface-to-air missile system. The spooked officer looked for any signs of a rocket but didn't see anything. Then, six seconds after the spike, he heard a signal like a car alarm, warning him that enemy

Close formation: Scott O'Grady and flight leader Captain Robert G. Wright were on routine patrol over Bosnia in their F-16 fighters when the junior pilot received a radar warning on his headset.

Ready to go in: American marines on the aircraft carrier USS *Kearsarge* in the Adriatic study maps before embarking on a rescue mission to retrieve the downed pilot.

target-tracking radar had locked onto his plane. His mind continued to race through all the steps he had been taught. At eight seconds a recorded female voice uttered two urgent words, "Counter! Counter!"

O'Grady saw a brilliant red flash to his right between his plane and Wilbur's.

Wilbur screamed, "Missiles in the air!"

But before O'Grady could hear him, in a fraction of a second he felt himself being swallowed by a thunderous force that engulfed his F-16 and blew it into flaming pieces that swirled all around him. The missile had struck his streaking plane in its soft underbelly, scoring a direct hit. And as the shocked flyer felt

> **❝ I saw the cockpit disintegrate ... I saw the ejection handle, the most glorious sight. ❞**
>
> Scott O'Grady

the murderous force, he reacted by reflex and with his left hand yanked the yellow handle jutting up between his legs with the "PULL TO EJECT" wording on it.

Will it open?

The Advanced Concept Ejection Seat, or ACES-II, of his F-16 was a state-of-the-art supersonic device designed to eject him as quickly as possible without tearing him apart, and luckily for him it hadn't been damaged; it functioned perfectly, rocketing him out into the frigid air at amazing speed.

So strong was the catapulting that he lost emblems from his G-suit and a heel from his boot, though at the time his focus was on his life-saving parachute. Would it open? When should he deploy it? Where should he land?

Worried that something may have been damaged by the explosion, O'Grady decided not to risk waiting until he had reached 14,000 feet (4,267 m) before deploying his parachute, and so, pulling the manual handle, he hoped it would work well enough to save his life.

To his everlasting relief he felt a jerk and heard the comforting sound of his nylon chute billowing.

By opening it at such a high altitude instead of waiting, he knew he would be more vulnerable to enemy eyes and fire, but he felt he had no choice: it was a chance he had to take. He had jumped from a plane ten times before, so he felt he could survive.

At 14,000 feet (4,267 m), the ACES-II seat automatically dropped away and released a floating rubber raft and other auxiliary gear. As he surveyed the scene below, he could see his plane wreckage smoking in the distance and he scanned the land for areas he should try to avoid and for woods that might provide cover.

Where to land?

He was trying to steer as best he could, straining to keep away from an idled military-looking vehicle that had caught his eye. The wind kept blowing him southeast, near a highway he needed to skirt. He felt dangerously exposed, knowing that his dangling body offered a fat bullseye for enemy marksmen and a visible target for the converging search parties.

Rescue mission: Armed marines deploy to their Sikorsky CH-53E assault helicopters on the USS *Kearsarge*.

Mission accomplished: A relieved Scott O'Grady emerges onto the flight deck of the USS *Kearsarge* having been rescued by marines.

Heading onto a small grassy clearing within the woods, the keyed-up flyer landed without injury and frantically struggled to free himself from the tangled chute and lines and survival bags that were encircling him like wild vines.

Although it took him only two seconds to break clear, he knew that he had no time to waste: the enemy would be fast upon him. And so, in the panic to get away, he left behind his auxiliary survival kit with its water and backup radio along with his limp nylon chute — all tell-tale evidence for his pursuers.

Time was running out.

Evading capture

Seizing his 20-pound survival rucksack as if he was carrying a fumbled football in the biggest game of his life, O'Grady ran through the grass as fast as his stiff legs would carry him and headed for someplace far enough away that would give him cover.

Upon settling on an overgrown spot, he threw himself down into the bushes and brought up his radio, placed it to his lips and pushed the button that would enable him to transmit. Then he whispered, "Hey, Wilbur, this is Zulu."

There was no response, so he whispered again, "Hey, Wilbur, this is Zulu."

Again getting no response, he immediately shut off the radio hoping that the enemy would not have been able to use it to track him.

No sooner had he turned it off than he began to hear voices headed in his direction. Lying face down, he burrowed his nose in the dirt, cupping his camouflaged flight gloves over his head and ears so he hopefully would not be spotted in the brush. He remained as still as he possibly could.

> ❝ **Most of the time my face was in the dirt, just praying that no one would see me.** ❞
>
> Scott O'Grady

five feet (1.5 m) but O'Grady stayed still and they didn't find him. Once more, his luck held out.

Weighing his chances of escape, he decided to wait to radio again for help because he didn't want to give away his position to the enemy. The minutes and hours turned to days and nights. The four eight-ounce bags of water were exhausted. From time to time the temperatures plummeted and his food also ran out, leaving him to wring a few precious drops of moisture from his socks and resort to digging for ants to eat.

"I'm alive. Help."

Finally, he knew he had to make one more desperate gamble. On June 6 he radioed for help. "This is Basher-52," he announced, using his code name in a rescue plea monitored by NATO officials. "I'm alive. Help."

The next day, just after 2 a.m., he spoke into the radio again and an American voice responded. The rescue plan was quickly set in motion.

Shortly after dawn on June 8, after six days and six nights, two AV-8 Harrier jump jet fighters swooped

Happy return: Scott O'Grady is hugged by his wife as he finally returns to Andrews Air Force Base.

Within minutes a teenage boy and a man wandered past. Then O'Grady glimpsed armed men searching nearby and he shuddered as they shot their rifles at something suspicious, aware that they probably were trying to kill him. He knew he could not surrender.

At one point the searchers approached to within

overhead and four CH-53E assault helicopters from USS *Kearsarge* filled with specially trained Marines, swept in amid a cloud of yellow signal smoke and scattered bursts of small arms gunfire.

The ramp of one copter had become jammed shut by a tree stump, leaving half the Marines stranded inside, as

12 others leapt from the other to take up cover positions on the ground. So now O'Grady emerged from his wooded, hilltop hiding-place and was led to the waiting chopper.

Asked if he was all right, the gaunt captain replied, "I'm good but I'm ready to get the hell out of here," and with that the copter whisked him aloft, shaking off some scattered machine-gun fire and at least one errant ground-to-air missile. Minutes later he was wolfing down some liquid and food. And two days later, he was being honored in the White House. "He is an American hero," President Bill Clinton declared.

"I am not a Rambo," O'Grady told reporters. "This is really amazing to me, all this attention I'm getting and everyone saying 'You're a hero, you're a hero.' Naah, I'm not a hero. All I was was a scared little bunny rabbit trying to hide, trying to survive."

O'Grady later recounted his experiences in two books, *Return with Honor* (1995) and *Basher Five-Two: The True Story of F-16 Fighter Pilot Captain Scott O'Grady* (1997).

> **"** Everyone is saying 'You're a hero, you're a hero' ... All I was was a scared little bunny rabbit trying to survive. **"**
>
> Scott O'Grady

Good news day: President Clinton was eager to hear good news from a war that many Americans believed to be Europe's, not America's, problem. Clinton called the 29-year-old "one amazing kid."

Hostage in Iraq

THOMAS HAMILL	**April 2004**

A Mississippi truck driver working as a contractor for U.S. forces in Iraq is taken hostage and fears that he may face the ultimate horror, to be executed on video. His only chance is to keep his cool, hope for the best and wait for the right moment to escape.

Thomas ("Tommy") Hamill, aged 44, was a third-generation dairy farmer from Noxubee County, Mississippi who went to Iraq as a truck driver for Dick Cheney's company, Halliburton, in late 2003. It was hazardous work when he signed on, but he supported America's mission and hoped to make enough money from it to save his family farm back home.

The danger level of his new job greatly increased on March 31, 2004, when Iraqi insurgents ambushed an American convoy at Fallujah, murdering and mutilating four Blackwater Company mercenaries in grisly scenes that were videotaped and broadcast throughout the world.

Hamill listened as President George W. Bush responded to the killings by saying, "This collection of killers is trying to shake our will... America will never be intimidated by thugs and assassins... We are aggressively striking the terrorists in Iraq."

Within days, the fighting reached a new level of ferocity, not just in Fallujah. Iraq was exploding.

On Friday, April 9, Hamill was working as convoy commander on a run to deliver fuel to American troops at Baghdad International Airport. About a half-hour into the trip, he noticed that traffic was unusually sparse and Iraqi cars were swerving to get out of their way. Then he saw abandoned gas cans along the highway, and although they had become a common sight during his six months in the country, their number and placement now struck him as an ominous sign — possibly

Outskirts of Fallujah: U.S. Marines in M1046 Humvees patrol behind a lead Nissan of the Fallujah Security Force, set up in 2004 to give an Iraqi presence to patrols.

Sitting ducks: Even more heavily guarded American convoys were attacked through 2004 near Fallujah. In this attack in May two servicemen were killed and five injured.

indicating the presence of improvised explosive devices (IEDs). He suddenly realized the convoy was trapped: there was no place to turn back.

"We're taking fire!"

The driver of one of his trucks behind radioed to say his engine was quitting. Unaware that the damaged truck had come under enemy fire, Hamill radioed the convoy's Army commander for one of his armed vehicles (known as a "bobtail") to provide gun support. But somebody in one of the gun-trucks radioed back to the lieutenant, "We're taking fire in the rear!"

Hamill instructed the gun-truck to pick up the stranded driver and just leave the truck.

But all at once others in the convoy were reporting they were taking fire. Bullets suddenly began smacking Hamill's truck, prompting the driver to smash the accelerator to the floor. The incoming rounds hitting his rig sounded like golf balls. Another truck caught fire.

One after the other the remaining convoy tried to veer through a hole in the guardrail in order to get off that lane of the freeway. Knowing that another convoy would soon be driving into the trap, Hamill grabbed his Qualcomm on-board satellite computer from between the seats and held it in his lap. He had just started typing, "convoy under attack" when a bullet ripped through the passenger-side door and struck his right forearm, knocking the computer out of his hands. In the adrenalin rush, Hamill had felt only a strong jolt, but he saw that a chunk of his arm had been blown away. Blood was gushing all over the computer.

In an effort to stem the bleeding, he reached for a pair of clean socks that had landed nearby and handed the radio to the driver, shouting, "You are going to have to run communications until I can get the bleeding stopped." He struggled frantically to exert enough pressure to stop the gushing, aware that gunfire was hitting them from all directions. He also heard explosions from rocket-propelled grenades and mortars.

The convoy had lost its formation. Trucks were careening every whichway. Now it was every man for himself. Suddenly a rocket-propelled grenade blasted Hamill's truck, nearly turning it over.

"We gotta keep going!" Hamill shouted. But diesel fuel had leaked over the road and some of the heavy fuel trucks were fishtailing out of control, flipping over and exploding. Others were stuck on the highway, erupting in flames.

Left behind

Given that Hamill's truck was still moving, he was surprised when Army Specialist Gregory Goodrich

Bolthole: Hamill was held at this farmer's hut, near Tikrit — Saddam Hussein's home town — before making his bid for freedom.

appeared from out of nowhere and jumped onto the running board next to him. To hold on, the soldier had wrapped his left arm around the side mirror and he was yelling, "We have got to drop this trailer."

But the gunfire was too heavy and there was no way anyone could stop the truck and disconnect the trailer.

The young soldier was shot in the arm but he kept firing away and trying to hold on, somehow managing to grab another clip, bump it, and slam it in his M-16. He swept the weapon back and forth, then clambered onto the hood to fire from a prone position.

The driver warned them their truck was about to die:

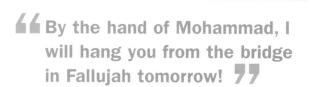

> " By the hand of Mohammad, I will hang you from the bridge in Fallujah tomorrow! "

Hamill's captors

they would have to bail. Goodrich fell to the ground just as a Humvee appeared and he ran to it and jumped inside. The driver did the same. But Hamill, who was wounded and weighed down by a four-pound helmet and a heavy flak vest, couldn't run fast enough, and he was left behind.

Although he tried his best to roll away and evade being spotted, bystanders pointed them out to the insurgents. The lone American looked back to see a fighter wearing a dark tan robe, crouched down, and pointing an AK-47 directly at him. Hamill dropped his satellite phone and surrendered. A group of boys and men proceeded to strip off his helmet, flak vest, wristwatch, wallet, ID badge, and pocket change. Then they prodded him up a short slope to a place near an alley.

It was then that a crowd of about 20 others charged at him, shouting in Arabic, and one of the young men struck Hamill across his right temple and ear with his rifle butt. The others acted as if he was their trophy. Was the mob going to kill him as they had done in Fallujah?

A small car raced up and four men started screaming at the crowd. Then they pushed him into the back seat and sped away, leaving the vicinity of the convoy. One of his captors was yelling, "Amreeky! Amreeky!" which Hamill assumed was signifying they had taken an American hostage.

Although he didn't yet know the official death toll — at least five drivers had been killed and two were missing — Hamill realized that several of his countrymen had died in the ambush. (The 724th Army Transportation Company had also sustained heavy losses. Goodrich had died a few minutes later and another soldier from their convoy was dead while another was missing.) And he might be next.

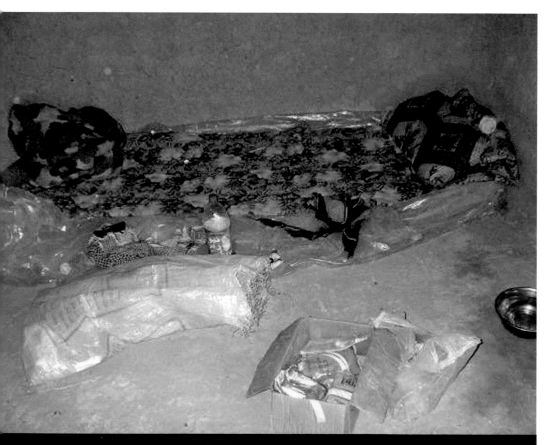

Uncertain future: Hamill was confined here for 23 days, not knowing whether he would be the latest Internet trophy killing of his violent captors.

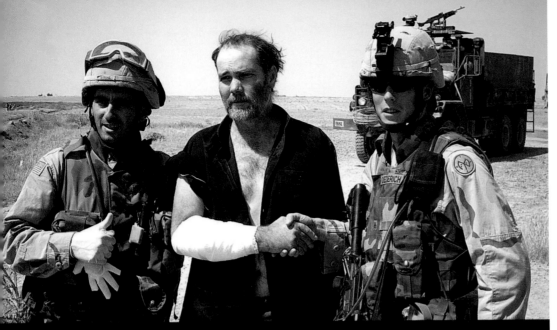

Safe at last: Hamill shakes hands with two soldiers from the 2nd Brigade Combat Team of the 1st Infantry Division shortly after making his escape.

Weak from his ordeal and the loss of blood, Hamill fell asleep. Over the next 23 days he was often moved from house to house. Generally speaking, his captors treated him tolerably well, except when they saw photographs of Americans mistreating prisoners at Abu Ghraib, after which they shackled his legs with a dog chain.

"I'm an American!"

Then, it happened: after 24 days in captivity, at a moment when his guards were temporarily distracted, Hamill took his chance and bolted away, running for a half mile (800 m) until he came face to face with an American patrol.

"I — I'm — I'm an American. I'm an American," he hollered. "I'm an American POW."

At last, he was free.

Hamill later co-authored a book, *Escape in Iraq: The Thomas Hamill Story*, and he returned to Mississippi, hoping to escape the war in his head.

Shown on TV

The next several hours were a whirlwind of activity during which Hamill never knew for sure that he would survive another minute. They put him in different clothes and examined his wounds. As they were driving him past burning trucks, they came upon a TV crew, which he at first assumed was from al-Arabiya or al-Jazeera. (He later learned the TV crew was from the Australian Broadcasting Company.) Thinking they were in league with the terrorists, Hamill refused to look at them out of anger that they were filming the carnage.

"What happened?" the reporter asked.

"They attacked our convoy," Hamill growled, turning and lowering his head. "That's all I'm going to say."

"Do you want to give us your name?" the reporter asked.

Finally, the hostage responded, "Hamill. Thomas."

With that, the gunmen slammed the door and sped off, taking him away once more.

Controlling his emotions

Realizing there was nothing he could physically do to control his fate, Hamill silently tried to control his emotions. His guards blindfolded him and took him to a compound where a doctor treated his wounds. One of his captors was about six feet four inches (193 cm) tall and missing his right arm above the elbow. The man shouted, "By the hand of Mohammad, I will hang you from the bridge in Fallujah tomorrow! By my hand I will hang you from the bridge in Fallujah tomorrow!"

Freedom: A grateful Thomas Hamill was flown for medical check-ups in Germany before going home. Nine days after being held by Iraqis he was watching the Houston Astros play the Florida Marlins.

Index

The Rock: Alcatraz Island viewed from a passing ship in 1892. Having served its purpose as a defensive fort, the island became a military prison from 1868 onwards. The large concrete cell block that dominates the island was constructed in 1909.

Limited means of escape: Russian convicts, dissidents and prisoners of war were shipped off to Siberia to work in the lead and gold mines. German prisoner of war Clemens Forrell was captured in 1944 but didn't make it home until 1952.

Emerging from the deep: After the rescue of the 33 surviving crew members, USS *Squalus* was salvaged, refitted and relaunched as USS *Sailfish* in 1940. It had a distinguished career in World War II, sinking the Japanese aircraft carrier *Chuyo* in 1943.

Picture Credits

Caption, page 2/3: A citizen of West Berlin waves from the roof of his car across the newly erected Berlin Wall. A similar three-wheel car was later used in an audacious escape attempt from East to West Berlin by Klaus Jacobi and Manfred Koster (see page 109).

All pictures for the book supplied by Corbis with the exception of the following images: Page 6 (top), Library of Congress, HABS PA,51-PHILA,354-114; Page 6 (bottom), Rex Features; Page 7 (top), Rex Features; Page 19 Getty Images/National Geographic; Pages 24 and 26, R. Mackley; Pages 30 and 31, Getty Images; Page 33, NASA; Page 35, Benjamin Marcus; Pages 40 and 42 Alaska Maritime National Wildlife Refuge; Pages 48 and 49, Getty Images; Page 50, Rex Features; Pages 57 and 58, Rex Features; Page 59, Getty Images; Page 76, Getty Images; Page 77 (bottom), Getty Images; Page 79, Rex Features; Pages 80 (top) and 81, Austrian Police News Service; Page 84, Rex Features; Page 87, Library of Congress, LC-USZ62-28755; Page 88, Library of Congress, LC-USZ62-10320; Page 90, Library of Congress, LC-USZC4-4659; Pages 93, 94 and 95 (top), Rex Features; Page 105, Getty Images; Pages 110 and 111, Rex Features; Page 117, Holly Reed Photography; Page 118, Library of Congress, HABS PA,51-PHILA,354-6; Page 126, Library of Congress, LC-DIG-ggbain-31293; Page 128, Library of Congress, HABS PA,51-PHILA,354-169; Page 129, Library of Congress, HABS PA,51-PHILA,354-163; Page 132, Library of Congress, HABS CAL,38-ALCA,1-1; Page 133, Library of Congress, HABS CAL,38-ALCA,1-I-3; Page 137, Library of Congress, HABS CAL,38-ALCA,1-E-1; Page 146, Rex Features; Page 149, Rex Features; Pages 169 and 171 Getty Images; Page 175, Getty Images; Page 178, Rex Features; Page 181, Getty Images; Page 183 (bottom) Getty Images; Page 186, Rex Features; Page 187, Janis Krums; Pages 188 and 189, Rex Features; Page 192, Getty Images; Pages 200, 201, 202 and 203, Rex Features; Page 212, Getty Images; Page 218, Getty Images; Pages 230 and 231, Getty Images; Pages 234, 235, 236 and 237, Rex Features; Pages 242 and 243, Getty Images; Page 249, Library of Congress, LC-USZ62-48870; Page 253, Library of Congress, LC-USZ62-123350.

Further Reading:

Chapter 1: Nature
Ernest Shackleton: *Endurance* by Alfred Lansing
Steve Fossett: *Chasing the Wind* by Steve Fossett
Aron Ralston: *Between a Rock and a Hard Place* by Aron Ralston
Vic Calandra: *Extreme Surf* by Benjamin Marcus

Chapter 2: Kidnappers
Entebbe: *Yoni's Last Battle* by Iddo Netanyahu
Iran Embassy: *Hostage* by Chris Cramer
Dr. Mary Quin: *Kidnapped in Yemen: One Woman's Amazing Escape from Terrorists* by Mary Quin
Kyrgyzstan: *Over the Edge* by Greg Child

Chapter 3: Regimes
Ellen & William Craft: *Running a Thousand Miles for Freedom* by William & Ellen Craft
Henry Box Brown: *Narrative of the Life of Henry Box Brown* by Henry Brown
Molly Craig: *Follow the Rabbit-Proof Fence* by Doris Pilkington
Dalai Lama: *Freedom in Exile* by the Dalai Lama
Jonestown: *Slavery of Faith* by Leslie Wagner-Wilson
Dith Pran: *Killing Fields* by Sydney Schanberg & Dith Pran
Gilbert Tuhabonye: *This Voice in My Heart: A Runner's Memoir of Genocide, Faith, and Forgiveness* by Gilbert Tuhabonye

Chapter 4: Prison and the Law
Henri Charrière: *Papillon* by Henri Charrière
Willie Sutton: *Where The Money Was* by Willie Sutton and Edward Linn
Billy Hayes: *Midnight Express* by Billy Hayes and William Hoffer

Chapter 5: Man-made disasters
Apollo 13: *Lost Moon, The Perilous Voyage of Apollo 13* by James Lovell and Jeffrey Kluger
WTC South: *Plucked from the Fire* by Hennessey William and Stanley Praimnath
WTC North: *Last Man Down: A Firefighter's Story of Survival and Escape from the World Trade Center* by Richard Picciotto and Daniel Palsner

Chapter 6: World War II
Gladys Aylward: *The Small Woman* by Alan Burgess
Colditz: *The Colditz Story* and *The Latter Days at Colditz* by Pat Reid; *Colditz, The German Story* by Reinhold Eggers
Rocky Gause: *The War Journal of Major Damon "Rocky" Gause* by Damon Gause
Stalag Luft III: *The Great Escape* by Paul Brickhill; *Moonless Night: Wartime Diary of a Great Escaper* by B. A. "Jimmy" James
Auschwitz: *I Escaped from Auschwitz* by Rudolf Vrba; *Escape From Hell* by Alfred Wetzler
"Clemens Forrell": *So weit die Füße tragen (As Far as My Feet Will Carry Me)* by Cornelius Rost and Joseph M. Bauer

Chapter 7: Modern warfare
Dieter Dengler: *Escape From Laos* by Dieter Dengler
Chris Ryan: *Bravo Two Zero* by Andy McNab; *The One That Got Away* by Chris Ryan
Scott O'Grady: *Return with Honor* by Scott O'Grady
Thomas Hamill: *Escape in Iraq* by Thomas Hamill and Paul T. Brown